Cover Photo:
"Courage Stone"
by SAJ Design Team
Shanksville-Stonycreek School
Memorial Gardens

Lower Photo:
"A Little Girl's Heart"
by Glenn J. Kashurba, M.D.
Shanksville Crash Site
September 20, 2001

On a bleak, raw day, a 5-year-old in a Sunday dress knelt at the crash site. She had suddenly become intensely interested in playing with the gravel. Her mother bent down next to her. Gently stroking her hair, she asked, "What are you doing?"

"I'm making a heart. Daddy always likes when I make him hearts."

The little girl kept working and furrowed a rather sturdy heart in the gravel. Temporarily satisfied, she stopped and began to look around.

She spied the flowers that were entwined within the long expanse of fluorescent orange mesh fence. Beyond the fence, 200 yards of September meadows stretched down a slope to the crater and charred trees.

She collected flowers and returned to her creation. The stones were soon covered with blossoms. She smiled, satisfied with her memorial.

Later, she knelt in the gravel with her nearly adult brothers, arms entwined on shoulders, weeping.

The legacy of a heroic father.

~ Glenn J. Kashurba, M.D.

Cover Design:
Atlas Printing and Creative Services/Cindy Breen
SAJ Design Team/Joe Kashurba, Alex Kashurba, Katie Keiser

QUIET COURAGE

The definitive account of
Flight 93 and its aftermath

Glenn J. Kashurba, M.D.

LIBRARY OF CONGRESS CATALOGING-IN-PUBLICATION DATA AVAILABLE.

Library of Congress Catalog Card Number 2006930919
ISBN 978-0-9721031-9-0

SAJ Publishing
113 S. Center Avenue, Somerset, PA 15501
www.sajpublishing.com

Book Layout: Cindy Breen/Atlas Printing Co. & Creative Services
421 W. Patriot Street, Somerset, PA 15501
814-445-2516
atlas@shol.com

First Edition

Printed in the U.S.A.
by Kirby Lithographic Company, Inc.

This book is dedicated to
the heroes and families of Flight 93
and all those who helped
in the aftermath.

Author's Notes and Sources

Notes:

I had the great honor and privilege to lend some small bit of support to a group of incredibly strong and wonderful people, the families of Flight 93. As we rode in the first set of buses to the crash site on Monday, September 17, 2001, those amazing people were already expressing their thanks to the citizens of Somerset County.

Despite all of their grief, amid the apprehension of seeing the crash site that claimed the lives of their loved ones, they kept repeating the mantra, "I hope the people here know how much we appreciate what they've done."

At the same time, many Somerset County residents expressed to me their profound gratitude toward the heroes for giving their lives to prevent an even greater tragedy. As a father of three children attending school less than sixty seconds airtime from the crash, I understand that feeling.

Courage After the Crash (SAJ Publishing, 2002) was a memorial to the courage of the heroes and the strength of their families. Additionally, the book was a thank you to the thousands of people who, in ways big and small, helped in the aftermath of the crash.

Courage After the Crash was published at the first anniversary of 9/11. Much has happened since then. America has been spared other attacks, but the world continues to be ablaze with conflicts. The *9/11 Commission Report* (US Government Printing Office, Official Government Edition, 2004) has shed light on the 9/11 plot, global terror and what happened on Flight 93.

In Somerset County, a unique relationship has grown between residents and the families of Flight 93. This has helped increase the popularity of the temporary memorial and progress toward a permanent Flight 93 National Memorial.

Quiet Courage: The definitive account of Flight 93 and its aftermath combines the oral histories of *Courage After the Crash* with those recorded through 2006. To that, I have added details of the 9/11 plot and what occurred on Flight 93. I feel that it is important to have the saga of Flight 93, from the plot to the memorial, all in one book. This will help readers understand the impact of the courageous acts of forty ordinary people.

This story is so important that it should never become an abstract historical event. To quote Ken Nacke, brother of Joey Nacke and member of the Flight 93 Federal Advisory Commission, "I'm not saying our country would forget. I'm not going to give them the opportunity to forget. I'm not saying they would, but it's worth reliving the pain that I have so people don't forget."

Sources:

PART 1 • SEPTEMBER 11, 2001

Nearly all of the oral histories in this section were recorded between November 2001 and May 2002. Exceptions are Ed Root, Gordon Felt, Ken Nacke, Pennsylvania Governor Mark Schweiker, Pennsylvania State Police Corporal William Link and the Congressional pages.

Over 100 people were interviewed during this time. Many of the accounts that appear in *Quiet Courage* are edited from longer accounts in *Courage After the Crash*. The original accounts were edited from nearly 2,000 pages of transcribed interviews. The accounts are memories and, in some instances, may be slightly inaccurate.

As with *Courage After the Crash*, I have attempted to concentrate the most essential information to a form that is sufficiently literary, yet still true to the speakers' oral style. Grammatical correctness has been sacrificed to achieve conversational fidelity.

Information on Somerset County history presented in the prologue is gleaned from a variety of sources available in Somerset County libraries. More information on Somerset County history is available at www.quietcourage.com.

Information presented regarding UAL 93 is based on the *9/11 Commission Report*. It is important for the reader to realize that video renderings of Flight 93 contain a certain amount of literary license. The actual record that we have of the flight of UAL 93 is based on information from the plane's Flight Data Recorder and Cockpit Voice Recorder, phone calls of the twelve people on the plane who spoke with someone on the ground and air traffic control records.

Material contained in the boxes and maps represents easily verifiable and publicly available information.

Details of what occurred at the New York and Washington crash sites were obtained primarily from the archives of the New York and Washington daily newspapers and the *9/11 Commission Report*.

The words of the hijackers translated into English are from the publicly released records of the Cockpit Voice Recorder on Flight 93.

Spellings of Arabic words, such as 'Usama bin Laden' and 'al Qaeda' are those used in the *9/11 Commission Report*.

The details of the NORAD/FAA plan and military response on 9/11 are both based on the *9/11 Commission Report*.

The alternate scenario of what may have occurred had Flight 93 not crashed in Shanksville is reconstructed from the *9/11 Commission Report*.

PART 2 • THE AFTERMATH

The vast majority of these accounts are edited from the original interviews recorded for *Courage After the Crash*. Exceptions are noted previously.

The details of the 9/11 plot and the history of Usama bin Laden and al Qaeda are based primarily on the *9/11 Commission Report*.

All names of the forty heroes are based on what is published by the National Park Service related to the Flight 93 Memorial. These names are different from how they were presented in *Courage After the Crash*. The names in *Courage After the Crash* were based on the bronze plaque placed at the site the week after the crash.

The brief bits of information provided on each of the forty heroes are based on newspaper reports, Jere Longman's book *Among the Heroes* (HarperCollins, 2002), or personal contact with families.

The description in the text of many events that occurred at the crash site, Seven Springs and elsewhere in Somerset County are based on my own experience and that of others in attendance.

The details of historical events in the timelines are based on newspaper archives, as is the historical information on anthrax. Specific issues regarding the medical implications of anthrax are based on internal medicine textbooks and consultation with infectious disease experts.

PART 3 • MOVING FORWARD

Some of these accounts are from the original interviews. Most of the accounts are edited from interviews recorded since that time. The timelines are based on the same sources as in the other parts of the book. Once again, the details of what occurred on the first anniversary that are not described in accounts are based on my own personal experience or that of others in attendance.

The information on the memorial design process is based on information available through the National Park Service and newspaper archives. The thoughts of Mr. Levy's journalism students are edited from comments they provided after returning from the crash site or other communications.

Further details regarding various ideas presented in *Quiet Courage* are available at www.quietcourage.com, including information regarding conspiracy theories.

The information presented in *Quiet Courage* is the best that was available at press time, prior to the fifth anniversary of 9/11. I expect that further information will come to light that will cause me to alter the book in subsequent editions.

Acknowledgements

Thanks to God for providing what I needed to complete this project. Thanks to my family for accepting the demands on my time and finances that started on September 11, 2001 and continue.

Thanks to the SAJ Design Team of Katie Keiser, Alex Kashurba and Joe Kashurba.

My sons, Alex and Joe, have spent long hours on this book over the past two years. Alex has grown into a first rate historical researcher, line editor and proofreader. Joe has become a great webmaster, concept designer and all-around 'I.T.' guy. My daughter, Sophie, has helped move this project along by accepting more responsibility in our home.

Katie Keiser has been my assistant for the past two years of this project. Katie has cheerfully accepted hour-to-hour schedule changes. She has transcribed interviews, researched, edited, designed, proofed, marketed and dealt with the media, all with great skill.

Thanks to Cindy Breen, the editor and layout designer for *Courage After the Crash* and *Quiet Courage*. She is a great artist and also has done a fine job of supervising production of *Quiet Courage*.

Thanks to Mary Fisher, my office manager, who continues her tireless work running my practice, proofreading and doing whatever else is needed.

Thanks to Kimberly Keslar, who was my assistant on *Courage After the Crash* and the first two years of *Quiet Courage*.

Thanks to former Governor Mark Schweiker and Flight 93 family members Ed Root, Ken Nacke and Gordon Felt for their help and commitment to this project.

Thanks to all of the contributors to *Courage After the Crash* and *Quiet Courage*.

Thanks to Hazel Yoder, John Shaulis and Henry Cook.

Thanks to Lisa Tristano at Marc P.R. and David La Torre at La Torre Communications.

Thanks to everyone that I thanked or forgot to thank in *Courage After the Crash*.

Thanks to Studs Terkel for pioneering the art of oral history.

Table of Contents

SETTING THE STAGE

Somerset County, Pennsylvania

Somerset County, Pennsylvania is somewhat larger than the state of Rhode Island. Its population is somewhat less than the number of daily visitors to the former World Trade Center Towers. It is situated an hour's drive east of Pittsburgh on the Pennsylvania Turnpike and one half hour south of Johnstown on US Route 219.

Somerset County is part of a beautiful area of ridges and valleys known as the Laurel Highlands. Not surprisingly, the number one county industry is recreation. The area abounds in State Parks, State Game Lands and four-season resorts. Residents of Pittsburgh, Baltimore and Washington, D.C. flock to the area to ski, golf, hike, whitewater raft, fish and hunt.

Somerset County's number two industry is farming. Dairy cows seem to outnumber humans. Other agricultural products include potatoes and maple syrup.

Somerset County has a long history of coal production. Enormous draglines, essential to strip mining, tower above the landscape. Miles of deep mining passages lie hidden beneath the surface. More recently, energy production has been expanded with an ever-increasing number of windmill farms.

During colonial times, young George Washington passed through the area on numerous military and diplomatic missions. In 1794, President George

Washington returned to the area leading the United States Army to quell the Whiskey Rebellion. The county was chartered the following year. For the next two centuries, little national attention was focused on Somerset.

Somerset Countians are a hearty sort. Referring to the county's reputation for farms, the highest point in Pennsylvania and occasional winters with 200 inches of snow, one political orator dubbed it "The Roof Garden" of Pennsylvania and its residents "those frosty sons of thunder." Many county residents are descendents of families that have lived here for generations. Others have moved to enjoy country living while appreciating the convenient proximity of city life. Children still have the opportunity to grow up relatively slowly. Schools are small. The 2002 graduating classes ranged from 218 at Somerset Area High School to 36 at Shanksville-Stonycreek.

Although pastoral and calm, Somerset County has had some experiences with disasters. Ferocious blizzards are generally taken in stride, but a freak winter rainstorm melted 10 inches of snow and led to a devastating flood in 1996. In 1998, two sets of tornadoes in the southern part of the county destroyed many homes and businesses in and around the town of Salisbury. Three residents died. A silver lining to the Salisbury tornadoes was that all aspects of the county's emergency response system became better organized and developed experience with large-scale destruction.

No one could possibly have imagined that those skills would be required in such magnitude and with such an audience as in September 2001.

Early September 2001 was generally warm and sunny in Somerset County. The residents of the Salisbury area had already rebuilt their community since the tornadoes of 1998. The county seat of Somerset anticipated a massive influx of emergency responders near the end of the month for the State Firefighters' Convention. Organizers predicted the largest crowd of visitors in the town's history.

Six miles northeast of Somerset, the tiny hamlet of Shanksville had settled back into obscurity after a brief brush with minor fame when a Pittsburgh newspaper article described it as a great community in which to live.

Chapter 1

Flight of UAL 93

September 11, 2001. Americans who lived through that day will always recall the details of what they were doing when the attacks on America unfolded. 9/11 became permanently seared in the American psyche, as had Pearl Harbor and the assassination of John F. Kennedy. September 11, 2001 became a great historic dividing line between the familiar past and an uncertain future.

In Somerset County, Tuesday, September 11, 2001 dawned as a warm, blue-sky day. The mood inspired by that beautiful September morning changed very quickly as residents reacted with helplessness, horror and disbelief to the terrible events unfolding in New York City and Washington, D.C.

Some Somerset Countians scrambled to contact friends and relatives near the initial attacks. However, living in a rural area so far from those centers of power and commerce, many observed with a strange sense of detachment and a feeling of personal safety. They did not know that a hijacked jetliner was headed toward them.

United Airlines Flight 93 (UAL93) had been scheduled to depart for San Francisco from Newark Liberty International Airport at 8:00 a.m. Due to typical East Coast air traffic delays, the Boeing 757 took off at 8:42 a.m. Four minutes prior, the FAA alerted NORAD that American Airlines Flight 11 (AA11) from Boston to Los Angeles had been hijacked.

Captain Jason Dahl and First Officer LeRoy Homer piloted Flight 93. They had not previously worked together but both had logged impressive flying resumes. Dahl had already achieved UAL's highest pilot qualification status in his 16 years with the airline. Homer was an Air Force Academy graduate who flew cargo planes during the Gulf War.

Five flight attendants completed the crew. Lorraine Bay, Sandra Bradshaw, Wanda Green and Deborah Welsh each had accumulated many years of experience. The least experienced flight attendant, CeeCee Lyles, was a former police officer.

In addition to the seven UAL personnel, 37 passengers boarded the jet that morning. Most of them looked forward to a pleasant flight and their plans in California. However, four passengers sitting in first class had no intention of touching down safely again.

Between 7:03 and 7:39 that morning, Saeed al Ghamdi, Ahmed al Nami, Almed al Haznawi and Ziad Jarrah checked in at the United ticket counter. Two of the men checked baggage. One of them, Haznawi, was identified for special scrutiny by the Computer Assisted Passenger Prescreening System (CAPPS). On the morning of September 11, 2001, CAPPS identified ten of the nineteen potential hijackers. However, the only consequence was that the checked bags of the selected hijackers were screened for explosives and loaded into the cargo hold only after the terrorists boarded. In September 2001, the United States of America had no plan to thwart an attack by hijackers who were eager to die.

The five-man hijacking teams on the other three doomed flights attacked when the jets reached their intended cruising altitude. This would have been

---

Aviation Acronyms

FAA - Federal Aviation Administration - is a section of the Department of Transportation that provides civil aviation safety and security. It operates 22 air traffic control centers often referred to as Towers (Boston Tower, Cleveland Tower, etc.).

NORAD - North American Aerospace Defense Command - is a cooperative organization between the USA and Canada that provides air defense of the airspace of North America. It was created in 1958 to defend against external Soviet threat and grew to 26 alert sites. By 2001, NORAD shrank to 7 alert sites in the U.S., supervised by 3 sector headquarters. Northeast Air Defense Sector (NEADS), based in Rome, NY, contained all 9/11 hijacked flights.

CAPPS - Computer Assisted Passenger Prescreening System - is a database established in 1998 by the FAA to enable air carriers to separate passengers into two categories: those who need additional security scrutiny and those who do not. It uses information from the passengers' itineraries to search for certain behavioral characteristics determined by the FAA (and now the Transportation Security Administration) to indicate high risk.

signaled to them by the pilots extinguishing the *Fasten Seatbelts* signs. The flight attendants would have begun their preparations to serve the passengers.

For unknown reasons, the four-man suicide team on Flight 93 delayed their attack by at least 15 minutes. Perhaps this was related to a delay in the opening of the cockpit door to the first class cabin or the absence of a fifth terrorist. Zacarias Moussaoui was frequently and erroneously referred to in the media as "the twentieth hijacker." However, the *9/11 Commission Report* concluded that Moussaoui received advanced flight training for a second wave of assaults or as a backup pilot for the 9/11 attacks. The terrorist pilots of Flight 93 and Flight 11, Ziad Jarrah and Mohamed Atta, frequently disagreed. Their relationship had deteriorated during the early summer of 2001 to the point that the plot planners feared Jarrah might quit the operation.

The most likely candidate for the fifth hijacker slot on Flight 93 was Mohamed al Kahtani. He was denied entry into the United States on August 4, 2001 by an alert immigration inspector at Orlando International Airport.

Whatever the cause, the delay proved crucial. During that time, the jet traveled an additional 125 miles along the flight path United had intended and away from the terrorists' target of Washington, D.C.

All existing evidence suggests that the first 46 minutes of the flight passed uneventfully. At 9:26 a.m., Captain Dahl confirmed that he received a cautionary transmission from United. The message informed all UAL transcontinental flights that two aircraft had hit the World Trade Center, and pilots should be aware of possible cockpit intrusions.

The terrorists attacked at 9:28 a.m. The jet began to dive from its cruising altitude of 35,000 feet. Eleven seconds into the descent, a radio transmission from the cockpit contained evidence of a physical altercation and a verbal

---

CVR - Cockpit Voice Recorder - is one of the 2 "black boxes" that the FAA requires on all commercial aircraft. It records 30 continuous minutes of voices within the cockpit and other sounds of interest, such as engine noise, landing gear, air traffic communications and alarms.

FDR - Flight Data Recorder - is the other of the 2 "black boxes" that the FAA requires. It records 25 continuous hours of operating conditions (air speed, heading, altitude, etc.)

NTSB - National Transportation Safety Board - is an independent federal agency created in 1967 and charged by Congress with the investigation of all civil air crashes in the US. During their investigation, the NTSB uses the FDR data to generate a computer-animated video reconstruction of the flight.

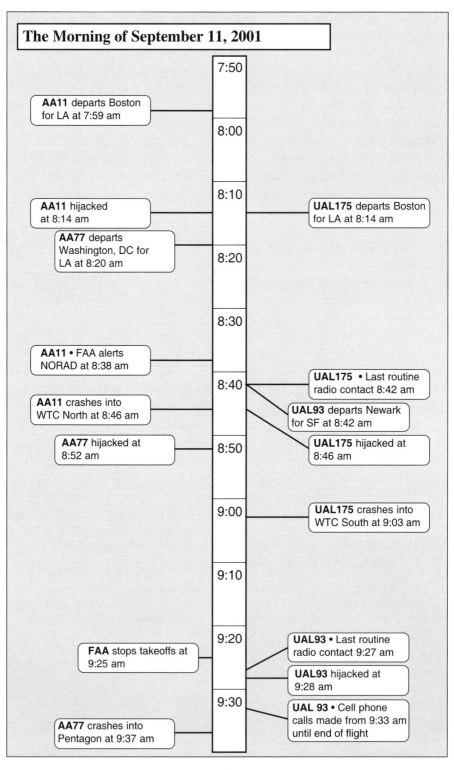

The Morning of September 11, 2001

7:50

AA11 departs Boston for LA at 7:59 am

8:00

8:10

AA11 hijacked at 8:14 am

UAL175 departs Boston for LA at 8:14 am

AA77 departs Washington, DC for LA at 8:20 am

8:20

8:30

AA11 • FAA alerts NORAD at 8:38 am

8:40

UAL175 • Last routine radio contact 8:42 am

AA11 crashes into WTC North at 8:46 am

UAL93 departs Newark for SF at 8:42 am

AA77 hijacked at 8:52 am

8:50

UAL175 hijacked at 8:46 am

9:00

UAL175 crashes into WTC South at 9:03 am

9:10

9:20

UAL93 • Last routine radio contact 9:27 am

FAA stops takeoffs at 9:25 am

UAL93 hijacked at 9:28 am

9:30

UAL 93 • Cell phone calls made from 9:33 am until end of flight

AA77 crashes into Pentagon at 9:37 am

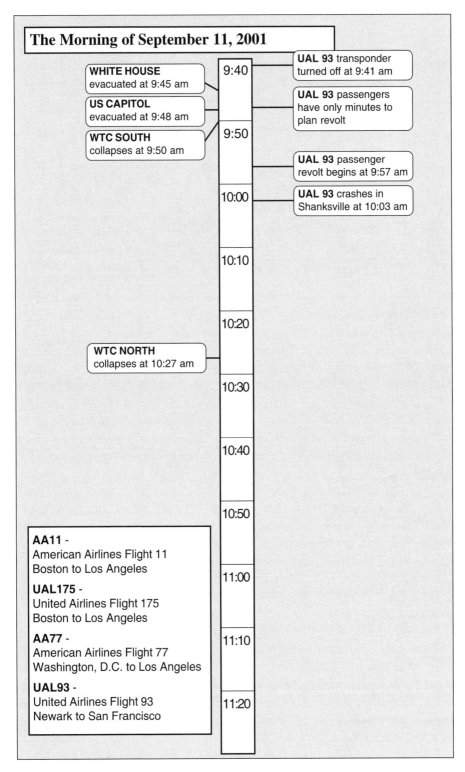

The Morning of September 11, 2001

WHITE HOUSE
evacuated at 9:45 am

US CAPITOL
evacuated at 9:48 am

WTC SOUTH
collapses at 9:50 am

WTC NORTH
collapses at 10:27 am

9:40

9:50

10:00

10:10

10:20

10:30

10:40

10:50

11:00

11:10

11:20

UAL 93 transponder
turned off at 9:41 am

UAL 93 passengers
have only minutes to
plan revolt

UAL 93 passenger
revolt begins at 9:57 am

UAL 93 crashes in
Shanksville at 10:03 am

AA11 -
American Airlines Flight 11
Boston to Los Angeles

UAL175 -
United Airlines Flight 175
Boston to Los Angeles

AA77 -
American Airlines Flight 77
Washington, D.C. to Los Angeles

UAL93 -
United Airlines Flight 93
Newark to San Francisco

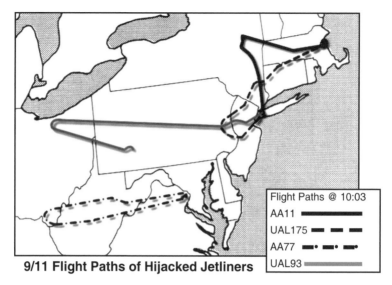

Flight Paths @ 10:03	
AA11	▬▬▬▬
UAL175	▬ ▬ ▬
AA77	▬• ▬• ▬•
UAL93	▬▬▬▬

9/11 Flight Paths of Hijacked Jetliners

"Mayday" call. A second communication 35 seconds later indicated that the struggle continued.

Three minutes later a hijacker inadvertently broadcast a message to air traffic control. Apparently, the man, who identified himself as the pilot, did not know how to properly use the cockpit radio. Instead of setting the system to the cabin public address mode, he continued to broadcast to Cleveland Tower.

The message warned the passengers that there was a bomb aboard, the plane was returning to the airport and everyone should remain cooperative. Immediately thereafter, the Cockpit Voice Recorder (CVR) indicated that a woman, assumed to be a flight attendant held captive in the cockpit, began to struggle.

She was murdered by her captors.

United notified the FAA of the hijacking while the jet climbed to nearly 41,000 feet and changed its heading from San Francisco to Washington, D.C. Within the next few minutes, Ziad Jarrah, the terrorist in the pilot's seat, broadcast to Cleveland Tower another message meant only for the passengers, "Here's the captain. I would like to tell you all to remain seated. We have a bomb aboard, and we are going back to the airport, and we have our demands. So, please remain quiet."

He then deactivated the plane's transponder, which emits a specific coded transmission allowing the plane to be easily identified by air traffic control radar. When the transponder signal disappeared, Cleveland Tower had to locate the uncoded signal of Flight 93 as a primary radar image. Air traffic controllers quickly identified the 757 from among the crowd of blips on their radar screens. Visual sightings from other aircraft in the area confirmed the location of the hijacked jetliner.

The 15-minute attack delay, once again, proved crucial. From the time of the hijacking, at least 10 passengers and two crewmembers were able to communicate with people on the ground via GTE airphones and personal cell phones. Two passengers reported the hijackers appeared unconcerned that passengers were communicating with the ground. This miscalculation allowed the captives to act and save thousands of fellow Americans.

The loved ones, operators and airline personnel they contacted informed the callers of the fate of the other hijacked flights. This information helped force a decision by the soon-to-be heroes to counterattack. Had this decision been delayed another 15 minutes, Flight 93 would have been only 10 minutes from Washington at the time of the counterattack.

The CVR indicates the heroes' assault began at 9:57 a.m. The terrorist attackers in their red bandanas had become prey. Jarrah began to rock the jet back and forth laterally to keep those who hunted him off their feet.

At 9:58 a.m., a terrorist in the cockpit yelled in Arabic, "They want to get in here. Hold, hold from inside. Hold from the inside. Hold!"

The counterattack continued.

Jarrah instructed another terrorist to block the door to the cabin. By 9:59 a.m., the resolve of the heroes caused the increasingly desperate hijackers to change tactics, and the nose of the plane began to violently rock up and down.

At 10:00 a.m., a passenger can be heard on the CVR yelling, "In the cockpit! If we don't, we'll die!"

The terrorist flight crew realized they were about to suffer the same cockpit intrusion and assault that they had just perpetrated against Dahl and Homer. Desperate and fearful, they hastily debated in Arabic when to crash the plane as it roared along at 580 mph only a few hundred feet above US Route 30 in Somerset County. The sounds of the attack continued until the CVR tape ended a few seconds later.

Terry Butler was removing a radiator from a junked car at Stoystown Auto Wreckers on the south side of U.S. Route 30. He had been watching coverage of the attacks on the World Trade Center and Pentagon in the company's office. He returned to work in a peaceful area of the sprawling junkyard, where he could occasionally watch deer feeding in an adjacent field. Terry knew that the FAA had already grounded all airplanes in the USA.

Butler: So I was down there getting a radiator out. I heard a plane, but I was looking the wrong way. I was looking down there because they usually fly that way. There was still some fog burning off. Then, when I turned around, right there it was, just coming above the treetops, flying straight. Maybe a little bit wobbly, but it was flying straight. Then it went up. I figured that he pulled up to miss that hill.

I didn't know what to think. I had never seen a jet that big. You know, this doesn't ever happen around here. I am from out in the boonies and never see any of this.

When it was coming across, it was probably a few hundred feet high. Then it went up probably twice as high. It definitely went up, and then when it got up so far, it just made that right turn. I guess they were aiming at that empty field.

I lost sight of it behind the trees. I thought it would pull up. When it went behind the trees, there were probably three or four seconds that went by. That is when I heard all of these booms. It shook the ground. I waited for the smoke.

When I saw the white smoke, I knew it was down. It was just like Boom, Boom, Boom, Boom! I mean it was just… [Stops.]

After that, it just got dead silent. I stood there for I don't know how long, just in shock. I called down on the walkie-talkie. I yelled and told them a plane went down. I guess they figured I was joking.

Then the second time, in my voice… [Chokes up.]

Chapter 2

'A jetliner went down'

The 757 rolled nearly upside down and slammed into the earth at a forty-five degree angle. The impact site was an empty field of a reclaimed strip mine. Had the battle lasted for another ten seconds and the plane continued on the same course, it would have crashed into the town of Shanksville. Over five hundred children, preschoolers to seniors, attended class at Shanksville-Stonycreek School District's only school in Shanksville that day.

Minutes before the crash, a passenger's cell phone call alerted the 911 Center in Westmoreland County, PA. The Emergency Management Agency (EMA) in that suburban Pittsburgh county notified the FBI. However, Somerset County's EMA 911 Center was unaware that Flight 93 was headed toward its jurisdiction until the plane crashed.

The last communication from Flight 93 may have been a dropped cell phone call into the Somerset County 911 Center at 10:02 a.m. Thirty-two seconds later, the first of numerous 911 calls reporting the crash of a large jet airliner between Lambertsville and Shanksville reached the EMA offices in the basement of the County Courthouse in Somerset.

Many residents in the Shanksville area clearly heard and felt the crash.

Anna Ruth Fisher and her mother, Anna B. Fisher, were visiting with other members of their extended Amish family at their farm on the outskirts of Shanksville.

Anna Ruth: I was reading the Bible that morning. Later my brother-in-law, David, and my sister came over to talk about some things. It was just after 9:00 a.m. [Many Amish use only standard time.]

Anna B.: We were sitting in the kitchen all together. We were visiting. Then there was a loud boom. It shook the whole house. We thought that maybe it was something that blew up on the Turnpike.

Alvin went to the neighbor's telephone, and that is when he heard about the Twin Towers. About then we saw this big mushroom smoke cloud going up.

Anna Ruth: It lasted near about half an hour. After the crash, another jet went near over to look.

Anna B.: Yes, we saw it.

Anna Ruth: I think they knew this plane was not right.

Anna B.: We were looking at the smoke cloud when we saw the jets circling up there. David climbed to the top of the silo. He looked over toward where the smoke was, but he couldn't see anything. Then somebody stopped at our roadside vegetable stand. They told us then about the plane crash.

SEPTEMBER 11, 2001: Calls to 911
Call #1 (10:02:06 a.m.)
911. What is your emergency?
(Cell phone.) Dropped call.
Call #2 (10:02:38 a.m.)
911.
... I live in the little town of Lambertsville in the suburbs of Stoystown. There was an airplane that crashed near Shanksville. Oh, my, it's on fire... and smoke. It's unbelievable!
OK, we'll get somebody out on that.
Call #3 (10:02:40 a.m.)
911.
An airplane crashed, Lambertsville! A jetliner went down in the wooded area or just in the fields down from the PBS strip. It would be half way between Skyline Drive and where Dr. Brant just built her new house, on Lambertsville Road.
Call #4 (10:02:40 a.m.)
911.
Was there an airplane that went down by Diamond T?
Where?
An airplane...Diamond T.
Diamond T Mine?
It was a big airplane, a big jet.
OK, we got some more calls on it. We'll get somebody out there right away.
I don't want to excite anybody, but it went down nose first, upside down!

Within two miles of the crash site, nearly 500 children, K-12, attended classes at the only school in the Shanksville-Stonycreek School District. J.P. O'Connor heard about the World Trade Center attacks while he was correcting papers in his fourth grade classroom.

O'Connor: It was toward the end of first period, and I had to pick up my students in art class.

I picked up my kids and went back to our room. I told the kids, "A terrible tragedy has happened in our country. I can't really show you a lot, but I will put on the TV for a couple of minutes and show you what is happening."

So I turned the TV on and talked to the kids a little bit. I explained that this was a very serious situation. Some of the kids understood that but others couldn't quite accept it. It was sort of a joke to them or something. Perhaps, it just wasn't real.

It wasn't long after that when Flight 93 crashed. The first thing was that we heard a large explosion. You could feel it. The whole classroom shook, and all of the ceiling tiles bounced up in the air and came back down. The students were scared. I told them that I would go find out what was going on.

I went out into the hallway. Mrs. Denner and some other teachers were already coming out. She said, "Look at that big black cloud over the playground!"

It looked like it was just below the playground. I couldn't believe how big and how black that cloud was.

Then somebody called in to one of the principals that a plane crashed. The first word we heard was that it was a small aircraft around Buckstown. Less than a minute later, the fire siren went off. People in the area have scanners. It was a matter of a few minutes until we heard that a large plane went down.

Brooke Piper was a sixth grader at Shanksville-Stonycreek School.

Piper: My class was in the gym. The whole gym started shaking. You could hear a rumbling sound. Our gym teacher went into the office, which is right next-door, and asked them what had happened. They said that a plane had gone down in the area.

Barry Lichty was the unpaid Mayor of Indian Lake Borough, a lake resort of nine hundred homes and four hundred full-time residents just north of Shanksville.

Lichty: My wife and I were watching CNN about what all was happening in New York and Washington. We heard this loud roar above the house that sounded like a missile. We both ducked. Shortly thereafter, we heard an explosion and felt a tremor.

My first reaction, as a former utility employee, was that maybe someone shot a missile into the substation over here. Then I began to worry about the breastworks of the dam. If we were being terrorized, that would be a natural target. So I called our police and told them that they better get out to the breastworks and keep an eye on it.

My wife was upset about me doing this, but I got into my truck to see if I could find out what was going on. I saw a plume of smoke. I ran into some of our borough employees, and we went over to the crash site.

Gerald Parry, Chief of the Berlin Volunteer Fire Department, was standing in the parking lot of Berlin-Brothersvalley High School, six miles from the crash site. He was speaking with a teacher and a custodian about a problem with the school's fire alarm system.

Parry: We were standing there talking in the corner of the parking lot when we felt and heard the explosion. If I had been turned the other direction, I might have seen it go down. We saw the smoke immediately. Before the call came in, I wondered if it was from a strip mine. But it felt too large to be a strip mine explosion; and, usually, we have some idea when they are going to happen.

Almost immediately, the tones started. It took about a minute or a minute and a half for all of the tones to get out. Shanksville was first; I think Somerset was second. Then Listie, Friedens, and Stoystown and additional ones after that. So I knew this was something big.

They said there was a plane down. I knew that we were going to get called so I headed toward the firehouse. The president of the fire company, Doyle Paul, showed up right after we got there, and some other fellows started coming in. It was less than five minutes and we were toned to respond to it, too.

Penny Reiman was the Supervisor of Radiology at Somerset Hospital. She lived just outside Shanksville. Her husband had previously farmed some of the land that became the crash site.

Reiman: I had taken a half-day off of work to take my mother to the doctor. We were on our way home and heard about the World Trade Center. My mom lives at Indian Lake. We were on Route 30, near Buckstown, when the plane crashed.

As we were driving along the Buckstown Road, many people were outside of their houses looking up in the sky. About that time, we saw the cloud of smoke. With the area being heavily mined, we thought that something exploded. When we got to her home, her neighbor came out and was very upset. She said there was a plane crash and that she saw the plane. I didn't have my car at the time so I took my mom's car. I needed to get to the hospital because I anticipated injuries. I continued down Buckstown Road and saw somebody near Indian Lake. I stopped and said, "Is it OK to go ahead?"

She said, "Something just flew into the lake."

They didn't know what it was. I continued on. I was very, very close to it. I just wanted to get to work.

As I was driving, I called into the hospital, and they said it was a passenger jet that crashed. When I got to the hospital, it was completely locked-down. I proceeded to do my job as far as canceling patients and coordinating things.

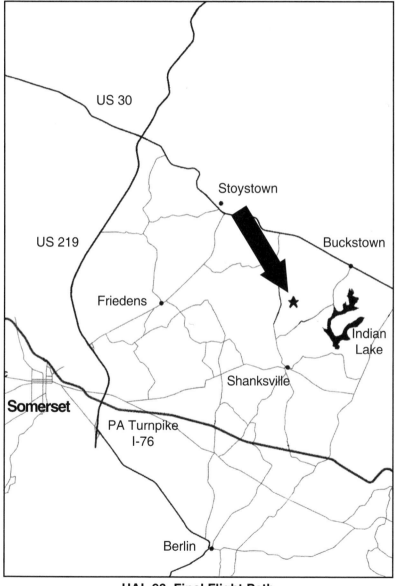

UAL 93 Final Flight Path

So many calls flooded the 911 Center that the phone system automatically rerouted some to neighboring Cambria County 911. An incredulous staff of Somerset County EMA dealt with a nearly impossible scenario of a commercial airline disaster during a national emergency. Despite this, the 911 audiotapes of that morning clearly demonstrate the EMA staff members reacting with professional cool. They dispatched eight volunteer fire companies to the scene and notified all the ambulance services in northern Somerset and southern Cambria counties.

The Shanksville Volunteer Fire Department received one of the initial calls and was able to muster four members to man the department's aged fire truck. However, this was more than usual since two members were unexpectedly home from work, one for a job interview and the other for his grandmother's funeral.

With only a general idea of where the plane had crashed, the Shanksville firefighters navigated to the crash site by way of the mushroom cloud of smoke visible from town.

Rick and Tricia King owned Ida's Store in Shanksville, the source of groceries, lunch and information for the area. The Kings and their two small children lived on the block between Ida's and the Fire Hall. Rick was the Assistant Fire Chief of Shanksville Volunteer Fire Department.

Rick: By about 10:00 that morning, the only family member who I hadn't talked to was my sister Jody. She lives in Lambertsville about two or three miles away from us. Just after 10:00, Jody called me. As we were talking, she said, "I hear a plane."

I said, "Yeah." No big deal.

She said, "No, Rick. It's really loud. It sounds like a big jet."

I had the phone in my hand. So I walked out onto my front porch. As soon as I walked out, I could hear it.

I said, "Oh my God, Jody. I hear it, too."

All of a sudden there was like a whining, screaming noise of the engines, and seconds later, it hit. The ground shook underneath my feet. I mean my porch, the house, everything just rumbled.

She said, "Oh my God, it crashed!"

I said, "I know, I heard it. I've got to go!"

I hung up the phone. I don't know where I put it. I don't know if I shut the door. At that point, my heart was pounding. I am the Assistant Fire Chief. In the daytime, our Fire Chief is at work, our Deputy Chief is at work, and we don't have a lot of people for a call. I had to get to the store and tell Tricia. I didn't know if she heard it or felt it. So I came running down and busted in through the door and said, " A plane just crashed!"

They were looking at me with this shocked look on their faces. There was a customer in the store, a local guy who is sort of a jokester. He started laughing, he said, "Yeah, right."

Tricia: I knew he was serious by the look on his face. He turned around, went out the door, and ran to the fire hall.

It was just crazy. We were all nervous wrecks because we didn't know what to do. We had no idea if there were people alive on the plane, if there were terrorists coming after us, or what was going on. We all wanted our kids. We ran to the school and got them.

Rick: I started to run up through the yards to the fire hall. I got about halfway and our fire siren started to go off. Somebody already called 911. I got up there and called Somerset 911 on the radio. They said, "Plane down, Lambertsville area."

There were only four of us that came to the station. Besides me, there was Keith Custer, Robert Kelly and Merle Flick. Merle is one of our older firemen.

I drove. We started down Lambertsville Road, and I was talking on the radio to County Control. I started thinking about a commercial airliner with two hundred or three hundred passengers. I was the incident commander because it was our fire district, and I was the highest-ranking person going to the scene. I told County Control that I wanted all available EMS units in Somerset and southern Cambria counties.

We didn't know exactly where it was. I was just driving to where it looked like the smoke was coming from.

I looked at Keith, and he looked back at the other two guys and said, "Get ready guys. This is like nothing we've ever seen before. Be prepared for anything."

The guys in the back were putting on their air packs. I was trying to think about what we were going to see there. I was thinking there were going to be fires and people trapped in a fuselage. I tried to reassure myself that we knew how to rescue people when they were trapped in cars and how to put out fires. We even have foam on our truck for the jet fuel. All of these things were racing through my mind.

Underlying all of that was, "What the hell is going on?" Because I was already so shook up seeing what was going on with the rest of the country.

I looked at Keith and said, "I can't swallow; my mouth is too dry."

He looked back at me and said, "Me, too."

Chapter 3

First Responders

Wells Morrison began September 11, 2001 at his desk reviewing the tasks that were scheduled to occupy his day. Within a few hours his plans would change as he would become site commander at the most productive crime scene of the most destructive criminal act in American history.

As the Supervisory Special Agent in Charge of the FBI's Mon Valley Resident Agency, Morrison supervised FBI activities across a large area of western Pennsylvania. When the second plane hit the World Trade Center, he summoned his agents back to their Charleroi, Pennsylvania headquarters and contacted his boss in Pittsburgh for instructions. The original plan was to be on high alert and standby for further orders. Morrison and his agents did not have long to wait.

Morrison: Shortly after that, I received a phone call advising me that there was an aircraft that was refusing to respond to radio traffic with Cleveland Tower. It appeared that aircraft was headed toward Johnstown. We supervise the Johnstown office of the FBI out of here. I contacted the Johnstown agents and instructed them to proceed to the Johnstown airport. We didn't know what we had other than an aircraft refusing to respond to traffic from the tower.

Then I get a call that we had a plane that crashed in Somerset County. I think a lot of people expect the FBI to know everything, but that is not the case. It takes a little while to be certain that the plane that was refusing to communicate with the tower is the same plane that had gone down in Somerset.

Right after that, I got a phone call advising me that there had been a call into Westmoreland County 911 saying that an airplane had been hijacked. I sent an agent over to Westmoreland County to pick up that original tape. We had agents heading to the crash site in Somerset. I also had an agent continue to go to the Johnstown Airport just in case there was anything else that might go on. I was in communication with our office in Pittsburgh.

We established a quick command post here. I requested of the Station Commander of the Belle Vernon State Police Barracks that he send a couple of troopers over here so we could be privy to all of their radio traffic. So we had a couple of troopers here as well as some FBI agents on standby.

I then proceeded to the Somerset Barracks of the State Police. I am familiar with those folks because we worked together on the kidnapping of a young girl two years ago. As a matter of fact, it was two years to the month because she was kidnapped in September of 1999.

At the Somerset Barracks I met with Sergeant Pat Madigan, the Station Commander. Shortly thereafter, Major Szupinka, who is the highest-ranking officer for the State Police in this region, arrived. Then the Major and I headed up to the crash site.

Flight 93 crashed within the boundaries of Stonycreek Township. There was no local law enforcement. The Pennsylvania State Police held jurisdiction and immediately responded with troopers from the Somerset Barracks who happened to be in the area on other calls.

Corporal William Link answered the phone that morning at the Somerset Barracks. Corporal Craig Bowman and Barracks Commander Sergeant Patrick Madigan were involved in a line inspection with Lieutenant Robert Weaver from the Greensburg Barracks. They learned of the attacks in New York and began to watch coverage on television.

Madigan: As we were watching, I made the comment to the Lieutenant, which I am sure was made throughout the county, "Well, at least there are no terrorist targets in Somerset County."

Not long after that, Corporal Bowman came in and said that we received information about a 911 call from a hijacked plane over Somerset with a bomb onboard.

I had two thoughts. My first was, "Now the rumors are going to start."

The second one was, "If there is a hijacked plane over Somerset, what am I going to do about it?"

Bowman: I walked out to communications to watch the television out there. Corporal Link was answering the phone. That was his duty for the day. I was just standing there. He was on the phone and another line rang, so I picked up the second phone. It was a truck dispatcher. He gave his name and said one of his drivers had just called and was certain that a large plane had crashed near Highland Tank. That is just north of the scene. So I immediately hung up and called 911.

At that time, I was thinking that this couldn't be related to New York. How ironic is this that we have a plane crash? But at the same time, I was thinking maybe this is related. In looking back, it just happened so fast. It was so surreal.

Link: Nick Pelc, one of our troopers who was off duty, called, in disbelief, and said, "Hey, Bill, what's going on?"

He lives just outside Indian Lake.

I said, "Hey, I know this is all crazy, isn't it?" thinking he was referring to the New York City stuff.

He said, "Man, my whole house just shook, my windows shook, my power went off, my TV, everything…"

I said, "What are you talking about, Nick?"

He said, "We just had something big happen out here. The ground shook. The whole house… and we lost everything."

So, I said, "Hey, Nick, we're getting some other calls. We don't have that many guys. Would you mind hopping in your car and see if you can figure out what's going on?"

So, I'm thinking, we have a plane down. Is it a big plane? A small passenger plane? What exactly do we have here? I'm hoping that it was not the worst. I'm having all these questions, and I'm trying to get people out to the area, locate the problem, and find out what's going on. It seemed like my mind was going a thousand miles an hour.

Bowman: I talked to the Sergeant. I am in the crime unit, so I am usually dressed in a shirt and tie. We changed into uniforms. While I was getting changed, the FBI called. Agent Paul Wilson of the Johnstown office said, "Do you have anything on a plane crash?"

I said, "Yeah. We're getting calls. One of the calls was from a trooper who lives nearby. He said his house just shook when something exploded."

The initial 911 calls led to a dispatch of emergency vehicles from the Somerset Ambulance main office in Somerset and the Stoystown substation on Route 30 near the site. Somerset Ambulance is a member-owned, private, non-profit organization with 25 full-time and 61 part-time employees.

Paramedic Jill Miller had been the organization's manager since 1991.

Miller: My brother, John Dickey, lives three blocks from the World Trade Center and works six blocks from there. So when the first one hit, I called him at work. He was OK and was planning on getting out of Dodge.

I was talking to the medic who was working at our Stoystown station when we got the dispatch for this crash. Of course, we were dispatched and everybody else in two counties was dispatched. I hung up the phone and went flying out there.

I had my cell phone and made a lot of calls on the way out. I called back to our station and had them get on the telephone and call everybody they could. I was trying to get information, but that was impossible because there wasn't any. I called all of the hospitals in the area (Somerset, Windber, Lee, and Conemaugh) and told them what was going on. They all activated their emergency procedures.

We thought there were going to be several helicopters coming. What we didn't know was that they all were grounded. Wherever they were, they had to land.

All the firefighters who responded to the crash were volunteers who were working or otherwise going about their lives when their pagers began to tone.

Gerald Parry, the Berlin Fire Chief, had been a volunteer firefighter since the age of 14 in different communities across Pennsylvania and Maryland. He donated time from the limited amount that remained after his family responsibilities and long hours of running his dairy feed business.

Parry: We went over in three vehicles. We had two members, who are farmers that live between Berlin and Shanksville, who responded directly when they heard us called.

We probably had 25 guys at the hall. The past chief and I discussed it, and we decided not to strip the tent because we did not know what else was going to happen. So when they called for manpower to assist the Somerset HAZMAT team, there were probably eight of us that responded over there total.

When you get a call like that, the first thing that is going through your mind is, what are we going to face? One of the first things that hit me is some fear. Being an officer, my primary responsibility is safety. Taking care of our people and trying to help anybody else. Then we worry about the environment and so forth. Some of the stuff I have seen in HAZMAT training was scary. So you just don't know what you are getting your people into.

Mike Sube was leaving the insurance office he owns. The married father of two young children had been a volunteer firefighter for 11 years and was the First Lieutenant for Somerset Volunteer Fire Department.

Sube: I got into my vehicle and had only gone about ten or fifteen feet when my fire pager went off. I expected it was an accident or something. Maybe somebody listening to all of this on the radio ran off the road.

The call came in, like, "Station 601 assisting 627, large commercial aircraft down in the area."

I couldn't believe it.

My initial thought was that there was something wrong with the FAA or the radar and that there were going to be planes falling out of the sky everywhere. How could this possibly have happened? Did they hit something?

We have been on plane crash calls before. Some have had fatalities. But when they said, "Large commercial," I was wondering, "What is large?" Maybe it was a commuter from Pittsburgh.

I was on our HAZMAT squad truck, which was the initial vehicle out. I believe there were eight of us. Then there was a brush truck because the calls that we had received when we were at the station said there were small brush fires. We had four people that responded in that. Then later on, they requested an engine from us, so we had three more people come out in the engine. Overall, we had about 12 or 13 people initially.

From the time I heard the call to about three miles away from the site, I was on the phone trying to track down my family. At that point, my daughter, once a week, went to a mommy's morning out for a couple of hours. My son was in preschool. So my wife could have been at the grocery store, at the gym or wherever.

I called her cell phone and the house and couldn't find her. When I finally got a hold of my mom, I was riding in the back of the HAZMAT vehicle, racing out Route 281 with the sirens blaring and the radio going.

I said, "You have got to find Tammy. I want the kids with her. I'm on my way out to this crash scene, and I don't know what we are going to be getting into."

The initial 911 calls led to the dispatch of numerous emergency vehicles from the main station of Somerset Ambulance, Somerset Volunteer Fire Department and the Somerset Barracks of the Pennsylvania State Police (PSP). All those vehicles raced from the county seat of Somerset and screamed toward Shanksville on Route 281 through the town of Friedens. The path took them past the National Guard Armory and Somerset County Airport. Friedens Elementary School lies between Route 281 and the runway.

Elizabeth Maul taught a fourth grade class at Friedens that day. She learned of the New York and Washington attacks that morning from the school secretary, Darlene Baumgardner. Darlene's son, Alan, worked for Somerset EMA.

Maul: I can recall vividly walking down this hall and thinking to myself, "OK, God, if this is it for me, please take care of my family."

Being so close to the airport, it has always been in the back of my mind that something could happen here at this building. I walked into my room and, within seconds, an airplane did go over the building low.

I remember saying, "Thank you, God. That one made it over."

I think that must have turned out to be one of the ones that they sent up. It was not the one that crashed.

It was just minutes until we heard the fire alarms. I didn't know there was a crash. A lot of fire trucks and ambulances were going down the road, and the kids kept looking out the window. They didn't know anything was going on at this point; and, of course, I didn't know about Shanksville. So I was saying, "We are all here and we are all safe. I don't smell smoke, so let's get our heads back on this math test."

Ruby Berkebile had taught at Friedens Elementary for 23 years. She tried to reassure her class of third graders.

Berkebile: Being this close to the airport, a crash has always been a concern of ours. The airplanes come in really low over our playground. I used to be in a back room with first graders, and there were times when I wanted to scream, "Hit the floor!"

They were really concerned. My room faces the front highway. Steady streams of emergency vehicles went by. Extremely fast. Sirens on. We were all pretty panicked just by that. But I said, "Oh, it is just probably an accident down the road and everything will be OK."

I tried to reassure them that no one's parents were involved in the accident down the road.

A little girl in Ruby's class and her twin sister in another third grade classroom knew otherwise. Their mother, Jill Miller, would be in an ambulance heading toward whatever trouble was down that road.

SEPTEMBER 11, 2001

Chapter 4

Confusion Reigns

Less than two minutes after Flight 93 plowed into the Somerset County earth, a military plane reported the crash to the FAA Command Center in Hearndon, Virginia. The plane was an unarmed Air National Guard C-130H cargo jet headed to Minnesota from Washington.

The C-130 had departed from the Washington, D.C. area at approximately 9:30 a.m. At that time, air traffic controllers at Dulles searched their radar screens for AA77. The 757 had departed Dulles bound for Los Angeles at 8:20 a.m. Hijackers commandeered the flight at 8:52 a.m.and turned off the plane's transponder at 8:56 a.m. Indianapolis Center had been tracking the aircraft. The controllers were unaware that two hijackings had just occurred in the airspace of the Boston and New York Centers.

With the transponder's signal lost, controllers at Indianapolis Center began to search for a primary radar return for AA77. Controllers looked to the west along the intended flight path and to the southwest, where the plane had turned prior to the transponder signal loss. They had no reason to look eastward where the jet sped out of their airspace toward Washington. Had they done so, they still would not have been able to see the plane's primary radar image. Although it was detected by the radar, due to a software glitch, the image was not displayed on radar screens at the Indianapolis Tower for over eight minutes.

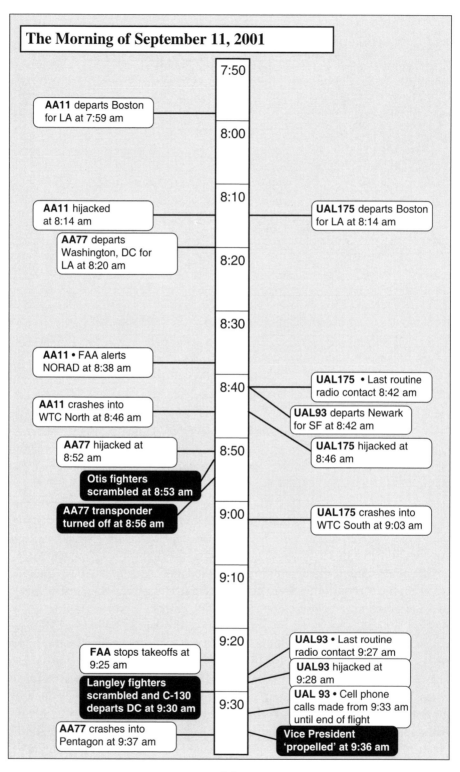

The Morning of September 11, 2001

7:50

AA11 departs Boston for LA at 7:59 am

8:00

8:10

AA11 hijacked at 8:14 am

UAL175 departs Boston for LA at 8:14 am

AA77 departs Washington, DC for LA at 8:20 am

8:20

8:30

AA11 • FAA alerts NORAD at 8:38 am

UAL175 • Last routine radio contact 8:42 am

8:40

AA11 crashes into WTC North at 8:46 am

UAL93 departs Newark for SF at 8:42 am

AA77 hijacked at 8:52 am

8:50

UAL175 hijacked at 8:46 am

Otis fighters scrambled at 8:53 am

AA77 transponder turned off at 8:56 am

9:00

UAL175 crashes into WTC South at 9:03 am

9:10

9:20

UAL93 • Last routine radio contact 9:27 am

FAA stops takeoffs at 9:25 am

UAL93 hijacked at 9:28 am

Langley fighters scrambled and C-130 departs DC at 9:30 am

UAL 93 • Cell phone calls made from 9:33 am until end of flight

9:30

AA77 crashes into Pentagon at 9:37 am

Vice President 'propelled' at 9:36 am

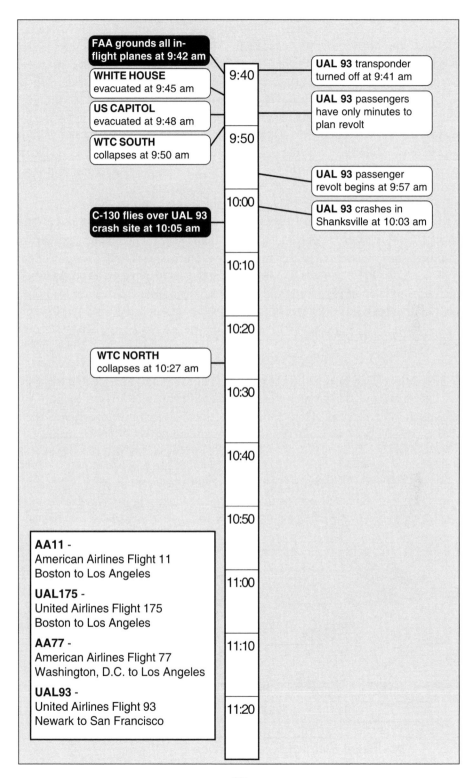

FAA grounds all in-flight planes at 9:42 am

WHITE HOUSE evacuated at 9:45 am

US CAPITOL evacuated at 9:48 am

WTC SOUTH collapses at 9:50 am

C-130 flies over UAL 93 crash site at 10:05 am

WTC NORTH collapses at 10:27 am

9:40

9:50

10:00

10:10

10:20

10:30

10:40

10:50

11:00

11:10

11:20

UAL 93 transponder turned off at 9:41 am

UAL 93 passengers have only minutes to plan revolt

UAL 93 passenger revolt begins at 9:57 am

UAL 93 crashes in Shanksville at 10:03 am

AA11 - American Airlines Flight 11 Boston to Los Angeles

UAL175 - United Airlines Flight 175 Boston to Los Angeles

AA77 - American Airlines Flight 77 Washington, D.C. to Los Angeles

UAL93 - United Airlines Flight 93 Newark to San Francisco

When air traffic controllers were unable to contact AA77 by radio, they assumed the most likely explanation of simultaneous transponder, radar and radio loss: AA77 had crashed. They informed the FAA regional center, Air Force Search and Rescue in Langley, Virginia and the West Virginia State Police.

AA77 continued to travel eastward undetected for over 30 minutes. During this time, passengers and crew used GTE airphones and personal cell phones. Among the callers was Barbara Olsen, nationally-known commentator and wife of US Solicitor General Ted Olsen. Olsen and the other callers were able to inform American Airlines of the hijacking but unable to pinpoint their location.

From 9:00 to 9:30 a.m., confusion reigned throughout the FAA. In retrospect, the only three facts known were that two jets had crashed into the World Trade Center, AA11 and UAL175 had been hijacked and AA77 was missing. They had not yet been informed by the airline that AA77 was hijacked.

At 9:32 a.m., air traffic controllers at Dulles discovered an unidentified aircraft approaching Washington, D.C. Controllers notified the recently airborne National Guard C-130H cargo plane about the unidentified intruder. The C-130 spotted the 757 and began to monitor it. The FAA also notified the Secret Service.

By 9:36 a.m., the plane began to bear directly toward the area of the White House. This information was relayed to the Secret Service. Quoting the *9/11 Commission Report* regarding the Vice President, who was monitoring the situation in the White House, "agents propelled him out of his chair." They then escorted him to the underground bunker beneath the White House.

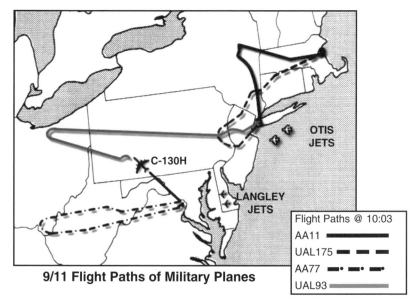

9/11 Flight Paths of Military Planes

OTIS JETS

C-130H

LANGLEY JETS

Flight Paths @ 10:03
AA11 ━━━━━
UAL175 ━ ━ ━
AA77 ━•━•━•
UAL93 ▬▬▬

The FAA contacted NORAD for the first time about the unidentified plane bearing down on the center of US government. The closest armed fighters were 150 miles east over the Atlantic Ocean. The NORAD fighters patrolling near Washington had taken off from Langley Air Force Base in Virginia at 9:30 a.m. They were ordered up in response to an erroneous report that AA11 was not one of the planes that hit the Twin Towers. Instead AA11 was reported to be heading southward toward Washington. NORAD had no knowledge that AA77 was the actual threat to Washington until 9:36 a.m.

The only other armed NORAD fighters aloft had been scrambled from Otis Air Force Base in Falmouth, Massachusetts at 8:53 a.m. to find AA11; seven minutes after AA11 hit the North Tower of the World Trade Center. Those fighters continued to patrol in the vicinity of New York City.

At 9:37 a.m., the C-130 that would later confirm the crash of Flight 93 watched AA77 slam into the Pentagon.

At 9:41 a.m., less than four minutes after AA77 struck the Pentagon, the FAA informed NORAD of another possible hijacking.

The jet was not Flight 93.

SEPTEMBER 11, 2001

Chapter 5

Scene of the Crash

Flight 93 crashed at the very end of a large field that had previously been a strip mine. When the bituminous coal was stripped from the site, over two hundred feet of soil and rock had been removed. The vein of coal was extracted and the land was replaced and replanted. Although work at this cut had been finished for several years, the ground was softer than unstripped earth.

When the plane slammed into the earth at nearly full throttle, the front third, ahead of the wings, disintegrated and was blown forward into a forest at the end of the meadow. As a result, the area beyond the impact point was scorched by the fireball and covered with small pieces of debris. The remaining two-thirds of the plane telescoped on itself and embedded directly into the soft earth of the old strip cut. The fuel tanks exploded and incinerated everything within the pit, leaving only a smoking crater.

Workers in the area and passers-by were on the scene almost immediately. Shanksville Volunteer Fire Department and Somerset Ambulance arrived shortly thereafter, followed by seven other volunteer fire departments and more ambulance units.

Rick King drove and Keith Custer rode across from him as the Shanksville engine screamed toward the crash site.

King: There were people on Lambertsville Road pointing down toward Skyline Drive. We turned up Skyline Drive and met the Somerset Ambulance coming from the Stoystown substation. They had missed the little dirt road that goes down closest to the site. They turned around and were motioning us to go down this little dirt road. They went ahead of us and we pulled in right behind them.

Custer: We turned in the road that went down to the crash, and as we were going down that road, there was total silence. We didn't know what to say to each other.

We got down to the bottom where it hit. I saw this big hole in the ground that was smoking. There were some spot fires. I remember looking around and saying, "Where is the plane?"

We stopped and I opened the door. The smell of jet fuel was so overpowering. I will never forget that smell; it is burnt into my mind.

When I got out, reality hit. It had actually crashed.

King: I had pulled into where the debris was laying. There were little puffs of smoke from the branches on the trees that were smoking and burning. Some brush was burning in the woods. I saw this mound of dirt, and I didn't really realize initially that that was the crater.

There was a tire there that was burning. We pulled our trash line, which is the line that is right in the front of our truck. We use it for car fires and things like that. I told our guys to go ahead and hit those fires where the tire was burning and where the crater was smoking.

Custer: I walked up, and there was a tire that was on fire, probably a hundred feet past where the crater was. It was a big tire. I was thinking this is no commuter jet tire. This is a big jet. I hit it good with the hose and put it out. I stopped and "poof," it just started on fire again.

King: I was looking around for other big parts of the plane. There was debris laying everywhere, but it still didn't look like a plane. I walked down to the edge of the woods. There was the same small debris there.

People started coming in. I tried to get through on the radio to Somerset 911. That was impossible because they were so busy with other departments coming and other agencies calling. It was chaotic there initially. Other companies' fighters came, and I told them to start a search down through the woods.

There is a power line there that goes down toward Barry Hoover's house. I walked that way, and there was mail scattered everywhere. I started thinking to myself that maybe this wasn't a commercial airliner. Maybe it was a mail plane or a Learjet or a commuter plane. But I couldn't put that together with the explosion I had heard and felt. It had to be something with a lot of fuel to make that sound and that rumble two miles away in town.

Guys were coming back from the woods and saying there was nothing down there. I was still trying to get through to County Control to tell them that there were no survivors. I was wondering where all of the people were. Maybe it was just a pilot. Maybe it was an empty plane.

I walked down the power line further and got my first glimpse of human remains. Then I walked a little further and saw more. I soon realized that whatever number of people there were on this plane, they were blown apart.

Somebody started hollering at me on the radio that there was a small fire at one of the cabins. I sent whatever engine was out at the end of the road to put it out. I think it was Central City.

Gary Thomas, the Chief of Somerset Volunteer Fire Department, was in Myrtle Beach, South Carolina on vacation that day. Assistant Chief, Jim Clark, commanded the department. First Lieutenant Mike Sube arrived on Somerset VFD's HAZMAT truck.

Sube: When we turned off the hard road and started back the dirt road, there were a variety of vehicles that were already there. There were a couple of coal trucks, emergency vehicles, pickup trucks, and all sorts of personal vehicles. We saw the congestion that was starting. We parked our HAZMAT rig across the road and shut it off to any other vehicles, emergency or non-emergency. We allowed enough room so that an ambulance could get by. We started setting up cones.

We left two of our guys back there. First Assistant Chief Jim Clark, Captain Bob Hayman and I continued up to the scene. I was thinking there would be fires, wreckage and chaos. It was not exactly coordinated. But it didn't come across to me that there was a frantic need for immediate care. That was what was somber and eerie.

When we walked up, the crater was to my left. Judging from the wreckage, we anticipated no survivors, but we still felt the need to make a sweep of the area. The captain and I started to make a sweep to give the chief an overall read on the brush fires and the scene itself. We started down into the woods through the wreckage and fires, relaying back what we found on our radios.

We made our way down into where the cabins were in the woods. There was debris in the trees and on the ground. There were small fires in the brush and trees. We made our way to a small pond. That is where I observed the largest piece of wreckage that I saw, which was a portion of the landing gear and the fuselage. One of the tires was still intact with the bracket and probably about three to five windows of the fuselage were actually in one piece lying there. It was only about twenty feet from this pond. I radioed to our chief that we were going to need some type of scuba team to confirm that there was nothing in the pond. I understand that later on in the week, they had to drain that pond to determine if there was anything there.

The most emotional time for me was after I had made my way down to the pond and saw that large piece of aircraft. We made another sweep where we went further down through the woods. I saw small pieces of human remains and occasionally some larger pieces. That was disturbing, but what was most disturbing to me was seeing personal effects. One of them was a doll, like a porcelain baby doll. That was when it really hit home for me, the point of realization that so many people died right there. That was what really affected me.

Jill Miller of Somerset Ambulance continued to try to coordinate a plan to provide medical care for hundreds of injured survivors.

Miller: We were probably less than a mile away when our Stoystown ambulance got there. Kevin Huzsek told us that he didn't think there were survivors but he was going down in the woods to check. When we got there and were able to determine that there were no survivors, we cancelled everybody. Then our biggest concern was what was on this plane and what we just exposed ourselves to.

We tried to keep anybody we could out of there. It was too late for us, but we were going in there still hoping that there were four hundred people that we could help.

We did a lot of head scratching and looking at each other for a little while. We were smart enough to figure out that this was not our game. We were going to have to be there to do what we were told to do, but our mission isn't search and recovery. So we just kind of waited.

Every fifteen minutes, somebody with a little bit more authority showed up. The FBI and all of those other 'initial' people just kept coming.

Somerset EMA managed to have someone on the scene with a GPS shortly after the crash. Bill Baker was heading toward Indian Lake when he passed emergency personnel headed the opposite direction. A Berlin fire fighter himself, Baker attempted to follow the emergency vehicles but lost them on the winding roads.

As he started down Buckstown Road, a car was approaching him, flashing its headlights. It was his wife. She had been visiting relatives nearby, heard the crash and went to the site. She informed him of what she witnessed, and he raced towards the disaster.

Baker: One of the first things I saw when I got out of my vehicle was a book. I looked down and kind of moved it with my boot to get a better look at it. It was a Bible. That was really odd; in all of this destruction, there was a Bible.

There was debris everywhere. You couldn't step without walking on a piece of plane part, fabric, or some kind of debris. When they said it was a 757, I looked out across the debris field. I said, "There is no way there is a 757 scattered here."

At that time, we didn't know that it was in the hole. The jet fuel smell was really strong, and it was eerily quiet. It was really unnerving and surreal.

I had initially walked down into the woods to survey the area. There were plane parts hanging in the trees. You couldn't see them right away. You had to kind of stand there and look for a little bit to pick them out.

The dirt was kind of piled up on the one side, and there was a hole. It was only six or eight feet deep. It wasn't any bigger than an office. It looked like it fit in a strip-mining job. There was a little bit of smoke coming out of the hole. There was some debris in the hole, and the jet fuel was puddled in different places. There were a couple of spot fires in the trees. The fire departments had handled a lot of them until I got there. The snags and clumps of brush were still burning. But there wasn't much fire.

The biggest piece of debris I saw would have probably fit in my pocket. I knew, with the size of the debris, that there weren't going to be survivors.

I called our EMA Center with the GPS coordinates. Then we started setting up a command post and getting organized.

Roger Bailey was the Second Lieutenant with the Somerset Volunteer Fire Department and arrived with the second wave of firefighters. He was asked to walk the extent of the debris field and report back to his Assistant Chief, Jim Clark, and the State Police.

Bailey: We started down through the debris field. I saw pieces of fiberglass, pieces of airplane, pop rivets, and mail. I guess there was 5,000 pounds of mail on board. Mail was scattered everywhere.

I didn't think about it at the time, but probably thirty feet from the crater was a piece of foam rubber out of a seat cushion. It looked perfect. It wasn't even burnt. We were walking down through there, and the one guy who was with us almost stepped on a piece of human remains. I grabbed him, and he got about half-woozy over it. So I said, "Maybe you better go over there and keep people out."

Sean Ibinson and I actually walked the whole debris field. We walked straight to see how far it went. It went a long ways, maybe two miles. We kept finding pieces of a gray type of sheeting that they put over the airplane frame and then put the fiberglass over top of it. We saw white fiberglass, different colored pieces of fiberglass and mail. It seemed like every piece of mail that I looked at was from Blue Cross and Blue Shield.

We walked straight down through the debris field and up through the woods where there was a home. They were in the yard picking up stuff. I had orders when we left that it was a crime scene and that nobody was to touch anything. If we saw anybody picking anything up, we were to tell them to lay it down. If they refused, we were to call back, and they would have somebody come over and arrest them.

At one point, I turned around and looked at Sean and said, "Sean, we have got to be out of our minds."

He said, "What do you mean?"

"A hijacked airplane crashed in Pennsylvania. How do we know there isn't a biological weapon on board? How do we know that there isn't a chemical weapon on board? How do we know that two days from now, we aren't going to fall over dead? Here we are walking through this debris field without even a mask on."

We continued walking and saw more people. I said to everybody, "Everything you touched, lay it down and go wash your hands. Do not touch your mouth."

They all asked why.

I said, "As a precaution. We don't know what we are dealing with. Please wash your hands for your own safety."

We went through a little further, and there was a family in their yard, with kids picking things up. I explained to them about the danger and that this was a crime scene.

After about a mile, we walked up on top of a hill, and there was a farmer there with a four-wheeler. He said, "How far are you going?"

I said, "As far as there is debris."

"There's debris up to the next road."

"Are you kidding me?"

"No, jump on the back of my four-wheeler, I'll take you up."

So we did and he took us up. On the way he said, "There are a hundred people in the field up there picking up stuff."

I said. "Oh, no!"

We got up into the field, and there were all of these people coming down the road, picking things up. I radioed back and said to our chief, "There are all of these people here picking stuff up."

The State Police came on and said, "Where are you? I am sending an officer there now. This is a crime scene."

I told these people what he said, and they heard my radio. Some of them just dropped everything. Some of them just handed it to me. I didn't want to touch that stuff, but I carried it and gave it to one of the Fire Police that they had sent up there to help.

Chapter 6

A Crime Scene

The first PA State Police on the scene were Troopers Patrick Stewart, James Broderick and Joseph Grove. They happened to be patrolling nearby at the time of the crash. At the Somerset Barracks, Corporal Link continued to man the phone, while Sergeant Madigan and Corporal Bowman responded to the scene with more troopers.

Bowman: On the way up, we encountered some PennDOT workers. We told them to follow us. We knew that we were going to need as much help as we could get with traffic control. PennDOT was great. They followed us up and worked with us from the beginning.

We pulled in and passed this long row of fire trucks to the area of the debris field. It was just a large area of destruction. I got out, walked around and looked at this debris on the ground. I saw these small pieces of what I later learned was insulation. It resembled a honeycomb type of material. I was walking on that.

Until that point, I had never been to a large plane crash. I was thinking I should be seeing parts of planes, seats, etc. There was nothing that was recognizable to me as a plane.

Something else that I will never forget was the strong odor of burnt fuel. Just horrendous.

I walked over and there was this big hole in the ground. Paul Wilson, of the FBI, was saying that he had gotten information from the Johnstown Airport. I knew only commuters flew out of Johnstown. I was thinking that this couldn't be a commuter plane causing a hole like this. Then someone said it was a commercial airliner with as many as four hundred people on board. The feelings that were going through my mind when I heard that!

It still was amazing to me that this was all happening.

Madigan: My first thought at the site was, "Where is the plane crash?"

There was a hole in the ground, the trees were burnt and there was smoke everywhere. But when I looked at the pit, I didn't realize that was where the plane had crashed. I thought, at first, that it was a burn pit from the coal company.

Then one of the firemen said that this was where it went in. I was amazed because it did not in any way, shape, or form look like a plane crash. You think of a plane crash, you think you would see recognizable plane parts. But at the pit, there was nothing that looked like a plane. There were some parts in the trees in the wooded area. But they weren't very big parts. I think the biggest part they found was maybe a four or five foot section of the fuselage. Everything else was pretty well disintegrated.

Link: Another thing I remember vividly about that day was a female caller who said, "There's a woman about 150 yards in front of the impact site where the plane went down! She's still alive and she needs help!"

"How do you know that?"

"Well, I can hear her."

"Where do you live? Do you live out near the crash site?"

"No, no. I can just hear her yelling. She's yelling."

"Were you driving by? Did you have a cell? Did you stop to help?"

"No, no. I'm a psychic. I'm calling from California."

You talk about a range of emotions. I'm glad it was me and not someone else taking that call. If someone had done something like that to a family member of one of those victims, I can't imagine…

After determining that there were no survivors, the firefighters concentrated on extinguishing small fires and assisting the Pennsylvania State Police. The FBI assumed jurisdiction since air piracy is a federal crime. The local fire chiefs, PSP commanders, EMA personnel and local FBI agents huddled to develop a plan to bring some order to the site.

Madigan: We told the troopers that we were going to treat this as a crime scene. We told the fire companies that we were going to keep one or two of their units handy in case any fires flared up. Then we just tried to move people back. Because, right at that point, we were all standing in the middle of it. We wanted to get everybody back from the scene itself and secure the perimeter.

The FBI was there soon after Corporal Bowman and I got there. It was Arnie Bernard from the Johnstown office. I remember seeing him walking around taking notes. Air piracy is a federal crime. That is why they were involved from the beginning. It was obvious from the beginning that this was a terrorist act. I don't know who notified the FBI, but the first agents were there soon after the incident occurred. Then, of course, they brought in more agents from across the country.

Soon after we were there, we realized that we were going to need a command post. I think it was Lieutenant Weaver who made that determination. So somebody, I don't remember who it was, went up to the coal company building up there. It was not being used or being used very little. They were gracious enough to let us come in and take it over. As it turned out, that was a perfect location for a command post. It was close to the scene. We took that over for three weeks or so. We got up there first, then Rick Lohr's County Emergency Management people came and started coordinating the recovery.

The first few hours seemed like constant phone calls. My cell phone was one of the few that worked up there at the beginning, so I was getting phone calls from Harrisburg and from the commissioner's office and everywhere else. But after the FBI got there, magically, all the cell phones seemed to work.

The main roads around the command center determined the outer perimeter. We wanted to make sure that no one would park along the road and walk through the woods to the site. PennDOT was very helpful. They showed up at the scene soon after the crash and put up roadblocks and signs.

We got the map out and determined which roads would be the outer perimeter. Then we stationed troopers at the intersections. As more troopers came in, they relieved PennDOT. We put them every hundred yards or couple hundred yards around the scene.

We determined that an inner perimeter was necessary. I don't know who made the determination of how far it went. I think it was a joint determination of our people and the FBI. So inside the wooded area, where those cabins were, we had a second perimeter, right at the outer limit of the debris field. That determined the crash site.

Bowman: I went back and got in the Lieutenant's car and started to take care of the radio. That is where your breakdown occurs, communications. We had a lot of phone calls coming in from our command staff, other stations wanting to know where to go and so forth. I stayed in that role until evening when our command post arrived from Harrisburg. They set up and assumed communication responsibility.

The way our radio system works, we have several radio channels that we can utilize. I had to go to a channel called mobile-to-mobile so that Greensburg station, Somerset station, the helicopters and our cars on the road could hear me. We don't use mobile-to-mobile often, because we are being broadcast everywhere, but, because of the magnitude of this crisis, we had to.

Fortunately, I had some instruction on how to do this. You go to an incident command center where you have one car at the scene. All communications go through that car. I took it upon myself to assume the incident command at the scene. As a result, I had Greensburg calling me, Somerset calling me, and the helicopter was calling me. I was calling the helicopters. Incoming cars were saying, "Hey, we are coming up Route 30. How do we get to you?"

I had a notepad and a county map open in front of me.

At the same time, we were trying to formulate some type of a rough perimeter. The command staff officers were trying to organize; they were looking at the big picture. Some of the guys from the Somerset station and I were looking at the little picture. Let's get this thing secured the best we can with the limited number of troopers we have. Then, as more people come, we can fill them in and expand.

I was extremely busy at the radio. It would have been easy to lose track of who was calling and how many people we had coming and so forth. At the same time, I was trying to keep contact with my boss, to make sure I wasn't making decisions that I wasn't supposed to be making. I made the decisions that I was comfortable with and the others I would check with him. He was usually within earshot. That is how we did it. Sort of orderly chaos.

We all knew what our goal was. But we had people who didn't know the terrain, and we didn't know how big this debris field was. The more we heard from troopers on the radio, the bigger it got.

During this whole time, I am worried about my family. I am thinking, how many more planes are going to fall out of the sky? Is this related to terrorism? Maybe. Maybe not. I remember hearing a report that there were six planes unaccounted for. My kids were in Berlin in school. My wife was at home. I was wondering to myself, do they need to be assured that this is just an isolated case? Was it an isolated case? I think that I tried to reassure myself. I was thinking they were targeting populated areas. Yet, why did one crash here in a field?

Terry Wilson was a criminal investigator with the Pennsylvania State Police. He lived in Shanksville, and his three children attended school there. Several years before, he worked the USAir Flight 427 crash near Pittsburgh. All aboard were killed.

Wilson: Gary Boyer and I came in from the Buckstown Road. As soon as we cleared the woods, I saw the first fire truck. I know most of the firemen. There were two or three of them standing there.

I said, "What is going on?"

They said, "The crash is back there a little ways."

So Gary and I started walking back. As we were walking back, we started to see the debris. We got back to where the power line went up through, and we could see the firemen in the woods putting out the fires. I was looking down, and the debris was getting bigger. Then we started to see human remains.

I worked Flight 427. I was up there the very first day, and I worked until it was cleaned up. I saw the remains coming out, the Ziplock bags, the whole bit. So I knew how this was going to be once I saw how the crash site looked. I said to Gary, "Man, this is just like Pittsburgh."

We walked up through the field, and there was a fireman standing there with a hose. I said, "Where is the crash site?"

He looked behind him. We looked behind him. All we could see was this black hole.

There was an access road that came down almost to the crash site. We walked up to it, and that is where Paul Wilson, Arnie Bernard and the guys from the FBI were. Craig Bowman and Sergeant Madigan were there from our barracks. They were all standing there, trying to decide what to do.

We were trying to take all of this in. It was just so amazing. About that time, Gary looked up on the hill. There was a dragline up there. We could see media crews setting up. The FBI wanted to get a perimeter set up because it was a crime scene. Gary said, "Let's get our car and go up there and get all of those people out."

So we did.

From that dragline, we could look down and see everything. The whole valley. Gary said, "You know, this is a good place. We ought to just stay here. Let's see if they will just let us stay here for our security assignment."

I told Gary, "We don't want any detail where we are going to be in the woods camping."

Trooper Mark Hogan grew up on Long Island. His family features a long line of New York City police and firefighters. One cousin was a lieutenant with the New York Fire Department and had just received a promotion. He was scheduled to receive his new equipment at Governor's Island in New York Harbor on September 11, 2001.

Trooper Hogan worked that morning dressed in coveralls, conducting truck inspections at the Somerset interchange of the Pennsylvania Turnpike. While inspecting a vehicle, he overheard a radio news report about the World Trade Center.

Hogan: I was hurrying up, trying to get the report done. I knew, with something like this, we were all going to be called back to the barracks. Just before I was ready to leave, we got the call for all cars to report back to the station, "Code #3."

When you get Code #3, something big is happening.

So I got back, still in my coveralls and my ball cap. The other truck inspector was there, Jack Baker. He said, "Put the street uniform on. We have to hit the road."

We got all of our stuff. We signed out shotguns. We got riot helmets, batons, and extra gloves. We got ready to roll for whatever might happen.

There was some indecision about what we were going to do. It wasn't our area of responsibility. It is Troop A's. Our Sergeant and our Lieutenant were already up there at the site. We wanted to do something, but we had to wait for orders. Then we got the call to establish some security areas. Some of us went to cover the interchanges. Some of us went to the tunnels. No one knew what to think. What are we going to do now? Is this the start of a war? Is this an isolated terrorist act? Everybody was on edge. We went out to patrol the tunnels, making sure no one tried to shut down the turnpike by shutting down the tunnels. We were listening to the news reports on the car AM/FM's. The anger was building.

We are the State Police. We are not the militia, but all of a sudden, it felt like the front lines. They didn't train me for this in the academy. They gave me a riot baton and told me how to handle riots. They didn't tell me how to handle a war.

All across the United States, police responded to the attacks by guarding potential targets or investigating specific threats. In Maryland, a bomb threat to an airport used by the Air National Guard reached Baltimore County Police. Officer Ken Nacke prepared to respond with his explosives-detection dog. Nacke's regular canine partner of nine years had been euthanized the day before.

Nacke: My dad always taught me to prepare for the worst and hope for the best. In my job, I hold that close to my heart. On my locker room door, I had a picture of every family member: Mom and Dad, my kids and wife, my brothers and my one brother's wedding picture that had all of us in it. I went through that mental check in my head. Mom and Dad were okay; they were in Ocean City. Paula and Doug and her kids are okay; they're not flying. My wife and kids are at home. Dale's in Atlanta, and he's not flying. I thought to myself, Joey never flies for work. You can count on one hand the number of times he has flown for work. Good. I was counting my lucky stars that they were all okay.

Outside Shanksville, as the State Police and firefighters began to set perimeters, the first media personnel arrived on the scene. WJAC-TV, the NBC affiliate in Johnstown, Pennsylvania, sent two teams to the crash. Reporter Jon Meyer and video journalist J.D. Kirkpatrick responded in one van, while reporter Sherry Stalley and video journalist Keith Hoffer traveled in another. In the confusion, only Jon Meyer got to the impact site while Hoffer was able to film the smoking crater. Hoffer's shots became the best video record of the initial crash scene.

Meyer: As I was leaving for work, I was thinking that we were relatively safe here because we live in central Pennsylvania. My family lives in a rural area. I had some relatives and friends in more populated areas that I was concerned about. I was thinking that this was going to be an interesting day to watch the national news, but we were not going to be doing much here except for local reaction.

I went to work thinking, "What is next? What city is going to get hit next?"

I walked in the door at 10 a.m. and went to watch a little bit more of the TV coverage about New York and Washington. That is when we got a call at the station that a big plane had crashed near Shanksville. One of our photographers, J.D. Kirkpatrick, and I jumped into our van and headed out to Shanksville. Our station is about 20 miles from where the plane actually crashed.

Driving out there, I was wondering why a plane crashed in Somerset County. I could understand New York and Washington, but why here? I was also thinking that this was just too coincidental not to be related.

I was also wondering to myself what I was going to see when I got out there. I had a mental picture of a broken up fuselage and maybe survivors coming out of it. I was thinking that we were going to have to help them first and then cover the story. The more I thought about it, the more I didn't know if I was ready for what I was going to see there.

Hoffer: I had the same reservations. [Nodding.]

Meyer: We pulled onto Skyline Drive and followed the emergency crews as they were going in. We stopped at the top of the hill there. I started running ahead of J.D. He went back to get his camera. I ran over the top of the hill and really couldn't see anything except this large field. There was a spot at the end where the emergency crews were gathering. I could see that it was smoking and burning a little bit. So I ran as fast as I could towards that.

I ran right up to the crater and was right there, standing a few feet away, looking into it. I was overwhelmed by the crater's depth and size, but there was nothing that I could identify as having been an airplane, except that there was this incredibly strong smell of jet fuel.

I went up on top of a mound that overlooked the crater and got out a little notebook. I started writing down everything that I saw. This was a big story, and I needed to remember everything that I saw. My adrenaline was pumping so much that I was afraid that I wouldn't remember it all.

I am six foot six and was standing on top of a ten-foot mound. It wasn't very difficult to spot me. The next thing I knew, I was surrounded by firefighters and police, telling me that I had to get out of there.

Later, when I looked back at my notebook, every word that I wrote was unreadable or spelled wrong. That shows how much my adrenaline was pumping at that point.

Once they pushed me back, I was about 150 yards away, where they decided to set up the first media barricade. The photographers hadn't made it past the barricade. I think I was the only one that got through.

At that point, we did a few eyewitness interviews of people that had arrived and then went up to our truck and started doing live phone reports. We were trying to set up a signal so that we could do a live report with video. About the time we had the signal established, the police came up again, surrounded us, and told us we had to move back even further.

We moved to a hillside nearby, where we could still overlook the crash site. They said that we would be fine there. I did a few reports there with the other reporter from our station, Sherry Stally. As soon as we were off the air, we were surrounded by police cars again. They were telling us that this was now a crime scene and we had to get out of there. We pleaded with them to let us stay for another few minutes to finish feeding our video and to go back on the air and say that we had to move back or be arrested and that we would bring more live reports as soon as we could. That was when we went over to what became the media staging area.

By then, other stations were starting to arrive from Pittsburgh and Altoona. Nobody was allowed in as far as we had been. There was no more opportunity to video the crash site or any of the efforts that we had been able to see before. We just had to wait for the FBI or the State Police to come out and give us what information they could. That was the way it stayed for the rest of the first day.

Hoffer: I was with Sherry Stally. Jon was with J.D.

Meyer: They got there right after I did.

Hoffer: We came in from the opposite direction. We pulled up within probably 75 yards of the crater, and I got about two or three good shots off before the State Police got to us and moved us back out.

Chapter 7

'If it's happening in Somerset ...'

John Peters, a big man with an incisive, dry wit, has a tendency to say what others are thinking but are afraid to verbalize. John is a geologist by training but has worked for many years with the Somerset County Planning Commission. He lived with his wife and two teenage sons in Friedens.

John and his co-workers were listening to the day's events on a radio in the Somerset County office building. They had no idea that next door, in the basement of the County Courthouse, the 911 Center was coordinating the initial phases of a disaster response.

Peters: We have little cubicles. I had my radio on WDVE. They didn't bother to interrupt the song; but right after, they said that there had been an accident at the World Trade Center. A plane had flown into the building. So, at that point in time, we figured that some dumb ass with a little Piper Cub had gotten disoriented and flew his plane into the building, and that was it.

Then they came on and said that it was a larger plane and that they would keep us updated, which they didn't. So we turned it to NBC. While they were telling us that this was an accident, the second plane flew into the second Tower. We started to think it wasn't an accident.

We all sort of forgot about where we were and what we were doing, and that became the focus of the day. The next plane was the Pentagon. So then we were starting to get a little nervous.

The guy in the cubicle beside me said, "Maybe living in the middle of nowhere does have some advantages because at least we are pretty safe here."

It wasn't too much later that Tom Brokaw reported to the world that, "Authorities at the Somerset County Airport have announced that a plane went down near Shanksville."

Up until that point, when they were talking about Somerset, we thought Somerset, New Jersey. Everyone just kind of looked at each other and wondered if planes were just going to start randomly falling out of the sky. Everybody got on the phone to see where their family members were.

Dennis Kashurba, a licensed psychologist, was on his way to work at the Children's Aid Home in Somerset. The Children's Aid Home began as an orphanage and foundling home in the 1800's. It grew to serve the mental health needs of children from many counties across Pennsylvania. Kashurba listened to the day's events on the radio of his car while pumping gas.

Dennis Kashurba: That's when I heard that a plane was down in Somerset County. Talk about shock!

I was just totally shocked at how incorrect my assumptions had been that we were safe here, a tremendous contrast to my initial feelings when I heard about the first plane. It was a reminder of just how human we all are. How we can be correct about something, but there are so many things beyond our control that we could not possibly have considered. So in Somerset, the chances of involvement in a terrorism attack, you probably couldn't put odds on it.

I went over to the Aid Home where, of course, the TV was on. That bunch of kids was also captivated by what was unfolding on TV. I saw the first Tower collapse. I was thinking that we have this mammoth structure that is built supposedly to withstand the force of a 747. How can that occur? It was that combination of intellectually being befuddled and emotionally having that sick feeling in the pit of my stomach.

I talked with some of the Aid Home workers whose family members lived or worked in the area where the plane went down. I tried to be of some comfort to them at that time of ultimate uncertainty.

I reflected later on the randomness of it all. It reminded me how some of the guys that I had gone to school with had died in Vietnam. There was no way of knowing who, when, or how, in those circumstances. It didn't matter how good of a soldier you were. Just like it didn't matter how good of a person the people in the World Trade Center or on Flight 93 were. It was the total randomness of it. We like to figure that we have a large amount of control in our lives. Something like this certainly makes us question that.

I just felt bad for the families of those people. I didn't know them and, in all likelihood, I wouldn't ever meet them. I knew a little bit about how those families must have felt. I knew that from having been with so many families in so many other tragic situations over the years. When you're with them though, you are still lost for words.

Christine Piper was working in Somerset at CME Engineering. Her two daughters, Brooke and Nicholle, attended Shanksville-Stonycreek School. Brooke heard the school gymnasium shake when the plane crashed. Nicholle, on the other side of the school, was unaware anything had happened. Christine's sister, Hope Neiderhiser, was home getting ready for work.

Piper: I was working. I was putting together an accounting spreadsheet at CME. We heard the sirens go off. One of the guys in the office is a fireman and has a scanner. At that point, there were supposedly three or four other planes down real close in Latrobe and Indiana [PA] and by Indian Lake.

When I heard that all of these planes were down, my friend Jamie called Shanksville School. Of course, the phone was busy. We knew about New York and Washington. So I just panicked. My sister lives in our guest cottage on our farm. She was less than five miles from the school, my husband thirty, and I was ten. So I called her right away on her cell phone and said, "Hope, go get the kids!"

At that point, we weren't sure of anything. Even on the scanner they said something like, "A plane is down in Shanksville, all medical personnel in Somerset County report to the site. Be prepared to resuscitate."

Right away, in my mind, that is meaning terrorists or whoever survived the crash. Hope and I just panicked. She got to their school in three or four minutes. She just went in and grabbed the kids and scared Nicholle to death. Nicholle was sure there was a death in the family or something. They all went back to my house and called me.

I guess it took her five or six times trying to call me until she could get through to tell me she got the kids.

Neiderhiser: I went up and turned onto Route 160 because I thought it would be quicker. They had already closed off Lambertsville Road. I was ready to go through a field.

I kept thinking at that time, what if they had to land the plane and there were still terrorists in control? What if they wanted to hit something on the ground? What is there in Shanksville? There is a school and that is just about it. I just kept thinking that if they were going to hit something, they were going to hit the school. So I was pretty nervous driving to Shanksville.

I went and got Nicholle and Brooke. They were scared, mostly because of the look on my face. They were panicking because they thought something bad had happened to some family member. When we got in the car, I explained what was happening. I was kind of freaking out too because I kept thinking, if it's happening in Somerset, it's happening in every small town across America.

Penny Reiman continued her work in the radiology department at Somerset Hospital.

Reiman: I have three children: eleven, seventeen and twenty. My twenty-year-old was working in Berlin. When the plane crashed, the guys at work said, "It's in Shanksville. You've got to go."

So he went. When he heard terrorists, the first thing he thought about was his brother and sister. He said he was going to take a gun with him. Fortunately, he didn't do that. He went to the school and walked in the office and said, "I want Greg and Kelly excused right now. They are to go to their grandmother's and not move until they hear from me."

Shortly after that, the school made an announcement over the local radio and TV stations that no one from Shanksville would be excused to anyone except a parent. Then he went and he checked on his other grandma and made sure she was okay.

Pennsylvania State Senator Richard Kasunic had represented Somerset County since 1994. He was familiar with Somerset County disasters. In June 1998, he drove into Salisbury as the tornadoes approached. He spent that night huddled in the school with many of his constituents. On September 11, 2001, Senator Kasunic was in Alaska on a hunting trip.

Kasunic: We left the main lodge and went out further into the bush. We had just been dropped off. Camp had already been set up. I was talking with the gentleman who would be guiding me. We heard the gentleman who just dropped me off coming back. We were wondering what he forgot.

He got out and was crying; just sobbing. He said that America had been attacked. He didn't have any details because all he had was one of those satellite telephones, and it wasn't very darn good. All he knew was that he had gotten into his track vehicle and was heading back to the lodge when he called his wife. She was crying hysterically. The best that he could get from her was our nation was under attack and we were at war. He didn't have a whole lot of details.

He was crying and we were caught up in the moment, too. The three of us were there crying and wondering what is going on. Then he further explained to me, "And I thought I ought to come back here to tell you because something happened in Pennsylvania, also."

You know, I am getting chills now talking to you about it.

He said, "A plane went down or was shot down or something happened around a town called Jonestown."

I said, "Jonestown or Johnstown?"

Immediately my heart really started pumping. I was afraid of what the answer was going to be.

He said, "Yes. Johnstown. That's it. Johnstown."

My heart just sank. My knees were like rubber. Something came over me that I had never experienced. What was I going to do? I was in Alaska and the crash was in Pennsylvania. I said, "That is my district. What can we do? I can't stay here. You have got to get me out of here."

Fenna Queer had worked for United Airlines for thirteen years. She had flown from Pittsburgh to UAL headquarters in Chicago on the morning of September 11. She was trying to find a way back home since all planes had been grounded.

Queer: I was standing in the lobby. There was a lady from our SAT Team [Special Assistance Team] who ran out to her car and came back with a big road atlas. There was a gentleman standing beside me. She said to him, "I don't know how I am going to find Johnstown."

I said, "Johnstown?"

"Yeah, do you know where it is?"

"Johnstown, Pennsylvania? Oh, I can show you that."

So I opened the map and showed her where it was.

"What is the closest airport?"

"Well, you have Pittsburgh here. Johnstown has a small airport, and Harrisburg."

"Okay."

"What is going on there?"

"We have a plane down there, we think."

That is how I found out. Then I was really anxious to get home.

Holly MacKenzie was a flight attendant for United Airlines. Her husband, Gregg, was a pilot with American Airlines. Holly had just returned to their home at Hidden Valley Resort after taking their four daughters to school in Somerset. Gregg was supposed to be flying into New York's JFK Airport from London that morning.

MacKenzie: I turned on the TV. I saw the World Trade Center on fire and watched 175 hit the second Tower. I got a call saying that the first airplane that went into the Trade Center was American Airlines. My husband was in the air at the time, on his way back from London. I was thinking that he was too far out. He could not have been in New York because he wasn't due in until 10:50 a.m., and this was like 8:45 a.m.

A few minutes later, I got another call saying that it was United that went into the second Trade Center. I was thinking that this was just impossible. This could not be happening.

I had this doctor's appointment to go to. I was thinking that I was just going to continue my life and go to the doctor. I was driving, and my cell phone was ringing continuously. People were asking me where I was. Why was I not at home? Why wasn't I getting my kids from school?

Then on the radio they said that an airplane had gone into the Pentagon, as well. I was starting to panic. I was thinking, "Where is Gregg?"

So I started calling his cell phone frantically and just kept getting his voice mail. Then my phone rang again and it was a friend of mine from Hidden Valley. She said that there was an airplane down in Somerset. I turned around right there because all I could think of was that Somerset is small and I have kids in school.

I kept listening to the radio. They were saying it was United Airlines that had gone down in Somerset. They originally said it was a 747. We have a 747 that does a Cleveland turn out of Chicago.

I was thinking how that flight is typically full with four hundred people. Then they were saying it could be a 767. We had a 767 inbound to New York.

At that point, I didn't know who it was. I didn't know where it went down, but I knew I had to get home. I called my girlfriend back and said, "Send your husband for my children now!"

Finally, I got home and turned on the TV. I was staring at the TV, still thinking that this was impossible. I called my girlfriend and told her that I would be over to get my kids. But I couldn't move from the couch.

My phone rang. It was Gregg's cell phone. I couldn't hear him and then it dropped. I hung up, and I was thinking, "All right, he's okay."

The next thing I heard on television was about all of these cell phone calls that came from Flight 93 and the other flights. So I didn't know that he was okay because I couldn't hear him.

I started frantically calling him again, thinking that he was calling from the air. I couldn't get through. At that point, I just completely lost it. I couldn't find Gregg, and I didn't know who all I knew on the United flights that had already crashed.

I felt like an airplane had crashed in my heart. [Stops to recompose herself.]

Chapter 8

What If

At 9:52 a.m., Lynne Cheney joined her husband in the underground bunker complex beneath the White House. The Vice President talked by a secure telephone with President Bush, who spoke from Air Force One on a runway in Lakeland, Florida. Due to the instability of the situation, Mr. Cheney advised the President not to return immediately to Washington from Florida. A reluctant President Bush agreed. Shortly after the call, Air Force One made a very fast and very steep takeoff to a high altitude. The destination of the executive jet was to be determined in the air.

Laura Bush had been escorted to a secure location outside Washington. She had gone to the Capitol Building that morning to address a congressional committee regarding early childhood education. Bush was met at the Capitol by her husband's nemesis, Massachusetts Democratic Senator Ted Kennedy. The First Lady and Senator Kennedy agreed to postpone the hearings due to the attacks. Bush waited in Kennedy's office, along with New Hampshire Republican Senator Gregg Judd, until the First Lady's Secret Service detail evacuated her to a safe house. The Capitol Building was hastily evacuated at 9:48 a.m.

Larry Eickhoff was piloting a plane for FedEx when the FAA ordered all aircraft in the US to land. His wife, Jeannie, watched the day's events at their home in Yorktown, Virginia. Their sixteen-year-old daughter, Nicole, had just started her second day at work as a House page in the Capitol Building. Pages attend school from 6:00 to 10:00 a.m. and then work in Congress until their House adjourns for the day. They live in dormitories near the Capitol.

Larry: I was flying, and they forced us to land close to Memphis. I've been flying for a lot of years and for me to hear, "US airspace is closed..."

I said, "What do you mean, 'US airspace is closed'?"

Then I heard something about airplanes crashing into buildings in New York City. So, we were all eager to get down on the ground. We were down in time to watch the Towers fall.

Jeannie: We hadn't heard from our daughter. We both thought, "Surely Congress has a plan. They have a bunker or something like that."

Then we found out what the plan was…

Larry: They just told all the pages and everyone else to run for their lives. They all took off.

Nicole Eickhoff, Patrick MacDonald, Julia Owen and Tyler Rogers were Congressional pages for the House of Representatives.

MacDonald: We started school early that day because Congress was supposed to come into session at 10:00 a.m. We had to be at work by 9:00 a.m.

I was scheduled to go to Annex 2, which is a building a couple of blocks from the Capitol. You have to wait for a shuttle. So, I was standing right outside the Capitol with two other pages, Chris Harrington and Eric LaLue. We heard this very loud explosion.

We looked across the river, and I saw the blackest smoke I had ever seen. We knew what was going on in New York, and we all looked at each other, with terror on our faces. We didn't say anything. We wanted to be in denial. I was thinking, "Please don't tell me that this has anything to do with what's going on in New York. It's a house fire, a structural fire, a construction accident, whatever."

A minute later, the press, who were camped out on Capitol Hill that day like every day, ran over to where we were. They're yelling to their cameramen, "Get this on film! Get this on film!"

We heard them screaming on their cell phones, "Pentagon, Pentagon!"

We were still hoping it's not a big deal and there wasn't anything really wrong. Maybe the Pentagon was giving a news briefing. Then some reporter looked over at me and said, "You know, I don't think I want to be standing next to this building. If they want to hit anything, they're going to want to hit this."

We were still trying to process all this, and it didn't make sense. Well, it made sense, but it wasn't supposed to be happening.

What prompted the evacuation of the Capitol was a lot of low-flying planes, because everything just got so screwed up trying to land the planes that day. Many large, commercial planes were flying directly over the Capitol. There was a big one that came over us; it was very low, like it was on a direct approach. Planes aren't supposed to fly over there. We looked up; it was moving really slow. The Capitol Hill police officers were looking up, too, and they just started running. They yelled to us, "Get away from the building! Get away from the building!"

We evacuated, and I don't think I ever ran that fast before. I don't remember what happened from the time we were told to get away from the Capitol until I got to our dorms about three blocks away. I thought that plane was going to hit the Capitol, like, now. You're just going on instinct and thinking stuff in your head like, find a ditch, so that when it does plunge into the building, you won't get hit by debris. I was thinking that stuff until I finally got to our dorm.

We still didn't know what was going on when we got there. There was chaos; 30,000 people who work on Capitol Hill hitting the streets, talking on their cell phones, being confused...

Nicole Eickhoff: I remember being so happy and excited that morning. It was my first real day of work, and I had memorized all of the faces and names, and where they were from. I came in and, I was like, "Hello, Congressman Portman. How are you? Congressman blah, blah, blah..." I was trying to be very professional.

I worked in the Cloak Room. In the Capitol they have two Houses, obviously, and on the floor of the House of Representatives there are two L-shaped rooms in the back where you can go and get refreshments, smoke or whatever. They are called Cloak Rooms.

I was upset when I saw the plane crash into the World Trade Center on television, especially since my father is a pilot. I was automatically thinking of my father. I was worried.

We didn't hear anything from the explosion at the Pentagon. We were inside the Capitol, inside a room with a bunch of people eating, bustling around and making phone calls. When we got the news that we were being evacuated, I went out onto the House Floor.

I remember the men's faces. They were scared. It was just as moving as seeing your father frightened. That put a lot of fear into my heart. I started moving faster.

I remember them pushing me in the back, just pushing me toward the exit, like, "Little girl, you get out first."

They had this protective kind of feeling.

As soon as I got outside, I could see the smoke. I didn't know what to do. I heard some other pages saying our instructions were to go home.

I remember running and saw my friend, Jennifer Shay. She was a Flag Page that day. She had this big crate on rollers with a huge box of flags that she was rolling down the street. She couldn't imagine leaving American flags in the street. She had seen panic before on newscasts, and she knew people would steal them.

She had the peace of mind to take this huge cart down the road. I ran by her and asked if she needed help. She looked at me with her big, expressive eyes and said, "No."

I kept running until I was back at the dorm.

Owen: In my Algebra II class that day, we had a word problem that still chills me today. It was… "In 1945 a plane crashed into the Empire State Building. Using this formula, how long did it take for the falling debris to hit the ground?"

Honestly. That was the word problem for the day in my Algebra II class.

We got out of school around 9:00 and walked across First Street to the Capitol Building. The sky was so blue. That whole morning, I just kept commenting on what a beautiful day it was.

We got to work and were there for just a few moments when Tyler came out of the House Cloak Room and said that a plane had crashed into the World Trade Center. We stood there in the Cloak Room and watched TV. It was scary and a horrible accident, but it really didn't hit home. I didn't actually feel threatened in any way.

Then the Pages' Supervisor came in and said, "I think everything is going to be fine, but there are rumors that a plane crashed into the Pentagon and there are fires on the National Mall."

When the actual reports confirmed that something happened at the Pentagon, I immediately got incredibly upset and worried. I thought I had to get out of the Capitol. I couldn't help but think that something horrible was going to happen. We were in a very public building and we weren't safe.

As soon as one of our supervisors told us to go home, my friend Robert and I were the first to leave. We literally ran out the door and down the stairs. We got outside, and I realized all hell had broken loose. The beautiful day I kept commenting on had been transformed into flashing lights and sirens and people running hysterically and Capitol police officers yelling expletives to get out of the building. There were fire trucks and emergency responder vehicles all heading west toward the Pentagon. You could look up in the distance and see the smoke.

I didn't know what was going on. I didn't know if there were other buildings being targeted. My dad worked for the Department of Energy. He had a lot of meetings at the Pentagon. He used to work there. I didn't know whether something happened to him. There were so many rumors: State Department bombed, fires on the Mall, government buildings destroyed. The rumors were running wild.

Robert and I ran down the street toward the page dorm. I fell and skinned my knee. Robert had to pick me up and help me. It was chaos everywhere. It was very clear that something was terribly wrong.

Robert and I were the first ones back to the dorm because of my paranoia and my urgency to leave immediately. I ran upstairs to my bedroom and turned on my TV. We didn't have cable so I was adjusting the bunny ears, but everything was scratchy. I couldn't understand what they were saying.

I turned off the TV, picked up the phone and there was no dial tone. Then I tried again and got a dial tone, so I tried calling my dad in his government building. They said all circuits were busy.

I was freaked out. I was convinced he was dead. I don't know why. I called my home in Annapolis and got the answering machine and left a hysterical message for my mother saying that I was okay but I was afraid Dad was dead. I called a very close family friend and got the answering machine. I don't think I left a message.

Then I called my grandmother in Annapolis. When she heard my voice and heard I was okay, she started bawling hysterically. She told me that she was sure Dad would be okay. She told me she loved me and God was with me and, you know, things grandmothers say to you. She said she would call my mother and the rest of the family.

Seventy-five years old. She really had her act together and was taking care of everything.

I went downstairs, and other pages were filtering in. I remember seeing Tyler coming down the sidewalk and exchanging a glance with him, like, "What's happened?"

He looked up, saw me and shook his head. Some people were crying, some telling jokes, you know, what human beings do to deal with something like that.

Rogers: I was in the Cloak Room that day.

There are these clocks with bells situated around the Capitol that ring to tell you what's happening on the floor. Built into the clocks from 9 to 3, there are 6 lights. Three bells ring, then it will light up and that will mean that we're adjourning or whatever.

One of the codes is '12 bells' which is a civil defense warning. No one knew what that meant. We were not trained about it. So, when they made the decision to evacuate the Capitol, our supervisor rang the 12 bells. We really didn't know what to do.

We went to the basement of the Capitol to get our bags, and we started running. The Capitol Hill police officers told us to take it easy. I went out on the west side of the Capitol, which faces the Mall.

I had been watching CNN earlier. On the ticker there were reports of fires on the Mall, so I expected to go out and see all that. I didn't see any fires. We walked down the steps of the Capitol, and right when we got there, other Capitol police officers started yelling at us to go faster. One yelled that there was another plane on the way. We just started sprinting.

That was when I saw the first fire truck go by. I remember all the officers, other pages and Jennifer Shay with all the flags.

I remember looking back over my shoulders, expecting to see a jet crashing into the Capitol.

But, luckily it didn't, thanks to other people's actions.

Conflicting information about other possible hijackings or unidentified planes continued to reach the national military structure. One concern was of a possible hijacked plane from JFK headed toward Washington. Another flight deemed threatening, although with little specific evidence, was Delta Airlines 1989. The Boston to Las Vegas 767 seemed to fit the profile of two of the hijacked flights: transcontinental 767's departing Logan airport early that morning.

At 9:41 a.m., the FAA reported to NORAD that Delta 1989 might be hijacked. Fighter jets scrambled from bases in Ohio and Michigan to find the jetliner. The 767's pilot aborted the flight over western Ohio, turned to the east and landed in Cleveland.

FAA / NORAD COOPERATION PLAN ON 9/11/2001

The last hijacking in US airspace was a 1993 Frankfurt to Cairo Lufthansa Flight that landed at JFK airport in New York.

Scenarios of aircraft being used to deliver weapons of mass destruction had been considered by NORAD. However, cruise missiles were thought to be of much greater potential concern.

In the event of a hijacking, commercial pilots were to notify air traffic control by voice or a code 7500 transponder message. FAA controllers were to report a hijacking up their multiple layer chain-of-command. The FAA hijack coordinator was to contact the Pentagon's National Military Command Center (NMCC). NMCC was to request from the Secretary of Defense (SECDEF) approval of military assistance in the hijacking. With SECDEF approval, NORAD was to issue orders for jets to scramble, find the plane and monitor from a distance of 5 miles.

No provision existed for a hijacked airliner that would attempt to disappear by turning off its transponder.

No provision existed for a suicide hijacking.

Order to shoot down a commercial jet had to come from the President.

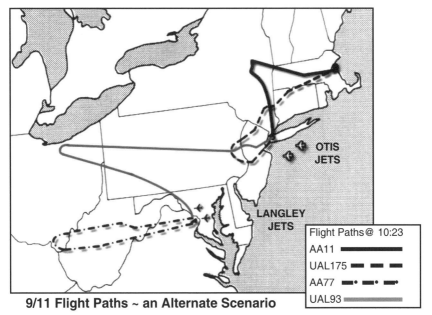

Flight Paths @ 10:23	
AA11	▬▬▬▬
UAL175	▬ ▬ ▬
AA77	▬∙ ▬∙ ▬∙
UAL93	▬▬▬▬

9/11 Flight Paths ~ an Alternate Scenario

Shortly after Flight 93 was confirmed hijacked, Cleveland Tower asked FAA superiors if NORAD should be informed of the Flight 93 hijacking. The *9/11 Commission Report* indicates no such notification occurred. The military did not know Flight 93 was a possible hijack until 10:03, the time that it crashed. The National Military Command Center in the Pentagon first heard that Flight 93 was hijacked from the White House Secret Service. The Secret Service had learned about Flight 93 from its own communication with FAA officials.

By 10:10 a.m., the Langley NORAD fighters arrived over Washington. These fighters were originally scrambled to protect Washington from AA11, which had already crashed in New York but was reported to be heading toward Washington. When AA77 crashed into the Pentagon, the Langley NORAD jets were 150 miles east of Washington over the Atlantic. The pilots were ordered to Washington when AA77 roared toward the nation's capitol. When the Langley fighters finally appeared over Washington, they were issued distinct orders not to fire on any aircraft in the area.

Reports of aircraft approaching Washington continued to reach the White House. One of the reports was of the eminent approach of a jet, presumably Flight 93, which had already crashed. A confusing series of discussions eventually led to 'shoot-down authority' orders. Those orders were not communicated to NORAD until 10:31 a.m..

If the passenger revolt had not caused Flight 93 to be crashed at 10:03 a.m., the plane would have arrived over Washington between 10:13 and 10:23 a.m. The military has asserted that NORAD jets would have been able to bring down the 757 if it had not crashed. *The 9/11 Commission Report* seriously questions this contention.

The 9/11 Commissioners point out that the earliest the Langley fighters could have learned of Flight 93 was at 10:07 a.m. They would have had only six to 16 minutes to take out the airliner. However, the pilots were unaware that the threat was a commercial jet. Some thought the smoking Pentagon had been hit by a cruise missile. In addition, NORAD had not yet located UAL 93.

Finally, there were no orders yet communicated to shoot down a commercial airliner. The shoot-down order from the President to the Vice President did not make it to NORAD until after Flight 93 would have arrived over Washington. Someone else in the chain of command, unauthorized to do so, would have had to give the order for the US military to destroy a US commercial aircraft with passengers onboard. The fighter pilots involved would have had to execute this highly unusual order with little time for confirmation.

If the passenger revolt had not brought down Flight 93, the 'best case scenario' would have been that the NORAD fighters would have intercepted and shot down the massive jet over the densely populated Washington-Baltimore metropolis. The resulting rain of thousands of tons of debris might have killed hundreds and certainly would have brought a demoralizing end to the day of hijackings.

A far worse scenario would have seen the destruction of the US Capitol Building, White House or another national landmark accompanied by many casualties.

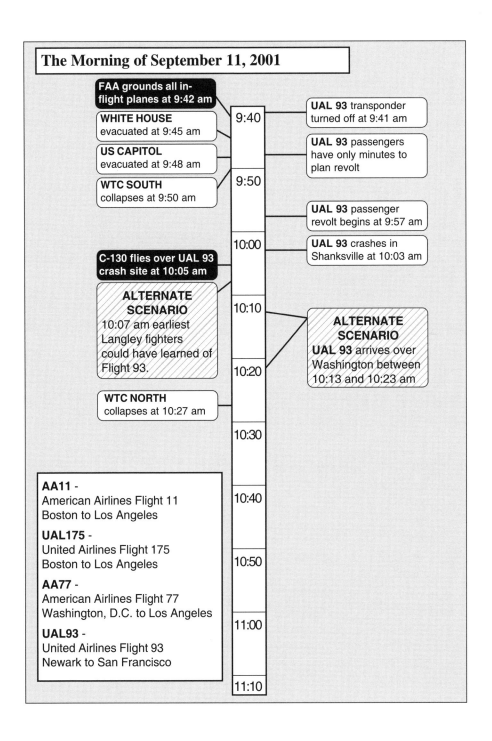

The Morning of September 11, 2001

FAA grounds all in-flight planes at 9:42 am

WHITE HOUSE evacuated at 9:45 am

US CAPITOL evacuated at 9:48 am

WTC SOUTH collapses at 9:50 am

C-130 flies over UAL 93 crash site at 10:05 am

ALTERNATE SCENARIO 10:07 am earliest Langley fighters could have learned of Flight 93.

WTC NORTH collapses at 10:27 am

UAL 93 transponder turned off at 9:41 am

UAL 93 passengers have only minutes to plan revolt

UAL 93 passenger revolt begins at 9:57 am

UAL 93 crashes in Shanksville at 10:03 am

ALTERNATE SCENARIO UAL 93 arrives over Washington between 10:13 and 10:23 am

9:40
9:50
10:00
10:10
10:20
10:30
10:40
10:50
11:00
11:10

AA11 -
American Airlines Flight 11
Boston to Los Angeles

UAL175 -
United Airlines Flight 175
Boston to Los Angeles

AA77 -
American Airlines Flight 77
Washington, D.C. to Los Angeles

UAL93 -
United Airlines Flight 93
Newark to San Francisco

Chapter 9

Taking Command

At 10:45 a.m., the Langley NORAD jets circling Washington were joined by other planes authorized to shoot down aircraft. The 113th wing of the District of Columbia Air National Guard contacted the Secret Service about protection from further attacks on Washington and was ordered to scramble fighter jets. By this time, however, all four of the hijacked jets had crashed.

The two groups of military aircraft with conflicting orders circled Washington as the Otis fighters patrolled New York. Soon, fighter jets could be seen above other major US cities. The confusion in the sky mirrored the confusion on the ground at the three crash sites.

In Pennsylvania, within a short time of the crash, few land or cell calls were able to penetrate the overloaded phone lines into Somerset County. State and federal officials improvised ways to contact county officials for more information.

From his Harrisburg office, Pennsylvania Attorney General Mike Fisher tried unsuccessfully to phone county officials. He eventually managed to contact Somerset County District Attorney Jerry Spangler by email.

Benedict Vinzani Jr., PhD, manager of Somerset Borough, received calls and emails seeking more information.

Vinzani: On September 11, 2001, the plane often was reported to have crashed in Somerset, Pennsylvania. Actually, the plane crashed approximately six miles outside of the borough. However, people began to call or otherwise contact us because they were concerned that the plane had crashed right here in the borough.

Probably the most chilling communication that I remember was an email from the Pennsylvania State Association of Boroughs, which read, "To anybody in Somerset, if you are still here and can respond to this email, please let us know how you are doing."

Even telling you this right now gives me goose bumps.

In the Commonwealth of Pennsylvania, the Lieutenant Governor oversees statewide emergency management. The Emergency Operations Center outside Harrisburg alerted Lieutenant Governor Mark Schweiker when the first plane hit the World Trade Center.

Schweiker: I was in the eastern part of the state on the Pennsylvania Turnpike. The first order of business was for both the Governor and me to return to the Emergency Operations Center (EOC) outside of Harrisburg. My car was already moving northbound on the northeast extension so the decision was to go to the helipad at the Bethlehem Barracks of the Pennsylvania State Police for my return to the EOC.

I first heard about Flight 93 while traveling at top speed in the left lane of the northbound Turnpike. I had two responses. First, it was gut-wrenching emotion. I thought of the size of airliners and the prospect of 300 passengers falling to their death. The other involved my predecessor, Mark Singel. After finishing our debriefing session during the transition back in '94, Mark said, "Good working with you. Only the best for you and Tom."

Then he added casually, "Listen, hope and pray that you never have to deal with a plane crash."

He had dealt with the USAir 427 crash in Pittsburgh.

In a short period of time, what had been a sunny Tuesday morning turned into a hellish stretch of weeks that didn't slow down until I left office in January 2003.

The Somerset County Commissioners, along with County Solicitor Dan Rullo, were scheduled to start their weekly meeting at 10:30 a.m. Their agenda included the typical items regularly discussed in a rural county of 70,000 residents. They convened quickly and moved to authorize any emergency expenditure of county funds to deal with the reported plane crash near Shanksville.

While the commissioners met upstairs in the county courthouse, EMA received confirmation from first responders at the site that there were no survivors. EMA Director Rick Lohr received a call from the Cambria County 911 Center to contact Cleveland Tower. Lohr learned from the FAA that the plane was a United Airlines Boeing 757 with as many as 400 people aboard. Lohr communicated this information to Bill Baker at the site.

People across Somerset County learned of the crash from the media or word-of-mouth reports. The news interrupted a meeting of pastors at Trinity Lutheran Church in Somerset. Among those attending the meeting were Pastor Ed DeVore of Friedens Lutheran Church and Pastor Robert Way.

Pastor Way had only recently been ordained and started his first assignment with the Good Shepherd Lutheran Ministry. He pastored St. Paul's in Buckstown and St. Mark's in Shanksville.

Way: When I found out about what had happened, I jumped in my car and headed toward Shanksville.

My son was in high school at the time in Johnstown. They were watching the events on television. When it came over the TV that a plane had crashed in Shanksville, he thought I was dead. All he knew was that I had gone to work that day in the office at Shanksville. I wasn't able to get through to my family until sometime early that afternoon. I felt bad that I didn't get through immediately. I never realized that they would think that I was killed.

I spoke to one of my secretaries on the telephone who told me of some parishioners that live near the crash. I checked first on one of our older members, who is in her late eighties with a lot of medical problems. Her property basically borders the field where the plane crashed. I met with her and we prayed. That is when I saw the first television coverage of what had happened. Actually, I didn't even have the radio on driving from Somerset to Shanksville. Don't ask me why; I just didn't.

I headed to the next family's home. They had the plane go down about a quarter mile away. They could look out the back door and see debris and smell jet fuel burning. They also had a family member who was in the military and were upset because they knew what was going to happen next.

I headed toward Skyline Drive. I didn't realize that I couldn't get through because that was exactly where the plane went down. When I got to the first intersection, there were Fire Police who had it blocked off. They were directing people back away from the site. However, they approached me, I guess, because I had clerics on. They said that they were looking for clergy at the crash site and would I mind going down?

To be honest with you, I didn't really want to go down. But I parked my car and began to walk down the road toward the crater.

Maybe a quarter of a mile down the road, a whole load of firefighters was coming back up on a truck. They said, "Pastor, you are not going to be allowed down there. They are not letting anybody else in. The FBI is pulling the plug."

It was an odd combination of feelings. There was some relief, and there was this determination that I was supposed to continue down there and do what I was sent to do. However, of course, it became obvious that the FBI had, in fact, "pulled the plug."

Soon after, Wells Morrison arrived on the scene to take command of the crash site for the FBI.

Morrison: One of the first really recognizable things that I saw as I walked towards the crater area was an open Bible. It was weird. Ironic. Sad. But it was lying there on the road.

Major Szupinka and I proceeded to the crater area, and the thought that kept going through my mind was, "Where is the plane?"

I didn't have an appreciation for things we learned later about the speed and the impact.

Right after the crash, there were probably four or five of us there, the guys from Johnstown and a couple of us from here. I contacted our Pittsburgh office. I started telling them what I believed we needed in the way of resources.

Of course, this crime scene was different from a lot of crime scenes, and it was different from the USAir crash of 1994. In that crash, there was a question about the cause of the crash. Was it sabotaged? Was it a mechanical problem? Was it pilot error? So it was a different animal in 1994 because the NTSB has standing if it is anything other than a criminal act. The FBI has the jurisdiction if it is a criminal act, particularly a terrorist act. At the USAir crash, it wasn't known, so we worked with the NTSB, but they really had the lead in that investigation.

In this investigation, we felt certain that it was an act of terrorism related to the New York and Washington, D.C. events. We immediately started thinking more along the lines of a criminal investigation, a crime scene versus a crash site.

By the time Morrison took command, most of the fire companies had already pulled out. Shanksville VFD Assistant Chief Rick King was joined by Chief Terry Shaffer, Deputy Chief Steve Yoder and several others who left work when news of the crash spread over the airwaves.

Yoder: When I got out there, the first person I saw was Rick. I asked him, "What's up?"

He said, "There is nothing here."

"Where is the plane?"

"There is no plane."

That is when the State Police were starting to move people back out of the way. As soon as they decided where the command center was going to be, Terry and Rick moved up there, and I took over fire ground operations down at the crash site itself.

While the FBI, the State Police, local fire chiefs and EMA tried to bring order to the site, Rick Lohr, Director of Somerset County EMA, continued to coordinate the disaster response from the Courthouse.

Lohr: Once everybody knew what had happened, I started getting calls from people offering all sorts of things. My first call out was to FEMA Harrisburg, who I answer to. They are actually PEMA, Pennsylvania Emergency Management Agency. It starts with the Federal Emergency Management Agency (FEMA), then the state, then the county, then the local. Later on that morning, I got a call from Lieutenant Governor Mark Schweiker. In Pennsylvania, the Lieutenant Governor is ultimately in charge of Emergency Management. Mark and I know each other pretty well, so it was, "How you doing? If you need anything, you know where to call."

I got another call from him early in the afternoon with a status report of what was going on throughout the state.

Our biggest thing at that point was starting to make calls to get resources coordinated. In an aircraft-down situation of this magnitude that is not considered a criminal act, PEMA and the county EMA would be in charge of the incident action. In this case, because it was a criminal act, the FBI was in charge. So we answered to the FBI. Our role in this was to help with the recovery by coordinating resources and manpower. We set up our operation at the command center and started coordinating resources.

The State Police set up the perimeter around the crash site. When I got there, Bill tried to get me in, but he couldn't. I didn't reach the actual site of the plane crash for two and a half weeks, when the FBI left and the site was turned over to the county coroner.

After witnessing the last seconds of the flight of UAL 93, Terry Butler decided to leave Stoystown Auto Wreckers and go home to recompose himself.

Butler: I came back and all of the news media was there waiting for me. WJAC from Johnstown, they were there first. They did an interview live from right there in the yard. Later, they had CNN, they had everybody, everybody. I don't know who all was there.

They were just all bunched around, and I just stood there. It was weird. Scary. It was scary because they had the big mikes that they can hold and point at you. It was just… [Trails off.]

Mayor Lichty returned to his Indian Lake Borough office from the crash site and began fielding calls.

Lichty: I had a couple of the news media calling me, saying that they had heard that there were remnants of the plane in Indian Lake. At that time, I hadn't received any report from anybody around the lake about that.

However, later that day, I started getting calls from people who were finding things like charred seatbelts, ledger sheets, papers, and lighter things like that. I called, and of course, the FBI came in and closed everything off into a crime scene. I also told them about what my wife and I heard going over the house prior to the crash. You have to understand that Flight 93 came from the west and did not come over my house. I don't know what we heard.

There were rumors that Flight 93 was shot down. I was at the crash site within fifteen minutes. If it were shot down, there would have been debris spread over a much wider area. The debris was confined to where it crashed, forward of that in the trees, and down wind here at Indian Lake.

The media reports of the Flight 93 crash did not reach everyone across the county, even some with a vital interest in what had just happened.

Despite flying an American Airlines Airbus into New York's JFK International Airport, Gregg MacKenzie knew nothing of what had happened in New York or a few miles away from his wife, Holly, and their four daughters in Somerset.

Gregg: I was finishing the second leg of my usual run. We were coming back from London, and we just passed Bangor, Maine. At that point, we had been aloft for almost eight hours. Generally, we are the first flight back in the morning. It was very quiet and a beautiful morning.

We were approaching Boston, which was actually in sight. We got a call from Air Traffic Control at the New York Center. They said, "American Flight 115. All of the New York Airports are closed. You need to find another place to land. We have a report that an airplane has hit the World Trade Center."

We were tired and blurry-eyed because we had been up since midnight eastern time. So it took a second to sink in. We were shocked. It was a beautiful, clear morning. It was surreal.

They didn't really elaborate, but our first instinct was that somebody in a small airplane had crashed into the Trade Center. There is a VFR Corridor that comes down the Hudson River. Private pilots can use that. They come in at

1,500 feet or something like that. We thought that some idiot in a small plane was sight seeing and flew into the Trade Center. So our initial reaction was that it was bad, but not that bad.

Boston was the natural choice of where to land. I was unaware that the whole thing had started in Boston. So I called our dispatch center in Fort Worth, and they were very reticent to give us much information.

I thought it was very odd. In fact, I was a bit upset because, in retrospect, it would have been nice to have a little information. At this point, I was still unaware that it was a terrorist thing. I guess it occurred to us, but not really. Things were happening so quickly.

So I just came back to them and said we would land in Boston. I think they told us to land once we got onto the approach. We began to notice that there was no one else out there. There was no one in the sky. No one on the radio. It would be like driving out of Pittsburgh on the parkway at rush hour on Friday evening and not seeing one single car.

It was spooky. It was like an Outer Limits episode or something. I think we both were beginning to get a very creepy feeling. But we didn't have a lot of time to talk because we were busy.

So we landed in Boston. It was dead quiet; no one was moving. It was beginning to sink in that something was very unusual. We attached it to the gate, parked the brake and shut the engines down. We have automatic direction finders, which work on the AM frequency band. I tuned in to WBZ, Boston, 1030 AM. Immediately, I heard about American Airlines Flight 11. I thought, "Oh, my God!"

The American people came on the airplane. They ushered us off and into the terminal. That is when we got all of the information. Those were Boston crewmembers that had gone into the Trade Center. So, things there were in an awful state. All of the employees were crying.

Apparently, one of the flight attendants on Flight 11 had just phoned one of the girls in operations and was speaking to her when they went into the Trade Center. She was practically catatonic. There were photographers and news people everywhere. They were saying that other things were still happening.

At that point, we didn't know what was going on. It was raining airplanes for all we knew. After they ushered us into operations, we sat there for about an hour. They found us a hotel. Once we got to the Sheraton at Copley Plaza, we went out and had a drink. Again, it was very odd that things were so quiet in Boston. No airplanes. The only thing you could hear was an occasional F-15 go by. That is an unusual sound. An F-15 doesn't sound like any other airplane. Everybody was in shock.

I called my wife from the airport. It was hard to get through on a cell phone, but I talked to her. I didn't know that the airplane had landed in

Shanksville, which was probably a good thing. I heard "Pennsylvania," and I thought, "What are the chances?"

When I talked to Holly, the first thing she said was that the kids were okay. Then she said that a plane landed in Shanksville.

I was thinking, this is… [Stops and shakes his head.]

Holly: I went over to my friend's house. They are a USAir couple. Her husband was sitting there bawling. This was just more than anybody could believe. I gathered my kids up and took them home.

I spent the rest of the afternoon watching TV and yet wanting to shield my kids from it. But I couldn't shield them because they knew. They were scared to death, and they were saying to me, "So you are going to quit your job, right? And daddy is going to quit his job? How is daddy going to get home from Boston?"

I couldn't sort anything out.

A USAir jetliner trailed Gregg MacKenzie's Airbus by several hours over the Atlantic from England. Ed and Nancy Root, a couple from eastern Pennsylvania, were on that plane after a vacation and business trip.

Ed Root: Well, we never got home because, halfway over the Atlantic, they rerouted our plane without telling us. I even asked a flight attendant. "You haven't handed out customs cards, yet."

She was real quick and made up some story, "Yeah, they gave us the wrong cards; they were in German."

I don't think they wanted to alarm everyone and get everyone upset by telling us what was going on. We never knew anything until we were about to land in Gatwick; that's when they told us that there was a security problem with airspace in the States.

We got a little bit more information when they said there was an attack in New York and Washington, and for a short period of time, I thought it was a nuclear attack. I really did. Our son works in New York so we had about fifteen minutes of stark terror because we had no idea what was really going on.

In Gatwick, I was able to contact my daughter, Emily, and she told us our son, Derek, was okay. He actually saw the second plane go into the Tower. After the first one hit, he and some of his co-workers went up to the roof of their building, and they were there when the second plane hit. He ended up walking to a ferry and taking that home hours later.

Our daughter didn't tell us about Lorraine then. She waited until we were back at the hotel. I guess she didn't want to tell us when we were standing in the airport. So, it was maybe an hour or two after that.

I never thought anything of Lorraine because she had no business being anywhere near Pittsburgh, and she didn't fly that often. She worked a few trips a month as a flight attendant.

We were in total shock. We just looked at each other and literally did not even react to my cousin's death on Flight 93.

In Baltimore County, Officer Ken Nacke had just emerged from a building where he had conducted a bomb search.

Nacke: When we search a building, we turn off all of the radio equipment, including our cell phones. You don't want to hurt yourself by having the equipment set off the device.

After sweeping the building and making it clear, we came back to our truck. I got my radio equipment and turned my phone on. Thirty seconds after it was turned on, my cell started ringing. It was my wife, who was hysterical. "Dad just called, and he thinks that Joey was on one of the planes that crashed."

I went straight to denial. "No. Can't be. He never flies."

I asked if one of the airlines had called Mom or Dad, and she said no. I asked if Amy, Joey's wife, had talked to anybody, and she said no.

I stayed in denial.

As the day went on, I was unable to get through to my parents. When I got to a computer, I checked the two airports closest to where he lived, Philadelphia and Newark. I knew what airline he was flying because Dad learned that information and gave it to my wife earlier. I tracked the two flights that he could have taken and found that one got diverted out of Newark. I didn't know if it was his flight.

I called United and spoke to someone who said they were not giving identifying information out. They were just trying to get a list of family members. They said they would call back. But, as the day went on, I got that feeling that something had happened.

They actually called my parents around 6:00 at night and told them that Joey was on Flight 93.

Near Adirondack State Park in New York, Gordon Felt was working at his summer camp for children with autism.

Felt: I had just come into my camp that morning and was doing our closedown for the summer. One of my maintenance men came over and said, "Are you listening to what's happening on the radio?"

I called my wife, and she brought up a TV so we could watch it unfold. I wasn't even thinking about my brother, Ed, at that point. I knew he was traveling that day, but those early reports mentioned a small aircraft going into the Trade Center.

Then we got a call from my sister-in-law, deeply concerned. She wasn't able to get in touch with my brother. I called his cell phone and left a message saying, "We're concerned. As soon as you touch down, call in and let us know what's going on."

69

Obviously, we never got that phone call.

The one call he made from the flight was to 911.

His wife, Sandy, got the call from United Airlines that he was on the plane and that the plane had gone down. She called and told me that Ed was gone.

I had to tell my mom. That was the hardest thing I've ever had to do. No parent should outlive his or her child, particularly when the child is murdered, and it is covered on national TV.

SEPTEMBER 11, 2001

Chapter 10

Creating Order

Seven Springs Mountain Resort is a large vacation community perched atop Laurel Mountain, 15 miles southwest of Somerset. Tens of thousands of skiers, golfers and convention conferees visit Seven Springs each year.

John Mates was the Director of Inside Operations on September 11, 2001. Kisa Valenti worked in the Sales Department.

Valenti: I got a call from Joe Marotta of United in the early afternoon. He wasn't sure what was going to happen, but he was looking for a site that would be secure for lodging some Flight 93 families. They were still trying to figure out what the best scenario would be.

His initial thought was to make the headquarters for United in Johnstown. He wanted to know if we would be able to give our facility exclusively to them. I explained that I didn't know what was going to be happening in the next few days, but it could not be exclusive. However, I explained that I thought we could handle most of their needs. I figured he didn't know the size and layout of Seven Springs.

He was thinking probably thirty some rooms for the families, plus his staff that would be staying here. But at that initial call, he was thinking that a lot of their staff would be staying in Johnstown. He was in Chicago, and at that point, United was working on special clearance to get a plane out. I told him we weren't their closest lodging facility if they were trying to get the families as close to the site as possible. Not that I was turning down business, but I just didn't think, being from Chicago, he realized how far away we were from the site.

He immediately said, "I know exactly where you are. We have everything right here in front of us."

They had already researched it. I said, "That's fine. You are going to need bus transportation to get your crew over here."

My immediate goal was to find out how many people and when they were coming. I knew we had to feed them. He didn't know if it would be five, seven, ten or fifteen days. So we were just flying by the seat of our pants.

The initial calls from the Chicago-based UAL Special Assistance Team (SAT) to Seven Springs represented one aspect of a standard response to an airplane crash in the United States. Congress mandates that the National Transportation Safety Board (NTSB) investigates all civil air disasters. Federal law also requires that the air carrier and the American Red Cross team to bring the victims' families to the site of the crash and attend to their needs. Although the unique circumstances of September 11, 2001 altered the usual chain of command at the crash sites, the Keystone Chapter of the Red Cross automatically began a formal response within 15 minutes of the Flight 93 crash.

Jack Humbertson, a three-decade volunteer, phoned Chapter Executive Director Janis Yingling at the Johnstown Headquarters. Humbertson, in addition to being chair of the Keystone Chapter's Disaster Committee, was also a volunteer firefighter. He learned of the crash within minutes and informed Yingling of the need to initiate a disaster response. Yingling, in turn, called Georgia Lehman, Director of Emergency Response. Lehman had traveled to central Pennsylvania that morning for a statewide conference. From this phone chain, the local Red Cross response began.

Marilyn Albright had been the Service Center director for the Salvation Army in Somerset for less than a year. She moved to Pennsylvania from St. Louis, where she had run a private, nonprofit food pantry. Albright received a call from her field representative, Chris Crowe, about the crash in Shanksville.

Albright: I went out there with Chris. I had gone to a training in August that was for a terrorist attack. There were hundreds of HAZMAT units, FEMA, PEMA, fire departments from all over. They used the vacant Greengate Mall in

Greensburg. I was still new, only a few months into working for Salvation Army. I followed some of the leaders, trying to learn as much as I could.

The main thing I learned was that you get down into the command area as close as you can because they usually try to hold us back. They don't consider us important enough. So our role is to get down in there as close as they will allow us and find out how many people are involved so that we can order enough food.

Firemen have all of this gear on. They need to replenish their fluids. So, through the years, we have always been there to help them with coffee, donuts, Gatorade, and all kinds of stuff. My field representative had never been to any kind of disaster, so he was saying, "Well, what did you learn at that training? What do we do?"

We were in a cornfield. We just parked the car. The next thing we know the crowd is multiplying around us. At first we figured 150. Then, within an hour or two, it multiplied into 300 people. I was wondering what all of those people were doing there? We went back and forth into the command post to find out how many people were there. They were starting to set up perimeters. The people that guarded the perimeters needed food. Chris called and made arrangements with the Salvation Army guy from Pittsburgh to get more people out to the site. He called the units that were closest. We had to have people twenty-four hours a day for the duration. We had to have staffing and scheduling of volunteers.

Later that first day, someone pointed at me and said, "You are in charge of food."

It was like 400 people three times a day.

I was scared.

Shanksville-Stonycreek School Superintendent Gary Singel learned of the Flight 93 crash while at a relative's funeral in Johnstown. The elementary and senior high principals supervised the initial response at the school. J.P. O'Connor and his fellow teachers watched their classes shrink in size as the day progressed.

O'Connor: Some parents were calling in. Others were coming into the building. They wanted to pick up their children. So many were picked up that, when we went back after lunch, the teachers got together and put the kids in one classroom. We decided to put in a movie, listen for their names and just keep dismissing until they were all gone. Most of the kids were out of there by probably somewhere between 1:00 and 1:30 p.m.

The kids who hadn't been picked up yet were all in one room watching *Free Willy*. They knew the situation was serious. They knew that all of their classmates were leaving. As far as any visible signs of anxiety, crying, or anything like that, there weren't any. I think the teachers were calm. We were just waiting for information as to how the day was going to play out.

Pastor Robert Way drove back to his office in Shanksville after being stopped from walking down to the crash site.

Way: I headed back into my office. I began to make phone calls to members to see how they were doing. I continued to try to have contact with these people regularly after that. Some, basically, were prisoners in their homes. They couldn't really go out and move the debris from their picnic tables, for instance. It was now evidence in a crime scene. They had to wait for the authorities to mark everything and take it away. If they did remove some things before the State Police and the FBI got there, they were supposed to put them in plastic bags and mark down where they found them.

After making some calls, I met with Pastor Ron Emerick of the United Methodist Church in Shanksville. He and I decided that we needed to arrange a prayer service.

Some time after that, I was able to get through to my home. My family was quite pleased to hear my voice. I apologized to them, explaining that I never even considered that they would have thought something happened to me.

I decided that I needed to do something a little bit more routine, so I walked back down to get the mail at the post office. In the process of walking to the post office, there were some kids sitting there. The kids had been excused from school, so they had been kind of milling around and gathering in small clumps here and there. I started talking to them and asking them how they were doing. Some of the kids knew who I was from church. Some I didn't know at all. They started asking questions about what was going to happen. Was this the start of World War III? Are we all going to die? Is this the end of the world?

I tried to reassure them the best I could. I told them that something terrible happened, but I did not feel that this was the end of the world or that their lives were threatened directly. I tried to explain that I thought that this was a misdirected flight and something had happened to bring it down here. At that point, nobody really knew what happened to crash Flight 93 near Shanksville.

There were two adults who were standing nearby where we were talking. They were paying close attention to the discussion. Before I left the kids, I told them that they could come talk to me if they felt the need to. As I was leaving, the two adults stopped me. They were a photographer and a reporter from *National Geographic*. They asked if they could do a brief interview with me. I don't know if that interview was ever used. They were respectful, but many of the other reporters were not.

As more and more State Troopers poured in from across west central Pennsylvania they established a double perimeter around the site. The inner perimeter contained most of the debris field. The outer secured the roads that broadly encircled the inner perimeter.

Members of the news media began to arrive within 30 minutes of the crash. As the crash site became a federal crime scene, they were moved further and further back. Immediately outside the outer perimeter established by the Pennsylvania State Police, they began to congregate off the last paved road leading to the site. Without any planning, this area rapidly developed into a several acre media village filled with reporters from around the world.

The company that had previously worked the mine still occupied some large metal buildings at the top of the hill overlooking the crash site. Somerset County EMA became the lead organization in building a command center around these buildings that would eventually host in excess of 2000 people a day. As more agencies arrived with their RV's and mobile command post trailers, local EMA staff arranged for their communication and power needs.

As more people flocked to the site, Marilyn Albright decided on a course of action to feed the site workers.

Albright: Well, I asked the media. I was telling everybody in the world that we needed sandwiches and pop. That was the wrong thing to do. Normally, what they do is they call a caterer and try to have uniform food service for everyone because it makes it easier to keep the food safe. You have to keep the hot food hot and the cold food cold or else you can get people sick.

Being inexperienced, I made the mistake of getting on the TV and saying we needed sandwiches, bottled water and pop. The next thing you know, we had a mountain of it that was overwhelming us.

It was good that we were getting it, but it got to the point where it was getting smashed. I was afraid it was going to rain. This stuff was starting to pile up way too much. We are supposed to have it all put away somewhere, but there was no place to put it until the disaster people got there the next day.

By afternoon it had become apparent that the plane that had crashed was Flight 93 with forty-four people onboard. It was also apparent that this plane was another terrorist-hijacked jet. What remained unclear, however, was why the crash occurred in this isolated location. No one at the site knew about the death struggle that had occurred just hours before in the skies above them.

Those at the site continued to be apprehensive regarding further terrorist attacks throughout the country and locally. Communications were very limited since the area was a dead spot for cell phones and the first responders all used different radio frequencies. The details of what was occurring in the rest of the country were unknown to most people at the site. Many had not even been able to contact their families until late that afternoon.

Sergeant Patrick Madigan continued to work at the site into the evening.

Madigan: With everything else on that first day, there was this strange incident. No one knew what all was going on in the world. It was rumored that eight or ten planes were hijacked and still missing. We were there at the site and an airplane started circling. It was a jetliner circling the crash site very low. It was so low you could see it was from United.

No one knew what to expect because we knew that all of the planes were supposedly grounded. People were starting to get pretty nervous. Everyone was looking and saying, "What is happening now?"

SEPTEMBER 11, 2001

Chapter 11

Night Falls

At 5:20 p.m. on September 11, 2001, the forty-seven-story skyscraper known as Building Number 7 of the World Trade Center Complex collapsed. Few people outside Manhattan noticed. Severely damaged in the attacks of the Twin Towers, Number 7 had already been evacuated, and no one was injured when it fell and added to the massive pile of rubble at the southern end of Manhattan.

In Washington, President Bush entered the White House at 6:54 p.m. Air Force One carried him to Washington from Offut Air Force Base (AFB) in Nebraska. The President had flown there from Barksdale AFB in Louisiana after the hasty and steep ascent from Florida. The First Lady had returned earlier to the Executive Mansion from her safe house. President Bush prepared for his 8:30 p.m. address to the nation.

Outside Shanksville, the United jetliner that Sergeant Madigan had seen repeatedly buzzing the crash site suddenly veered to the north. Onboard, Joe Marotta continued his series of phone conversations with Kisa Valenti and John Mates at Seven Springs.

Valenti: There were at least six or seven more calls between Joe and me that day. He called when he was getting ready to get on the plane, while in the plane, and when they were circling Johnstown. So we were pretty much in contact that whole time until they rolled in here about 9:00 p.m.

During the calls, Joe was passing around the phone because their plane trip was their organizational meeting. This woman was in charge of this, and this other woman was in charge of that. Now, it wasn't just Joe; I had all of these people.

This one lady gave me a shopping list over the phone. Toothbrushes, toothpaste, shaving cream, razors, contact lens stuff. Those people had literally

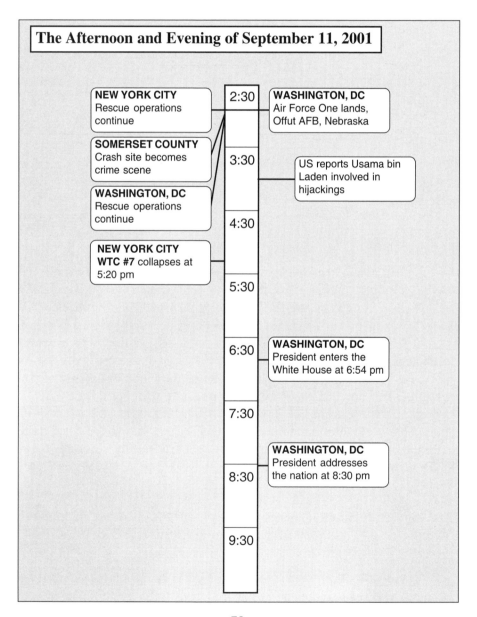

The Afternoon and Evening of September 11, 2001

NEW YORK CITY
Rescue operations continue

2:30

WASHINGTON, DC
Air Force One lands, Offut AFB, Nebraska

SOMERSET COUNTY
Crash site becomes crime scene

3:30

US reports Usama bin Laden involved in hijackings

WASHINGTON, DC
Rescue operations continue

4:30

NEW YORK CITY
WTC #7 collapses at 5:20 pm

5:30

6:30

WASHINGTON, DC
President enters the White House at 6:54 pm

7:30

WASHINGTON, DC
President addresses the nation at 8:30 pm

8:30

9:30

gotten up from their desks and boarded the plane. They didn't bring anything. These things were just to get them going for the next morning. They literally walked in, took a key, had ten minutes to go to the bathroom and went down to the meeting room. So we got that shopping list together, and Joe Cummins went out.

Mates: He was just hired as our human resource director. We told him to go to Wal-Mart, and he came back with all these big bags of stuff.

Valenti: They didn't have clothes, but they had the amenities that they needed to bathe and brush their teeth.

The community began to mobilize within hours of the crash. Somerset County businesses and individuals began to collect supplies for workers at the site.

Michelle Zarefoss taught kindergarten at Friedens Elementary. When the crash occurred in Shanksville, many media outlets reported that it happened near the Somerset County Airport. Zarefoss hurriedly contacted her husband who was in Nebraska on business to let him know she was safe.

Zarefoss: After school, I didn't really want to be at home with just my six-year-old son. So I went to my brother's restaurant. My brother, Jeff Latuch, owns the Chuckwagon Restaurant across from the Courthouse. The rest of my family was also in there. We were trying to figure out what we could do from the restaurant to help. We gave our names to people who were going to the site and told them, if they needed anything, we would come into the restaurant and cook.

We ended up that same night coming back and making sandwiches and things for Verizon. They were putting in lots of lines, and they needed food. So we went up to the site through all of the roadblocks, but we finally got their sandwiches and drinks to them.

The next day we went into the restaurant at 4:00 a.m. to make breakfast and took it out. You wanted to do something, but you didn't know what to do, so you tried anything that would help.

Other emotions began to surface in county residents such as John Peters of the Somerset County Planning Commission.

Peters: Once it became apparent that everyone was relatively safe and it didn't look like any more planes were going to fall from the sky, my emotions turned really quickly to a state of anger and rage that someone would have the audacity to do this to us. Also, anger that the government, our own government, was so complacent. People believed that no one would ever touch us. We were safe. Well, we were more vulnerable than we ever thought we were.

I remember feeling that the world changed forever that day. People made the analogy of Pearl Harbor, but that was a military base. This time they hit us right in our own backyard. I felt like I lived in Israel. Like I was going to see something similar to this each day on the nightly news, just like they do there.

Megan Evans moved to a farm outside Shanksville in the 1970's. She has a Master's of Social Work degree and worked as an educational consultant with Intermediate Unit 08 (IU-8). IU-8 provides specialized educational services and programs for Somerset, Bedford, Cambria and Blair County school districts.

During her time near Shanksville, she has seen her area de-electrify and go back in time as more and more adjoining farms have been bought by Amish families. Her farmhouse has become an important meeting point for the Amish. Her phone and freezer have become the Amish community's phone and freezer.

On September 11, she worked in Somerset. However, she received a detailed description of how her farmhouse rattled and shook from the Amish man who had entered her unlocked and unoccupied farmhouse to use the phone at the time of the crash.

Evans: That evening I was walking in the grove by the Shanksville School. There were helicopters overhead, so it was somewhat frightening. I took my grandson with me. I took the loop around, the usual route that I walk.

There was a panel truck that had pulled up. When I came out around the corner, my grandson was being interviewed. They were interviewing him without me present, talking to him about what he had thought occurred and photographing him. It felt scary.

In Shanksville, you saw television cameras or reporters standing on the corner. I was interested in who they selected to interview. I was dressed in professional clothing. I wouldn't be somebody they would select. They selected somebody that they thought represented Shanksville. So they looked for people who had a certain way of talking, a certain look, a ball cap or their idea of who lives in a rural area.

Americans watched the carnage on their TV screens, interrupted with international expressions of condolence or, alternatively, jubilation from certain parts of the world. British Prime Minister Tony Blair declared, "As for those that carried out these attacks, there are no adequate words of condemnation. Their barbarism will stand as their shame for all eternity."

Initial FBI follow-up of domestic leads about the hijackers matched the conclusions reached by the CIA from their international investigation. Americans had been attacked by a Middle Eastern terrorist organization. Americans commenced their education in a vocabulary of Arabic words and names such as jihad, fatwa, al Qaeda, and Usama bin Laden.

Patrick MacDonald, Nicole Eickhoff and the other Congressional pages received their own intelligence briefing.

Eickhoff: That night Congresswoman Wilson came up.

MacDonald: She was on the Intelligence Committee and had been at the Pentagon earlier that day.

Eickhoff: She said that some of her friends were injured and she didn't know where some of her family members were in New York.

She was frightened, but very strong. I remember she came to us and said, "You people are the beacons on the Hill."

Literally. "The Hill."

I remember thinking to myself of this responsibility, and thinking, I can't go home. I can't be afraid.

At 8:30 p.m., Americans sought solace and understanding from the President as he addressed the nation.

Later that evening, Somerset County residents began to hear reports of the death struggle that raged over their heads that morning. A list of the 40 non-terrorist passengers and crew was released.

Night fell on the site in the same surreal fashion that characterized the day. High intensity floodlights illuminated the crash site, while the surrounding forest was shrouded in blackness.

In those dark woods, State Troopers maintained an inner perimeter every 150 feet. They also maintained an outer perimeter on the roads around the site. The media village continued to grow as satellite trucks and reporters converged. The Salvation Army and Red Cross had already begun to feed the hundreds of people who were already at the site and prepare for the thousands who were expected the next day.

Jean Croyle was a freelance writer who helped obtain and deliver donations to the site workers. She first saw the site on Tuesday night.

Croyle: It was dark. There were lights all over this big, big field. I wasn't entirely familiar with the area, but you didn't need to be because there were signs telling you to stay back.

I was in shock. People were very willing to put an arm around another person and walk up to the point where you were allowed to walk. It was as though everybody knew they needed each other.

There was fear. I don't think anyone got the feeling that another plane was coming immediately but more that, all of a sudden, we were vulnerable to something we had never seen before.

We just all stood there and stared and wondered what those people went through. My heart ached as I thought how awful it was for them to have known that this was going to be it, in such an unknown place. In such a dark, big field.

Terry Butler returned to the site that night.

Butler: It was dark. I don't know how close to the site I was. It was an eerie thing because the fog was coming in. I just went out to take some supplies. They had to check me out up there, check my load.

I had supplies, like paper towels and bottled water. I just bought them. I figured it was the least I could do.

Address to the Nation by the President,
8:30 p.m., September 11, 2001

For Immediate Release
Office of the Press Secretary
September 11, 2001

Good evening. Today, our fellow citizens, our way of life, our very freedom came under attack in a series of deliberate and deadly terrorist acts. The victims were in airplanes, or in their offices; secretaries, businessmen and women, military and federal workers; moms and dads, friends and neighbors. Thousands of lives were suddenly ended by evil, despicable acts of terror.

The pictures of airplanes flying into buildings, fires burning, huge structures collapsing, have filled us with disbelief, terrible sadness, and a quiet, unyielding anger. These acts of mass murder were intended to frighten our nation into chaos and retreat. But they have failed; our country is strong.

A great people has been moved to defend a great nation. Terrorist attacks can shake the foundations of our biggest buildings, but they cannot touch the foundation of America. These acts shattered steel, but they cannot dent the steel of American resolve.

America was targeted for attack because we're the brightest beacon for freedom and opportunity in the world. And no one will keep that light from shining.

Today, our nation saw evil, the very worst of human nature. And we responded with the best of America – with the daring of our rescue workers, with the caring for strangers and neighbors who came to give blood and help in any way they could.

Immediately following the first attack, I implemented our government's emergency response plans. Our military is powerful, and it's prepared. Our emergency teams are working in New York City and Washington, D.C. to help with local rescue efforts.

Our first priority is to get help to those who have been injured, and to take every precaution to protect our citizens at home and around the world from further attacks.

The functions of our government continue without interruption. Federal agencies in Washington which had to be evacuated today are reopening for essential personnel tonight, and will be open for business tomorrow. Our financial institutions remain strong, and the American economy will be open for business, as well.

The search is underway for those who are behind these evil acts. I've directed the full resources of our intelligence and law enforcement communities to find those responsible and to bring them to justice. We will make no distinction between the terrorists who committed these acts and those who harbor them.

I appreciate so very much the members of Congress who have joined me in strongly condemning these attacks. And on behalf of the American people, I thank the many world leaders who have called to offer their condolences and assistance.

America and our friends and allies join with all those who want peace and security in the world, and we stand together to win the war against terrorism. Tonight, I ask for your prayers for all those who grieve, for the children whose worlds have been shattered, for all whose sense of safety and security has been threatened. And I pray they will be comforted by a power greater than any of us, spoken through the ages in Psalm 23: "Even though I walk through the valley of the shadow of death, I fear no evil, for You are with me."

This is a day when all Americans from every walk of life unite in our resolve for justice and peace. America has stood down enemies before, and we will do so this time. None of us will ever forget this day. Yet, we go forward to defend freedom and all that is good and just in our world.

Thank you. Good night, and God bless America.

THE AFTERMATH

Chapter 12

The Next Day

What had begun as a warm day on September 11, 2001 evolved into a cool night. A thick fog shrouded the area beyond the harshly illuminated impact site with a numbing peacefulness. For the rest of the week, that same fog would reappear each night and then be burned away by the rising sun to reveal a startling landscape.

Jon Meyer of WJAC-TV remained at the site throughout Tuesday and returned on Wednesday.

Meyer: I was there until about 11:00 p.m. I had to go back in the next morning at 3:30 a.m. I went back to Johnstown and didn't sleep at all that night. I hadn't seen anything of what happened in New York City after 10 a.m. because we were out covering the Shanksville site all day.

Someone had said that the World Trade Center collapsed. I pictured in my mind that, perhaps, the top fell off. When I got home, I couldn't believe what I saw. I couldn't go to sleep because I had this need to see what happened in the rest of the country. That is when the whole day hit me. It was so overwhelming. I never did fall asleep.

That first night when the 11th rolled into the 12th, I probably got back out to the site at about 4 a.m. A fog had rolled in, and there were all of these

State Troopers around on horseback. It was so quiet and peaceful. I had just watched all of the coverage of what happened on the 11th, and then I went out there and saw the peacefulness of that spot. A lot of people that I have talked to since have said that if this plane had to crash, this is one of the most tranquil places it could have gone down.

Jeremy Coughenour received some of the first calls reporting the crash to the Somerset County 911 Center. He was one of the many EMA staff to work overnight at the crash site.

Coughenour: I went in at midnight and relieved somebody, so I couldn't see anything. The next morning, it was just an unbelievable sight. Nothing was picked up, and they weren't doing any kind of recovery work yet. We went down to the crater. What struck me was that, for a plane that big, there were only fragments.

The State Police had a perimeter around the crater. They had light towers set up, and we were sent down to shut those light towers off. They put them on every night when it got dark to shine on the crater. That way it was lit up and they could watch so nobody could sneak in.

On the morning of September 12, 2001, the US woke to a nightmarish new reality. The nation reeled in shock and horror. Unknown thousands were dead. Smoke rose from the crumbled wreckage of a section of the Pentagon. The two tallest buildings in New York City lay collapsed upon themselves. Airplanes remained grounded. The stock exchanges did not open. Americans feared more attacks from an amorphous enemy that few understood.

In New York, rescue workers worked to free victims entombed alive in the enormous pile of smoldering rubble. Many families searched hospitals and morgues for loved ones who did not return home from work. The only reliable early figures on casualties from the World Trade Center attacks were the number of first responders who were lost. Those catastrophic totals vastly surpassed any event in United States history.

World Trade Center 9/11 First Responder Deaths	
New York Fire Department	343
Port Authority Police Department	37
New York Police Department	23
Total Lost	**403**

In Somerset County, residents helped to transform an abandoned strip job into a massive crime scene. Hundreds of reinforcements from outside the county continued to converge on the site. Some order had evolved from the chaos of the previous morning.

The initial perimeter established by State Police from the Somerset County Barracks, volunteer firefighters and PennDOT workers had become a double perimeter of troopers summoned from throughout the southwestern quarter of the state. The inner perimeter consisted of officers standing 150 feet apart around the primary debris field. This area became known as the hot zone. Soon, a decontamination (DECON) line was established to serve as the sole gateway to the hot zone. The outer perimeter consisted of troopers in cars, on horseback and on foot, lining the ten miles of roads that encircled the site.

Troopers Terry Wilson and Gary Boyer continued to help secure the crash site.

Wilson: The first day, we were right in front of this huge dragline. We looked at this boom. We thought it would be nice to hang a flag from the top.

Gary said, "I'll get the flag if you will climb it."

I said, "You get the flag and I'll do it."

So we found a piece of steel rod. The next day, when we went into the barracks, we got one of the flags. I climbed the boom the whole way up to the top and hung a flag up there. It is a real narrow stairwell and very steep the whole way up. When you get up to the very top of it, where that huge pulley is, there is a small platform. Then all I had to do was take wire ties and strap the pole to that.

From our vantage point, we could see crash site, everything to the left of it, everything to the right. You could see the workers when they came in their white suits. You could see the hill where the helicopters landed. You couldn't see any of the command center. Behind us was Route 30. We were there to maintain the security of the site. We could see people on the Buckstown Road. If a car parked up on Buckstown Road and people would try to enter through the woods, our job was to intercept them.

About the fourth day or so, it died down. They started to get the idea. Because they would walk the whole way in from Route 30, and then we would make them walk the whole way back. We were there from 6:00 a.m. until 8:00 p.m. There was no need to have anybody up there after dark because you couldn't see anything.

The area around the old mining buildings overlooking the site became the command center. Vehicles from various agencies began to congregate there. An improvised heliport occupied the top of the hill overlooking the command center, while a media village sprang up just outside the outer perimeter.

The National Transportation Safety Board (NTSB) is charged by Congress with the investigation of commercial air disasters. In the case of Flight 93, there was a presumption of air piracy from the beginning. As a result, the FBI headed the investigation and recovery efforts. FBI investigators converged on Somerset from Pennsylvania and several surrounding states. The FBI supplemented its investigative team with members of the Bureau of Alcohol, Tobacco and Firearms (ATF), NTSB and the Pennsylvania State Police.

The volunteer fire companies had extinguished most of the fires on September 11, 2001. However, hot spots continued to be a problem. When they would flair up, the Shanksville Volunteer Fire Department would be recalled to douse them. These firefighters also were required to perform other functions.

Terry Shaffer, Shanksville VFD Fire Chief, supervised his company's involvement.

Shaffer: The FBI was the incident commander, definitely. They called the shots on everything. You didn't do anything without their approval. But when it came down to fire level, they'd call me or call the station and say we need you to do this.

They had a briefing for all of the heads of the departments twice a day, in the morning and the afternoon. I attended the majority of them, and if I couldn't be there, either Rick King or Steve Yoder was there.

There would be twenty to thirty people sitting around long tables. They'd give us updates as far as what they had found that day, what they were going to be looking for, and how long they thought it would be. They'd go around the tables and ask if there were any issues with any of the departments, if there was anything we needed.

Rick Lohr and Bill Baker represented Somerset EMA at those briefings.

Baker: Rick and I were standing there the first time we met with the brass of the FBI, State Police and all of these other agencies. There we were in jeans and T-shirts. I was dirty because I hadn't been home or had a bath for I don't know how long. The FBI said that they were in charge and that we should all leave only our skeleton crews. They said they could handle it all themselves.

Rick and I were kind of bumping each other and wondering if they knew what they were in for. We told them that they had to have some decontamination and they were going to need people to do that. They said they could handle it.

They soon realized that they needed us.

The next day, we had Somerset Fire Department DECON team there to decontaminate their people.

While Somerset County residents responded to the crash of Flight 93, the US Government worked to respond to the terrorist attacks.

Nicole Eickhoff, Patrick MacDonald and the rest of the Congressional pages went to work in the Capitol Building.

Eickhoff: The next day, we went to school, and I asked our principal, "We're going to work today, aren't we?"

She said, "Of course. We'll see you at 9:00."

MacDonald: That day was the longest day ever. Literally.

Eickhoff: From 9:00 in the morning until 9:00 the next morning on the 13th. And we had already gone to school for 3 hours before that. We would take a couple hour-long naps on the couches in the back.

MacDonald: Congress was in session early because all 435 members wanted to get their remarks part of the record. That's understandable. Representative Heather Wilson told us the night before, "When we go to work tomorrow, we plan to sponsor a resolution condemning the attacks."

That's all well and good, but there was such a sense of helplessness. We're under attack. So many civilians just like us were murdered and here's what we're going to do. We're going to push papers that condemn the attacks, vote yes or no, and I wonder who's going to vote no on this. That was all we could do. But, then again, I also felt proud.

It was very eerie that morning going in because normally you don't have all the members of Congress there when we open up in the morning.

The Australian Prime Minister was there. We were scheduled to have a joint session of Congress with him that day. So the Speaker of the House says, "In light of what happened yesterday, we will not be having the joint session. The Australian Prime Minister is here and, on behalf of the people of Australia, he expresses their solidarity with America."

There were these one-minute speeches. I don't really remember any of them specifically, but they were moving and wonderful.

But to see these grown men. Not only were they grown men, they were leaders of our country. And they were scared. And crying. They had terror on their faces. It was not comforting at all. I felt nervous. And not only that, we were in a building that was a target.

I don't really know how to express that feeling that I had for about a week or two after 9/11. It came back periodically after I started getting over it. And I said it's so hard to express to people what terror does to you. To be in a building that you know can blow up any minute. A building that's marked as a terrorist's target.

The anxiety, knowing the building you are in could blow up. I don't know how to articulate it right now; but, I always tell people, you don't know what it was like unless you experienced it.

Eickhoff: Are they coming back for us? That was one of the questions.

MacDonald: We're not in a war zone. I mean, we are civilians; we're wearing ties, not uniforms.

Then you start asking the question, "Why do they want to kill us?"

It just didn't make sense. Why?

The 12th was very, very hard. I don't think I cried at all on 9/11, but I finally did after I read the resolution condemning the attacks.

I read it all the way through. It didn't get me until the last line, "Be it known that when this session of Congress adjourns, it adjourns in solidarity and with respect to all those who have lost their lives during this terrorist attack." Or something like that.

Then I lost it.

I broke down and cried. For some reason, that really got to me. It must have been a combination of being thankful to be alive, the enormity of the whole thing, and that there were so many people who were dead. So many moms, dads, kids, that didn't have that family member anymore. They were just like you and me. They just went to work that day. It wasn't a military installation. Even the Pentagon, lots of civilians work at the Pentagon. So, that was a hard, hard day. There was a sense of helplessness and a sense that our security was gone.

On September 12, President Bush met again, as he had after his speech the previous night, with his top security and military advisors. They continued to sort through the intelligence available to them.

All evidence pointed toward Usama bin Laden and al Qaeda as the perpetrators. Based in Afghanistan, they were protected by the extremist Taliban government. The Taliban was recognized and supported by their nuclear-armed neighbor, Pakistan. Primarily Muslim, Pakistan constantly faced off with its nuclear-armed, Hindu rival, India. A combination of delicate negotiations and overwhelming military force would be necessary to make good on the President's promise to punish the perpetrators and anyone who would protect them.

International diplomatic efforts began to yield dividends almost immediately. Article 5 of the North Atlantic Treaty Organization (NATO) Charter states that an attack against one member is an attack on the entire group of nations. For the first time in the 52-year history of NATO, the body's governing council voted to invoke Article 5.

Domestically, the FBI had already pursued numerous leads regarding the hijackers, who had not even bothered to use fictitious names. Working with the Immigration and Naturalization Service (INS), a total of 768 'special interest detainees' were identified. Some were already in custody. Of the total detainees, 539 were eventually deported or remanded to federal custody.

These detainees provided further leads and information regarding the hijackings. Perhaps more importantly, these actions may have prevented further attacks. Khalid Sheikh Mohammad, the mastermind of the 9/11 attacks, was captured by Pakistani forces eighteen months later. During his interrogation in May 2003, he conceded that the immigration dragnet and other initial government measures significantly impaired al Qaeda's operation within the United States after September 11, 2001.

Usama bin Laden and al Qaeda

1980 Usama bin Laden, 23, arrives in Afghanistan to join the war against occupying USSR. He was born the 17th of 57 children to a wealthy construction company owner. Bin Laden attended Abdul Aziz University in his homeland of Saudi Arabia.

1980's Bin Laden's combat experience was limited, but he helps develop the "Golden Chain" of funds from around the world to support the war against the Soviets. Bin Laden does not receive money from the US government.

1980's Bin Laden and Palestinian cleric Abdullah Azzam establish Mektab al Khidmat to recruit fighters for the Afghan war. Al Qaeda develops from this group.

1988 USSR agrees to withdraw from Afghanistan. Bin Laden and Azzam continue with financial and recruitment organizations for future operations.

11/24/89 Azzam and his two sons are blown up by a car bomb, the perpetrating group is uncertain. Bin Laden becomes the undisputed head of al Qaeda.

1990 Bin Laden continues operations in Afghanistan but moves back to Saudi Arabia.

8/90 Saddam Hussein's Iraqi Army invades Kuwait and Bin Laden offers Saudi Arabia his help to wage a guerilla war against Iraqi occupiers. When rebuffed, he becomes loudly critical of the Saudis for allowing the US military onto Saudi soil.

1991 The Saudis revoke Bin Laden's passport, but he flees the country to Sudan with help from a member of the royal family. The US-led coalition drives Iraqis from Kuwait.

1991 In Sudan, Bin Laden and al Qaeda help in the fight against African Christians and expand international connections to other militant Islamic organizations.

Usama bin Laden and al Qaeda, continued

1992   US troops land in Somalia. Al Qaeda works with other groups to develop a plan to push them out.

12/92   Two hotels used by US servicemen going to Somalia are bombed. Two non-Americans are killed. Al Qaeda's involvement is suspected.

2/26/93   The first World Trade Center bombing occurs. Six people are killed and 1,000 are injured. Al Qaeda is linked to the perpetrators, as well as to those who are plotting to blow up tunnels and other New York landmarks.

10/93   Two US Black Hawk helicopters are downed in Somalia. Al Qaeda training and support of assailants is suspected.

1994   US troops leave Somalia.

11/95   A car bomb kills five Americans and two Indians in Saudi Arabia. Al Qaeda's involvement is suspected.

6/95   There is an attempted assassination of Egypt's President Mubarak by the Egyptian Islamic Group, who are protected and aided in Sudan by al Qaeda. Resulting pressure by the US, Egypt and other countries on Sudan creates problems for Bin Laden and al Qaeda.

5/19/96   Bin Laden flees back to still-functioning camps in Afghanistan where fighting rages between warlords and other factions.

9/96   The Taliban takes over the Afghan capital of Kabul and establishes control over much of nation. Bin Laden and Taliban forge an agreement to allow al Qaeda to continue operations with support from the Afghan government.

1996-
9/11/2001   Al Qaeda camps in Afghanistan train 10,000 to 20,000 terrorists for militant Islamic movements around the world.

6/96   Massive truck bombing of the Khobar Towers apartments in Dhahran, Saudi Arabia kills 19 Americans, with 372 wounded. The Saudi Hezbollah group, supported by the Iranian government, is responsible and al Qaeda involvement is suspected.

3/97   A Bin Laden interview is aired on CNN.

Usama bin Laden and al Qaeda, continued

2/98   In a London Arabic newspaper, Bin Laden and four other non-clerical militants issue a fatwa (an edict interpreting Islamic law, reserved for respected clerics), calling for indiscriminant killing of Americans anywhere in the world.

5/98   Bin Laden explains his reasoning for the declaration of war against the US in an ABC-TV interview from Afghanistan.

8/9/98   Massive truck bombing destroys US embassy in Nairobi, Kenya, killing 12 Americans and 201 others. Five thousand people are injured. Five minutes later, a truck bomb, killing 11 non-Americans, damages the US embassy in Dar es Salaam, Tanzania. This marks the first attack conceived, planned and executed solely by al Qaeda.

1998-99   Strains on Bin Laden/Taliban relationship lead to series of meetings between Iraqi and al Qaeda officials. Bin Laden reportedly considers moving al Qaeda to Iraq. However, Bin Laden/Taliban difficulties are resolved and al Qaeda stays in Afghanistan.

1/2000   Al Qaeda-connected operatives plan attack on a US Naval ship in the Port of Aden. The suicide vessel, overloaded with explosives, sinks undetected.

10/12/00   Another explosive-laden suicide boat explodes next to the USS *Cole*; 17 sailors are killed and 40 injured in the attack on the destroyer.

2001   Bin Laden helps Islamic groups fight against Kurds in northern Iraq and to form Ansar al Islam, a terrorist group that later fights against the US-led coalition in the Iraq war.

5/12/01   Bin Laden's first choice for the "Planes Operation" which would become the 9/11 attacks.

PART 2

THE AFTERMATH

Chapter 13

City Builders

The FBI required materials, facilities, utilities and support services to proceed with the investigation and recovery. This required Somerset EMA to supervise the building of a town surrounding the crash site in less than two days. Mobile command centers, incident management trailers and vehicles of all types converged on the site. Somerset EMA found a way to connect them to power and communications. The EMA personnel then toiled continuously to establish and maintain the flow of resources to the two thousand people who worked at the site daily. Local vendors provided everything from ice to Chapstick. EMA staff became experts at creative procurement.

Rick Lohr, Director of Somerset EMA, supervised the operation.

Lohr: We handled nearly 300 resource requests in two and a half weeks.
FBI, State Police, HAZMAT, anyone. They had to build things like sifters, so we got the wood. There were requests for everything from Tyvek suits to twenty wheelbarrows. That Saturday, we cleaned out Lowe's in Johnstown of those heavy wheelbarrows and those white plastic chairs. We cleaned every county in western Pennsylvania out of recycling bins.

We even had to have PennDOT pave the road the whole way down to the hot zone and all around the command center. We started to call it I-93.

We had some things delivered. Most of the time, our staff used their own vehicles to pick up supplies.

People from our local office staffed the command post out there. We had other county coordinators that came in from Cambria, Fayette, Westmoreland and Bedford counties. We were staffed 24/7 for two and a half weeks. We were working twelve and sixteen-hour shifts. All of that for procurement of resources and making sure that those resources got to the party that made the request.

Bill Baker continued to work at the site each day.

Baker: We would call local vendors if we could. We got requests for three hundred tubes of lip balm for the FBI agents working down at the crater. We went to Wal-Mart. For stainless steel tables, we called PEMA in Harrisburg. Things that we were unable to get locally we left up to PEMA.

We had to be creative. We needed a half dozen kiddie swimming pools. They are hard to get in the middle of September around here, so Wal-Mart had to have them shipped in from stores further south. The same way with sunscreen.

I think the FBI felt that anything that they needed we could just go get. But they didn't take into consideration that you don't buy kiddie pools in the middle of September in Somerset County. You had to have a good relationship with the vendors so that if they didn't have it, they would find it for you.

The FBI had a piece of electronic equipment that required special batteries and cables. Well, the only place to get it was Kansas City or somewhere in the west. The guy out there said he would drive it to Somerset County. The whole country was aware, and the whole country was willing to give anything they could. We just had to make enough phone calls.

Tents were at a premium around that place. Everybody wanted a tent. The helicopter pilots wanted a tent so they could sit and do their paperwork. The troopers needed tents to be out of the sun and the rain. The Red Cross brought a vanload of tents. They were all shoved in the back. I looked in and thought, "Who are we going to get to pound stakes?"

Most of the tents we had were just able to pop up. These had to have stakes. So we contacted the Stoystown and Friedens Fire Departments and asked for a dozen guys with sledgehammers to drive stakes. They came out and hauled tents around and set them up for whoever needed tents. We kept a list of those guys in case we needed more tents set up.

If we authorized personnel for something like that, all we had to do was let the State Police know who was coming and what they were there for. They would have a trooper escort them. If you didn't have an ID, you had an escort.

There were three dragline buckets near the command center, and we needed a place to keep all of our stuff. We had a tent that didn't have any stakes, so we just threw it over one of those buckets. We were able to keep all of our stuff in this huge dragline bucket that was half the size of this room, and everything stayed dry and was out of the way.

Jeremy Coughenour of Somerset EMA also worked some day shifts at the site.

Coughenour: During the day, we were really busy. We coordinated all requests for supplies that the FBI and the ATF needed. When they called you, it was like they needed this yesterday. Try to find two hundred pairs of size thirteen rubber boots in Somerset. It was really stressful. They were just doing their job, but they needed stuff, and sometimes I think they thought that we were in a big metropolitan area with all kinds of resources instead of a rural area. We didn't have a simple way to get a lot of the stuff that they needed. We really tried. We made phone calls as far as California and had stuff over-nighted. It was just nonstop.

We used the Internet, found some places that might have what we needed and made some calls. When we told them who we were with and what we were doing, a lot of people were so generous that they just gave us the stuff. I believe the boots were flown to Cleveland, and then a man in Cleveland drove here as soon as he could get them. He dropped the boots off, turned around and drove back to Cleveland. We had to get them in less than twenty-four hours. It was pretty amazing that we did.

We got a lot of stuff from Quality Farm and Fleet. The manager was so nice. We would call him at 3 a.m. at home, and he would go open the store. He tried to get everything he could. We had our employees that weren't working in the dispatch center work as runners with their pickup trucks. They were going to Lowe's, Wal-Mart, Lincoln Supply, Home Depot, everywhere.

One item that stands out was the recycle bins, the plastic ones that were color-coded. They needed hundreds of those and they needed them now. We couldn't find them anywhere. We called everybody. Then one of the dispatchers in another county got a hold of somebody in Centre County who had a couple hundred of them. She brought them down, free of charge, in a big delivery truck. We lucked into some stuff, and a lot of stuff was just hard detective work.

We got a lot of requests that we thought were silly at the time. One hundred tubes of Chapstick. The Feds were getting chapped lips, so we got them the Chapstick. It went a half a day and it was hot. The Chapstick was melting in the stick, so they needed it in a cream or in a can. I worked three hours getting them a hundred tubes of Chapstick because Wal-Mart was already cleaned out. We had to go to every little store in Somerset and gobble up what they had. Now that was not good enough. That happened to us more than once.

At first, we thought we would just get slips for everything. I don't know how many slips we brought back but there were a lot. Finally, I said we need a credit card. So we had one credit card, and the runner would take that and pay for it all.

Reefer trailers. We needed refrigerated trailers at the morgue. It was hard to get a reefer trailer because they wanted to know what we needed it for. We were going to use them for the storage of human remains. People didn't want to give them to us for that, which is understandable.

Dumpsters. The big dumpsters that they load on the trucks; we needed lots of them. We were filling them before we could get them emptied.

At night, it was more relaxed, and we had time to go over to the snack tent. There was even a movie once in a while inside of the PEMA command post. They had a TV and a radio in there. It was pretty slow at night, but then as soon as the ATF and the FBI came in for the morning, it got busy again. They started showing up right at daylight in personal vehicles. They were staying at hotels in Johnstown and Somerset.

The rapid growth of support services at the command center allowed the FBI to concentrate on organizing its investigative effort. The first goal was to find the black boxes.

Little was known on September 12, 2001 of how the plane crashed. As a result, it was unclear where the black boxes might be found. Investigators were initially unaware that so much of the plane had actually been swallowed up by the earth into the relatively small crater. There was speculation that the black boxes could have been blown into the forest in front, and downwind, of the crater. There was also some concern that the explosion could have actually carried them beyond the forest into Indian Lake.

As a result, the FBI deemed a large area beyond the crater a crime scene and developed a thorough search plan. However, many people lived within the crime scene and their lives remained disrupted.

Pastor Robert Way continued to attend to his church members near the site.

Way: From the people I talked to, the most inconvenient thing was that, for four or five days, they still had to show identification to get into their own driveway. I guess there was a constant turnover of State Police early in the week, and so they didn't recognize any of the people or the cars. Of course, it happened to me a number of times when I went to check on people over those first couple of days.

One of the biggest disruptions for me personally during that time was that I could not walk out of my office without somebody from the media stopping me and asking, "Can I talk to you for a minute, Pastor?"

It was okay at first. But after a while, it became harassment. I ended up parking my car on the other side of the church so that I would have fewer steps between the church and my car. The questions seemed ridiculous. "How do your parishioners feel?"

How do you think they feel? A plane fell in their backyard. They are scared, and they don't know why it happened. They are worried about what will happen next.

Pastor Ed DeVore led the Friedens Lutheran Church. He attended the clergy meeting in Somerset on September 11 with Pastor Way.

DeVore: I knew we needed to do a service. We needed to get together as a community of faith. We decided that we couldn't get it together for Tuesday night but we'd do it the next night. So we called all the TV and radio stations to get the word out that we'd be having a service at Friedens the next night.

As a pastor, I've always prayed that I'd be ready whenever a crisis came to individual people or the community. I was through the flood of Johnstown in '77. So many people were killed. I was in seminary at that time. I remember how the churches rose to be the anchor for people. I felt that it was important for us to offer hope with this crisis. So we quickly got the service together.

The focus was John 1:5 "The light shines in the darkness and the darkness did not overcome me."

We always ask, "Why?" but I sometimes think we should ask, "Why not?"

As Americans, we live very insulated lives. I've had the opportunity to be in Kenya twice with Lutherans over there, to see what they put up with day in and day out. We are so insulated. This was a little reality therapy for us. We see what the people in Israel have put up with for decades.

So I started to talk in the sermon about, first of all, "Why not?"

Look at what is happening in the world. Then how, as Christians, our task is to stand up and say, "But the darkness does not overcome us."

Not politically, not militarily. We have a God who shines a light even in the darkest of times. We find strength there.

The service was well attended. It was a short service. There were about 120 to 150 people there, mostly from the Friedens congregation. It was interesting to see the faces of inactive people there. That was true all over after September 11, 2001. Inactive people came to church for a couple of weeks. The churches were full that next Sunday.

I had a couple from Moxham, John and Sandy Swick, come that night because Moxham only had a daytime prayer service. We talked after the service about what we could do. I think we were planning a meal for the workers. A relative of Sandy's has a store in Carlisle, Pennsylvania. She belongs to a group that is called Good Bears of the World. They send these teddy bears wherever there is a tragedy, like Columbine. I thought that was kind of different. I said they could give her my name and number and she could call me.

The next morning, she called and asked if we could use some bears. I said sure. So then I called Justin Beal. He is a member here, and I knew he was very involved with counseling workers at the site.

I almost was, embarrassed isn't the right word, but I wondered, with such a tragedy, what good are teddy bears?

PART 2

THE AFTERMATH

Chapter 14

Meals and More

The hundreds of people at the site around the clock had to eat. The American Red Cross and Salvation Army established command posts and began feeding workers on September 11, 2001. They continued to feed people throughout the entire duration of the operation. Hundreds of local businesses and individuals also contributed enormous amounts of food. This eventually made its way to the Shanksville Volunteer Fire Department, where volunteers distributed it by pickup truck on late night runs around the outer perimeter.

Janis Yingling and Georgia Lehman of the Red Cross helped coordinate their agency's food response.

Yingling: We initially set up a temporary headquarters at the Best Western in Somerset. Then we had to make arrangements to feed all of the site workers that had come in. We were trying to get information on who would be able to serve 800 meals.

Lehman: In disaster services, we divide into different areas. We have a Mass Care Officer who has been out on numerous jobs. That officer gets an estimate. How many State Troopers? How many FBI? How many volunteers do we have? How many volunteers from other organizations? Then they coordinate our numbers from that.

Every day we do a count. How many meals are we going to need? The first day we worked with a local restaurant to get that meal set up. We had Burger King, or whoever, give us so many meals at a certain time. Then we went to a contractor who would provide us breakfast, lunch and dinner. We went around the clock with our feeding vehicles, which we call ERV's. Breakfast, lunch, dinner and snacks to all the areas. The morgue, the site itself, the perimeter. The first night the food came from anybody, Burger King, McDonald's. We said, "Can you do anything?"

Yingling: "We need 200 burgers right away."

We do that with any type of situation that requires the firefighters being out for any length of time. They will call us and request Mass Care. We will get an estimate of numbers and call the local fast-food restaurants because they can produce that in a short amount of time.

Lehman: That first day, I believe all of that was donated. Then we went to a contractor, and it was a specific amount per meal. We contracted this assignment to Nutrition, Incorporated. They work with school districts and senior centers.

Marilyn Albright of the Salvation Army continued her on-the-job disaster response training after her televised plea for food on the evening of September 11.

American Red Cross
Flight 93 Disaster Response

- 300 plus volunteers and 29 paid staff assisted with relief efforts.
- 169 individuals from Cambria and Somerset counties volunteered.
- 30 local clergy attended Red Cross training to assist with spiritual care support.
- Volunteers served over 65,000 meals and snacks in addition to providing cots, blankets, rain ponchos and other gear.
- Volunteer mental health workers made over 1,700 contacts to provide support to family members, volunteers, disaster workers, school students and community members.
- Physical health assessments were made on 298 persons.
- Two memorial services and crash site visits were planned and implemented for the families of the crash victims.
- Approximately $250,000.00 was needed to cover the costs of this operation.

Albright: The disaster people showed up the next morning. They brought a refrigerated tractor. We kept getting things in and out. We had to rotate or use certain things right away, like anything that had mayonnaise on it. When it looked like it was going to rain, we had to make sure that we got the stuff off the ground and put it under cover. It was like camping.

There was a van that pulled up that had AT&T Disaster something or other on the side. The driver was on his way across the field. I stopped him and asked if we could get phones donated to us to use just for this operation. He said he was going to call his supervisor to make sure. He asked how many, and I just guessed ten. So he called somebody, and he said he would bring them tomorrow. The next day we had ten phones that actually worked.

I thought we would divide these among ourselves because we had units at the morgue and at the command post and the perimeter. People ended up getting my phone number because they heard I was in charge of the food. I started communicating more with Annie Daniels of the Shanksville Fire Department Auxiliary down at the fire hall. She would give people my phone number. I would receive phone calls from a church two counties over. Some church wants to make fifty pieces of chicken. I was trying to piecemeal things together. It was real frustrating because somebody promised to bring fifty pieces; somebody else said they would bring a hundred pieces. Then you have got to try to get somebody to do the potatoes. It was horrible.

Salvation Army Flight 93
Disaster Response

Meals Served	22,850
Emergency Vehicles	16
Canteens	7
Support Units	6
Operations Trailers	3
Nights Lodging Provided	128
Counseling Contacts	345
Individuals Prayed With	320
Bibles Distributed	1,000
Employees On Site	36
Volunteers Utilized	274
Total Volunteer Hours	13,864

We started ordering food as soon as I found out I could. Because I was new, I asked some of the more experienced Salvation Army people what they would do.

Captain Carney made a good suggestion. He said to call Meals On Wheels and find out how many they could do and ask them to do just one meal. I called Art DeLoretto from the Area Agency on Aging and asked him if he could do breakfast. He said yes without even batting an eye. That was a godsend.

He also had a meal plan. You would get scrambled eggs one day, french toast the next day, then oatmeal. So you would have a little rotation. The first day the portions were too small because they are used to feeding seniors. We had big, hungry State Troopers.

So then we asked them to not put the food in individual containers. We had them put it in a great big tub so that we could do the dipping.

One guy would come by in a van. They had these big tubs that were on shelves. I helped him unload the food. The minute the guy left, we had these roving vans that would pull up. We put the stuff into the vans, and they would take off with it. They would drive around the perimeter and deliver to whoever was out there. We ended up having units at the DECON area, the command post, the media staging area and, for a while, at the morgue.

Mark Santas, from the Emergency Disaster Services Department in Pittsburgh, was on the phone with the Eat'n Park Corporate office. They offered to provide, from their restaurant in Somerset, all of the lunches and, from their restaurant in Johnstown, all of the dinners. When you are talking four hundred meals, you almost have to hire more staff to do that much.

Eventually, we had three different places doing three different meals.

There is a man from Camp Allegheny, Chuck Wagner. He came every day, and he was willing to take our trash. Then we ended up ordering a dumpster. Chuck got to where he was picking up an Eat'n Park meal for us each day. Then Camp Allegheny ended up going to pick up both Eat'n Park meals every day. After that they were taking our utensils, like our dippers and spoons and stuff, back to Camp Allegheny. They would wash them and bring them back to us clean. By the very end, they offered to cook all of the meals there. They also took in our out-of-state staff since there were no rooms left at the hotels.

Terry Shaffer, Shanksville Fire Chief, watched the food from a generous community fill his fire hall and displace his engines.

Shaffer: Something else that needs to be told is the story of the community and how they responded to all of this. The food, I tried to keep clear of that because I had enough problems with what was going on up at the site. I was trying to keep control of how many different people went up to the crash site. I thought that the fewer people that had to go up there and experience that situation, the better it would be. Once you've experienced it, it's something you're never going to forget.

What went on down here was a completely separate story. It was just overwhelming.

We knew that there was this group of ladies that was starting to gather drinks and food around lunchtime that first day because they brought them out to us. That evening, when we came back, they were starting to set the tables up in the first truck bay here at the fire hall. Then they just kept working and took over all of the bays the whole way across the hall. By the end, we had this big refrigerated tractor-trailer and another tractor-trailer that came from Cumberland. It was just unbelievable.

We have letters upon letters from the State Police praising us for how well we took care of them. That was pretty awesome. The three ladies that organized this were firemen's wives. They showed up and decided they needed to do something. They took charge of getting it started. Then the other Auxiliary ladies came in. They had this place covered twenty-four hours a day. We couldn't put the trucks away for about a week.

The first few days after the crash, county residents attempted to help with the crash site in any way they could. For those residents away from the county on September 11, the main focus was to return home.

After landing in Boston on September 11, Gregg MacKenzie remained there with other AA pilots.

MacKenzie: We stayed there for a few days. They wanted us to stay together. After two or three days, they realized that they didn't need me to ferry the airplane because there were a lot of pilots there. I went down and got a ticket on Amtrak. They had plenty of seats.

We left Boston for D.C. My dad was going to meet me there. So, I got on the train and I was reading. We were going through Providence and the train slowed down. The train engineer came on the intercom and calmly said, "Ladies and gentleman, we have run over a guy jogging on the tracks and killed him. So we are going to be delayed for a while."

I was reading my book, and finally the train starts creeping along. I looked out the window, and there was this poor guy in a body bag, right outside the window, not five feet from the train. The cops were standing there, disgusted looks on their faces, filling out all of their forms.

We pulled into New York, and the Trade Center was still smoldering. So we were all gaping out of the window at that.

We left Penn Station and pulled into D.C. My dad picked me up and drove me past the Pentagon. It was still smoldering.

It was quite a day. I saw everything in one day as a casual observer. I was nobody, just in the background, but passing through all of these places where all of this stuff was happening.

State Senator Kasunic waited on September 12 for a bush pilot to land at his campsite so he could start his long journey home from Alaska. The guide who first notified him of the attacks showed up instead.

Kasunic: He came back the next day to tell us that he couldn't get me out of there because nothing was flying. Everything was shut down. In Alaska, even after they lifted the ban, because of the Air Force bases and the pipeline, the ban stayed a little longer.

I said, "I don't believe I am here. Why did I do this? Why did I decide to take this trip? I should be there with the people that I represent."

I didn't know what I was going to do back in Somerset, but my feeling was that was where I should be.

So we were stuck there with only this satellite phone and, half of the time, we couldn't get anybody on it. Rumors were just running rampant. The guide would sometimes get information from his wife. You have to understand that she was in their lodge, but still in the middle of nowhere. So she was not getting much information

There were seven of us there. We were sitting around, huddled up, and wondering, "What is going on? Is this a major attack? Who attacked us?"

Because we didn't even know that it was a terrorist attack. Is this World War III? Is this China? Is this North Korea? Has some enemy actually launched a full-scale attack?

It was pure misery and guilt. I can't explain to you how guilty I felt that I was there while this happened.

PART 2

THE AFTERMATH

Chapter 15

Hot Zone

Somerset Volunteer Fire Department runs the Somerset County Hazardous Materials Response Team. They had to develop a procedure for decontamination of site workers before the FBI crash site investigation could proceed.

There were three significant concerns regarding contamination for anyone working at the crash site. First, the area reeked of jet fuel. Second, human remains were strewn throughout the entire area. Third, the terrorists could have intentionally contaminated the plane with biological agents.

The area inside the inner perimeter of Pennsylvania State Police became designated as the hot zone. Anyone entering this area had to don a HAZMAT suit before entering and go through a decontamination procedure before exiting.

The DECON line became the gateway for the hot zone. All personnel and materials entering the site and all items recovered from the site passed through the DECON line. Somerset VFD manned the big blue tent marking the DECON line during the entire investigation. Without the expertise of this HAZMAT team, the FBI's investigation could not have proceeded.

The first step in the investigative process at the site was to map the entire area into a grid. After this process, the investigation and recovery work began in earnest. By that point, the FBI had assembled an investigation team of several hundred. They also obtained heavy equipment and operators from local businesses to begin the laborious process of searching the crater.

By the end of the week of September 11th, investigative and recovery efforts were well underway. Investigators who had come from several surrounding states stayed in local motels and hotels in Johnstown and Somerset. They would arrive on site each morning and separate into investigative teams with specific areas of interest.

One team focused on the crater. These agents would arrive before sunrise to dress in their HAZMAT suits prior to passing through the DECON line into the hot zone. This team's mission was to identify and recover every item that could be found. Recovered items included airplane parts, human remains, personal effects of the passengers and crew, materials of evidentiary value and 5000 pounds of US mail stowed in the belly of the plane.

The second investigative team concentrated on the area of the tree line and forest. These agents also were required to wear HAZMAT suits. Their mission was to search for all recoverable materials that could be found in the stand of evergreens and still-green deciduous trees. Because of the thickness of the forest canopy, a local tree service was eventually drafted to remove some of the trees and search others.

A third investigative team searched the area of Indian Lake. This involved a land search consisting of lines of agents walking through the properties of the resort homes and collecting recoverable material. Also, agents conducted a water search of Indian Lake by pontoon boat.

A fourth investigative team conducted interviews with witnesses in the area of the crash. At that time, it was still unclear what occurred during the last seconds of the flight.

After spending September 11 as FBI site commander, Wells Morrison continued as second in command for the duration of the investigation.

Morrison: We have, in every FBI division, what we refer to as Evidence Response Teams. They are agents and support personnel who have their normal jobs, but when there is a major crime scene, they come together as a group and process that crime scene. What we ended up doing was bringing in the Pittsburgh and West Virginia Evidence Response Teams, as well as six other Evidence Response Teams from surrounding fields.

We had about 150 agents working the crater, the woods, the pond and Indian Lake. The entire area. We augmented those agents with State Troopers from what they call their R&I, Record and Identification, the State Police crime scene people. We deputized them as special federal officers because they might be recovering evidence. We wanted them to do it in that capacity to facilitate the investigation process. We brought in an additional twenty or thirty agents to conduct interviews of witnesses on the ground. We probably had a total of 200 agents performing different functions.

We already had in Pittsburgh a Joint Terrorism Task Force supervised by the FBI. The ATF is a member of that, just like the State Police, IRS and a number of agencies. The ATF came out and offered their assistance. They assisted in the crater recovery effort.

Everything recovered out of the crater would be brought to the command post. We would photograph it and log it in. You have chain of custody issues here.

Personal effects and human remains from the crater would be taken over to the morgue. Evidence Response Teams at the morgue would take possession of that. They would sort out the human remains from the personal effects. Personal effects being rings, watches, things like that. Then they would log in anything that might be evidentiary in nature.

Certain things we thought were of particularly important evidentiary nature, maybe passports and documents of some of the hijackers, things like that. We had FBI agents who are pilots at the command post. They had a plane that was at Somerset County Airport. They would literally fly down to Washington daily, taking evidence that we thought was of particular significance. Sometimes they would make more than one trip a day.

We did the gridding, but the NTSB are the experts on aircraft. So they gave a lot of insight as to why things were where they were and where things might be. But our Evidence Response Team people did the individual gridding.

We had a separate trailer and separate support employees who are evidence control technicians. They were responsible for ensuring the evidence was documented correctly and logged in.

We had a lot of people working the crater. They got it down to a pretty smooth running machine. The first couple of days are usually your toughest. Getting organized. Getting set up. They just got it organized and set up and running smoothly out there.

The people who were in the crater, a lot of those Evidence Response Team members, had been through Kosovo. They had worked major crime scenes, death scenes, major disaster scenes. They had worked the bombings of the two American Embassies over in Africa. These folks weren't learning what to do. I think their experience helped this thing move along. It wasn't like somebody had to spoon-feed and walk them through things.

Terry Shaffer and the Shanksville VFD continued to aid the FBI throughout the investigation.

Shaffer: Once the FBI came in and took over, we figured they would tell us to hit the road. But that was the furthest from the truth. At one time or another, we were involved in just about every aspect of what was done up there, other than the criminal investigation.

We extinguished the brush fires and the other small fires on the first day and for several days after that. They called one afternoon and said they needed our Jaws. They found the nose cone of the plane and needed to pry it open.

They were surveying the area so that they could map and grid where different things were found. So they needed us to clear that out for them. In the interim, the guys would spot remains or personal effects and point them out to people who were flagging, or they'd carry flags themselves and mark them.

Mayor Barry Lichty and his Indian Lake community continued to live within a federal crime scene.

Lichty: The FBI showed up and started searching everything around the lake. It took them several days, and they did it several times. They marked everything they found with red ribbons. State Police had all of the roads blocked, and you had to identify yourself to get in here.

They lined up thirty or forty people in a row. They started at the lake and walked in a line all the way through the woods. They looked everything over pretty closely. My wife was home by herself when they came through the one time. They were still looking for the black box. We have a small fishpond that has about ten or twelve fish in it with a filter. One of the agents had her pull the filter from the bottom of the pond so that he could determine that it was not the black box.

There were rumors that they were going to ask us to drain the lake, which would have been a last resort. It would have taken us probably a month to do that to a level where they could do anything with it. But those were only rumors, and nobody in a position of authority ever discussed that with me. They did get boats and search from those.

After spending September 11 walking the debris field at the request of the Pennsylvania State Police, Roger Bailey spent several days working on the DECON line during the investigation.

Bailey: Tom Brown, one of our assistant chiefs, went out for a meeting with the FBI. They asked what we could do for them in regard to DECON. Tom and Dan Buck, Sr., went out the next morning to set up the DECON station. Whatever we needed to bring and however many people we needed to have was okay.

We made up a schedule. There were probably ten or eleven of us who worked out there. I think I worked there three days.

We set up our blue tent where the dirt road went down to the crater. There was a wash station, and there were dumpsters there. Inside of the tent were rubber gloves, booties, coveralls, water, whatever we felt was needed.

The workers would come in the morning. A lot of them would get dressed at the FBI trailers. They would walk down and already have their Tyvek on. They would go do their jobs, and then at break time, they would come out. We had those white plastic chairs set up for them. They would come out, strip their rubber gloves off, wash their hands, and sit down. They didn't need to come out of the DECON area.

They had a crate of water that they brought in and sat behind the tent. It was warm so I said, "Let's get some ice."

We requisitioned that through United.

We actually were "DECON and Requisitioning." Whatever they needed in the site, they came to us to get. We had a radio, so we would call up to the command center and say we need more boots, chairs, rakes, whatever.

When we went in each morning, we signed for a radio. Anything we needed, we called up and told them. They would ask who was authorizing this. There was an FBI agent who said, "If you need something, just tell them I said so. But if I find out you got something you didn't need…"

United had a tent with supplies, as well as EMA and the FBI. They had a woman going back and forth all day. All we had to do was say, "Sherry, I need this," and it would be there. So I told her I needed ice. She asked me how much I needed. For some reason, I asked for twenty-six bags. She came back in about an hour and a half with twenty-six bags of ice. So we started breaking this ice up and putting the water in coolers. Those guys thought we were great.

When they were coming out of the crash site, there was a wash station and then our tent. Then there were four kiddie swimming pools. Two rows of two. When they came out, they would form two lines and do a boot wash. They would walk through the first swimming pool, take the scrub brush and scrub their boots off a little bit. It had the heaviest concentration of chlorine. Then the next swimming pool had a little more of a dilution of soap and chlorination. The last one was a fifty-five gallon drum that was cut off. That was the rinse.

They took the suits off before they even came out. There was a dumpster on the crash site side of the tent where they threw their Tyvek suit. A lot of them didn't wear anything on their heads, but they had respirators. They would remove their respirator, take off the Tyvek suit and take off their rubber gloves. Then they could go over and wash their hands and their face at the sink area. There was stuff there to disinfect their masks. When they went back in the next day, we had replacement cartridges for them.

They actually would have one of those John Deere Gators with a little flat bed on the back. We made a barricade the first day I was there because they weren't coming out where they were supposed to.

I said to one agent, "I hate to be a pain, but we are here."

He said, "You are in charge. Anything you see that isn't to code, you tell me and we'll take care of it. I want it done right. You are the boss."

"Okay," I said.

So we set up horses and put a sign that read, "You must go through DECON," with an arrow. We put up another sign that said, "Do not enter site through this area."

When they brought things out of the site, they would bring them to a point and stop. They would set them down. We would call and say that we had stuff from the site that needed to come up. They would send a Gator down. The driver would turn around, we would load whatever it was onto the back, and they would take it where it needed to go. They had a Gator inside, too. Sometimes they would just carry things up to us. There was a big dumpster for plane parts. I guess United had it hauled away. I didn't see any plane parts come out. They were all put in that dumpster.

What did come out was HR (human remains), personal effects, evidence and mail. They had different color recycling bins for different types of things. One color would be only mail. When they had so much mail, they would call the post office to send a mail truck in. They would back it in, load the mail onto it and take it away.

HR was all bagged and tagged. Any little piece of remains was individually bagged, no matter what size. They would individually bag them and mark on the bag the grid area. The whole site was gridded off into areas, numbered and lettered. Then that was put in a red bag. When the red bag was full, they would tie it shut and bring the bag to the end of the DECON and say, "I've got HR here."

They would set it there. We would call on the radio. The FBI would come and take everything to the FBI trailer. The only people I saw pick up, other than FBI, were the mail carriers, and the FBI was there when the mail was loaded onto his truck.

Everything had to come out through that point. Clothing, personal effects, pictures. That was really sad. It didn't hit me until that first day when I actually started seeing the stuff.

When I loaded that first Gator, I bent down and picked the bin up. I was not even thinking about it, but I looked down and there was a wallet picture of a child. And uh… it does bring back a lot. [Stops and restarts with tears.]

How could you lose an airplane in so many pieces and have a wallet picture survive, not even torn? Family pictures, pieces of clothing, pieces of jewelry.

The first day, when I was walking through that debris field, I realized that there was nothing left. The remains that I saw, I could hardly even identify. The trauma that those people went through. I don't think I will ever fly on an airplane because I don't think I could ever handle that thought. They probably figured that they were going to crash. But did they know that they were going to be… [Stops and recomposes himself.]

After you worked the site for a while, you wanted to know every detail. What did you find today? Oh, we found one of the hijacker's passports. The one day that I was working there, they found a necklace from one of the hijackers. That was packed in a baggy, sealed in an envelope and hand-delivered. That kind of stuff was taken out through DECON, but we didn't actually handle it.

Barry Kister was a Somerset volunteer firefighter who worked full time at an industrial plant and part time for Somerset Ambulance. He worked for the ambulance company at the first aid station in the command center area of the crash site.

Kister: Our station had probably the best view of the entire little town. I called it an instant community. We were right on the end. I could sit there with my binoculars and watch them working in the crater.

On Thursday, they were digging; but by Friday, they had a sifter. They had an excavator in at the crater and a high-lift. Friday afternoon, they were to the point where the excavator would take a scoop of dirt and dump it into the high-lift bucket. They had part of the field marked off with flags. This high-lift would go over to the flagged area and start to dump the dirt very slowly. There would be a couple of FBI guys going through it with their hands as it was dumping. They ended up with these little piles of dirt.

The Shanksville Volunteer Fire Department was called in occasionally because somebody would dig into a hotspot and that would cause a little fire.

There was a scuba team there. They were going to dive the pond, but then they decided to drain it. I talked to those guys; they were very interesting. They were just there hanging out and waiting to see if they were going to dive.

No one had any clue, at that point, how long we were going to be there. There were rumors that we would be there for weeks or months. I called work, and someone talked to the plant manager about it. He said to stay as long as I needed to and do what I could to help out.

Thursday was pretty much getting organized and handing out Band-Aids, aspirin and allergy pills. Then, Friday, it was business as usual, and we had a State Policeman who fell and scraped his knee. We didn't have anything serious.

Friday, towards the end of the day, was when the first families came in. Kyle Ware and I were working. One of the FBI guys came down and told us to load our equipment onto our Gator and go up above because some families were coming in. So we loaded our equipment, went up and stood there with a group of other workers.

This little bus arrived and these people got out. There was a large garage that we were standing near. The families went around that garage and stood by a straw memorial built for mementoes left for the people that were on the plane.

They just stood there and looked at the hole. Sorry for calling it the hole, but that is what it was. So they were up there standing, and we were just around the corner of the garage, waiting. People would go up and peek around the corner. I walked up and looked around the corner.

At that moment, I became so sad that I couldn't cry. My dad was killed when I was twelve years old. I thought the world stopped.

This was worse for these people because they stood there, looked, and left with absolutely nothing other than the realization that their family member was somewhere in that ground.

THE AFTERMATH

Chapter 16

Support

Mental Health therapists from Pittsburgh Critical Incident Stress Management (CISM) and Somerset County Mental Health/Mental Retardation (MH/MR) Critical Event Response Team (CERT) worked at the crash site from the beginning of the operation. These counselors provided an opportunity for site and morgue workers to discuss the strains of their gruesome tasks. The stress associated with the aftermath of a mass casualty disaster was intensified by the frightening, uncertain circumstances of that time and being away from home for days or weeks. Often these mental health interventions were very informal.

Justin Beal worked for MH/MR during the Salisbury tornadoes. He helped develop Somerset County's CERT. In the aftermath of the Flight 93 crash, he was stationed at both the crash site and the morgue.

Beal: An excellent opening for us to communicate with people was to talk about their children, and immediately, "I haven't seem my child in fourteen days," or something like that.

My pastor, Ed DeVore of Friedens Lutheran Church, was able to get something like a thousand teddy bears. They were donated from the Good Bears of the World. We were able to give them out. That was the biggest hit. People would come to get those for their children and then talk.

For them to be able to take something positive back to their children was one of the best things that we could do. I know some of the best interventions I performed personally were handing someone the phone and providing a quiet place to talk to his or her family or a place to lie down or something like that.

I remember, when I was entering the field, wondering what to say in those kinds of situations, what is the psychology behind it? But then realizing that it is very practical and not very psychological sometimes.

It never ceases to amaze me how some of the simplest things are the most significant to some people. The bears were one of those. When we went down and picked up fourteen boxes of bears, I thought we would probably have them forever. They were gone within hours. As fast as we could give them out, they would take them. It was something positive, and it was an excellent icebreaker. It was like, "Stay away from those people over there, those mental health people. But they got the bears."

Tom Bender already knew crisis situations. He was a crisis counselor for years at MH/MR before teaming with Terressa Walker as a Family-Based Mental Health Services team. Tom was also familiar with disasters. During the freak Somerset County tornadoes of 1998, Tom was counseling victims of the first set of tornadoes when the second set destroyed his own home. Fortunately, his wife and children were spared by taking refuge at a neighboring farmhouse.

Bender: Justin Beal took Sharon Griffith and me out to the site. When we were quite a ways from the crash site, maybe two miles, we saw the first State Police checkpoint. We stopped and they called in our names. They were confirmed from the list, so they told us to go on. I don't know how far it was to the next checkpoint. The State Police were standing along the road maybe every 150 feet.

I had a sense of awe driving through there. The troopers were standing along the road. Some of them had little fires built to stay warm. It was pretty cold in the morning. Some of them had cars close to them. Some of them were just standing alone.

At the media checkpoint, there were acres full of satellite trucks from every TV station I could think of. They called our names in again, and they told us we were okay to go down. Then we turned there and went down the dirt road to the strip job. We went probably a quarter of a mile, and there was still another checkpoint. In front of that was the road that goes down to the crater, with a different checkpoint. They called our names in again. This was the third time they did that.

Maybe a hundred yards or so, the dirt road went into the strip job. There was a little scrap yard for the old equipment, some old drag buckets and some warehouses for parts. That is where the main staging area was for the State Police, ATF, FBI, NTSB, FAA, Department of Environmental Protection, Department of Natural Resources, Red Cross, Department of Transportation, United Airlines and Salvation Army. It was staggering. We pulled in, and there are all of these large RV-type trailers and mobile command centers.

I started seeing people who I knew from crisis work. I've gotten to know a lot of the firefighters and ambulance people from around the county. I saw some of the Red Cross people I had worked with at the tornadoes before my place got hit. It was strange saying hello to them there under those circumstances. Also, it was strange there, seeing all the State Police and the FBI with their weapons. That first day that I got there, it was very sobering.

It was amazing to me how solemn and tense it was at the site. I remember somebody ran. I don't remember who it was or where they were from. They ran from one trailer to another, across the staging area. I was standing at the end. Pittsburgh CISM had a surgical trailer, like a MASH unit, set up with two surgery rooms and a little office. I think it was from Allegheny General Hospital. That was our office area and counseling rooms. I was standing in the doorway, and I remember seeing this guy running.

Some FBI agents just stopped. Their hands went down to their weapons. Nobody pulled any weapons, but I thought, "This is not a place to be running around right now."

There was a lot of authority there.

We could see search teams working shoulder-to-shoulder, walking along the ground, picking up tiny pieces and putting them in bags. Also, there were people standing at the top of the crater, looking down in while the digging was being done.

The Evidence Response Teams that were in the woods were on their hands and knees. Most of the time they seemed to be picking up little pieces and marking or bagging what they found.

There was one agent who had problems after finding some piece of jewelry. I think it was a ring or a necklace. The realization that this belonged to somebody, that this was somebody's loved one, that made it suddenly too real. Also, several of the agents had said that this was the first crime scene that they had ever been to.

There were several people who came around to our trailer from the State Police, FBI, Red Cross or Salvation Army. They wanted to see our trailer. They said it looked like a cool trailer. They would end up spending forty-five minutes talking about past traumas, past accidents they had been on, past disasters, how many nights they have gone without sleep now at the site, etc.

With the State Police, there was a theme that they were doing fine but they were worried about their kids. Some said their kids weren't doing well because daddy hasn't been home for a week. They know he is at a crash site and they think he is going to get hurt. Several of the guys said they were fine when they were working but when they called home and tried to talk to the wives, they couldn't. One said, "She wants me to come home and I can't come home. I don't know how to deal with that."

The most common way we talked to people was when they came to our trailer because they wanted to look at it. The next most typical thing was when we would go and eat lunch. When we went to the picnic tables, we were just trying to build relationships so that people felt comfortable talking to us. Typically, we were 'the Shrinks.' So, there were the usual jokes about, "Oh, we are going to take you to see him," while we were eating lunch. The standard 'Shrink' stuff. Then we could really talk after some of that stuff was done.

There were a couple of people, brought to us by someone else who was concerned they weren't doing well. They had said they were not going back down to the hot zone anymore or they were not coming back to the site. After being on their hands and knees for I don't know how many days, picking up remains, they sort of lost it for a little while.

Eric Haglund was director of Family-Based Mental Health Services at Bedford-Somerset MH/MR. His wife, Pat, taught in the Meyersdale School District. They had three small children.

Haglund: The one day, I was talking to an agent who was very homesick. She was away for a week prior to September 11 at another crime scene and then immediately got called out to Shanksville. She was feeling bad and like it was time to go home. Her family felt it was time to come home, too. We were having a good conversation when another FBI agent came up and said that we should go up for a helicopter ride.

We flew from the helicopter pad straight down toward the crater. This area is all a field; from the air, it looks like one big possible landing strip. I wondered whether they were trying desperately…

Ironically, the impact site was at the very end, but at the exact center of that field. I was wondering if there was the struggle to put the plane down in the field. We all looked at each other. This is the last thing that the passengers saw before they hit the ground. What those final moments must have been like for the passengers. Another deep sense of empathy and sympathy. What that must have been like knowing that this is it. You heard the interviews of people who talked with their loved ones from the plane. They were very aware of what was about to happen.

It was shocking to see a pinhole in the ground looking down from the helicopter. Even flying low, it looked like a pinhole. That was it. You could see that the trees were very burnt and charred. You could see where the debris had sprayed. You could see that there was a very specific area of impact.

The rest of the site looked like a little campground from the air. It was very busy. There were a lot of guys still at the site with their HAZMAT uniforms on. That day, they were more in the woods on their hands and knees. You could see them in lines, fanning out in small numbers, going in different directions. You could see clearly how they had excavated the site. At that point, they were back-filling a lot of it. They were also draining the nearby pond. So the water level in the pond was down. We could see clearly that there was debris scattered right to where the pond was and through the pine trees.

Mental health workers felt it was important to provide emotional support to the local community. However, residents frequently sought less formal interventions.

Local clergy played an enormous role in and out of their houses of worship. Community members benefited from natural community supports, such as congregating and talking in groups or preparing food for delivery to site workers. Even the simple act of flying the flag or putting up a "God Bless America" sign helped those who displayed and those who observed.

Teachers at Somerset Area School District's Friedens Elementary School faced a different and unique situation. Five miles from the crash site, Friedens Elementary sits on the main route from Somerset to the Shanksville crash site. On September 11, 2001, this was the path of many screaming emergency vehicles. For two weeks after that, hundreds of site workers in scores of official vehicles passed by daily.

The school also sits on the edge of the Somerset County Airport. This normally calm facility hosted heavy helicopter and plane traffic during the crisis despite the flight restrictions on most aircraft.

Additionally, many of the Friedens students and teachers had to pass the temporary morgue at the National Guard Armory less than a mile from the school, while many of the students' parents worked at the crash site.

Michelle Zarefoss, who taught kindergarten at Friedens Elementary, spent the evening of September 11 at her brother's restaurant making food for site workers. She later developed a plan to decorate the vast expanse of chain-link fence separating the airport from Route 281.

Zarefoss: You wanted to do something, but you didn't know what to do, so you tried anything that would help.

That is where the signs came from. I just wanted to do something. I pulled out at that intersection every day and looked across at the airport. I got in my mind that I wanted to do something that would show.

So I went to the airport and asked for permission to decorate the fence. Our school was already decorated, so I thought of somewhere else that was close to the Armory. I knew that we had hundreds of site workers go by here each day. We started with all kinds of ideas of what we could write. We wanted it to be a thank you for all of the people who were going by and helping.

So that is where we started with the "Thank You." Then we got, "We the People Thank You." We then started thinking of all of the agencies. We tried to make as many as we could after school each night. Every night we would be there painting. It was funny because I would get the sheets out, and somebody would come one night, and then another person would come the next. I think almost everybody in the school came down and tried to help at least one night. We filled the fence pretty full.

Our school is right beside the airport. My room is on the back corner of the building, right off the runway. For the next two weeks, we had these big helicopters landing. It sounded so loud in that corner. Every time that one of those would land, with, like, Laura Bush or someone important, the kids would say, "Is that a plane? Is that a plane?"

I still was jumpy, and I would look out. I tried to reassure the kids without letting them know I was nervous. The next few weeks were that way.

Sue Foor, Ruby Berkebile and Elizabeth Maul all taught at Friedens Elementary.

Foor: Four or five of my children had either EMT's or firefighters or somebody working at the crash site. They would come back each morning and talk about what their mom or dad said. It couldn't be ignored.

I think they did extremely well. I was surprised how much they wanted to talk to me or to each other about it. They came with a lot of insight from their parents, because some parents, as I said, had been at the site. They really gave me more information than I would have gotten otherwise. I was impressed with how caring third graders could be.

A couple of the kids brought patriotic songs in. As we were working on some artwork, they asked, "Mrs. Foor, can we listen to this?"

I said, "Sure."

It was Lee Greenwood's song "Proud to Be an American."

I said, "If you know the words you can sing along," thinking I would have a couple of whispers or hums.

I was truly overwhelmed. They were loud. They knew every word and sang as proudly as if they had written the song. I started to cry, listening to them sing. I never dreamed that third graders would know that song. I was truly overwhelmed.

They were really surprised and tickled with the letters and the bears people sent them. I said, "Do you understand why they are doing this for you?"

120

I explained how we tried to do things for the crash victims and why people sent things to us.

I said, "Many of your parents were there, and they made everything go as smoothly as it did. Thank God for them."

Berkebile: The staff was sort of numb. We just tried to go about our jobs. We were told to listen to the children and if they needed help, we could get it for them. I didn't have anyone that needed any help. My major concern was for a little girl whose mother was a first responder and then remained very busy at the site. I asked her several times if she needed to talk to someone. She was fine. I think Mom had everything covered for her and her twin sister.

By the next day, we were wondering what we could do. The terror had turned more to concern. What can we do to help? We started putting the bows out and decorating the building.

I was putting bows along the fence, and one of the high government officials pulled in and watched me doing it. He thanked me. I was amazed that he noticed, being a man. We started to put ideas together. Someone called for the bows. I didn't have duty, so I ran out and put them on. Then we got the ideas for the windows. Just being able to feel like you were doing something helped. I think it helped the kids. It gave us all a connection to the families.

Maul: The kids had asked a lot of questions. They wanted to know if we were going to war, if we were safe here, why other people don't like America, and why they would do something like that to Americans. I tried to answer them the best I could.

They were very sensitive over it. They were amazing. Their hearts just broke for all of those people that were killed. They saw it on TV. I can remember, as a kid, seeing the events around President Kennedy's assassination on TV. I have never forgotten those visions.

My kids were wonderful. I have a very sensitive group of kids. They wanted to know what they could do. Was there something we could plan to do for people? We did several different things. I had showed them the video that had been on TV about Flight 93.

They saw the picture of the baby, and they were just so upset that Jeremy Glick has this little baby. They were thankful that they could write something special to Jennifer Glick, his sister, for the baby.

A lot of their families are from Shanksville. This happened in the backyard of some of their grandparents. Many had someone who was working at the site. So I think that it was an interesting metamorphosis for them.

They were saddened by it, and they were moved by it. But I don't think they were destroyed by it. There were many people to reassure them. I don't think the parents got as hysterical as they could have, being so close to this as we were. They were pretty panicked at that moment, but I think they got a good handle on it quickly.

We started right away making signs, having programs, singing patriotic songs, and observing moments of silence. I think, from the very beginning, that was built-in therapy that helped them express themselves and then move on.

These kids changed, very quickly. The world changed and they had to open their eyes to a lot of things that maybe ten-year-olds shouldn't see. But then again, at a very young age, they got to learn who the real heroes are. So, in the long run, the change may have been very positive.

PART 2

THE AFTERMATH

Chapter 17

Seeking Answers

By Friday, America had suffered no other attacks on its homeland. The nation still reeled in shocked sadness but began to make some initial moves toward recovery.

Some air travel restarted on Thursday, September 13, from airports that could meet newly developed security procedures. However, travel demand remained low as many Americans huddled around their televisions with their families. From high school football to the NFL, events were cancelled in fear that public gatherings would create targets for terrorists or copycats.

Frustrated rescuers recovered only bodies at the smoking World Trade Center ruins. The total of missing people in New York City stood at 4,763. Loved ones posted flyers and visited morgues. A five-mile-square section of southern Manhattan remained restricted. The rest of the city tried to return to work amid dozens of bomb threats and evacuations.

Over a third of the Pentagon remained closed as the President plotted strategy with his top military, diplomatic and security advisors. The State Department worked to isolate Afghanistan and its ruling Taliban government. At a National Security Council (NSC) meeting on Thursday, Secretary of State Colin Powell reported that Pakistan would comply with all US government requests regarding the Taliban. The President and his NSC then began to focus on options to destroy an enemy hidden in camps and caves on the other side of the world.

While a military response to the attacks developed, officials planned remembrance ceremonies in New York, Washington and across the nation. In Somerset County, a small memorial service for local residents was hastily arranged for Friday evening on the steps of the Courthouse.

Organizers expected five hundred local people to attend the service. Instead, over five thousand came. Governor Tom Ridge spoke and clergy prayed from the Courthouse steps. Bill Cowher and the Pittsburgh Steelers arrived in buses to lend support. In the audience sat the first of the heroes' families who had begun to arrive in town. They were astounded at the show of support.

Somerset County Judge Kim Gibson is a graduate of West Point. While on active duty, he was a Tank Platoon leader before attending law school and joining the JAG Corps. After active duty, he served in the Army Reserves before being activated for Operation Desert Storm. He retired from the Army Reserves as a full Colonel.

Gibson: We had been asked earlier in the day to make my chambers available for Governor Ridge because he needed a place to go before he spoke. So that day, his security people arrived about the middle of the afternoon. We met them and found out what security arrangements were needed. Of course, this was before he was appointed to his federal position.

My two youngest had some concept of what was going on, but I am not sure they totally grasped everything. Of course, they knew who Governor Ridge was. They were kind of excited that he was coming.

At the service, we stood just to the side of the Courthouse steps. That was the biggest crowd I had ever seen in Somerset.

It was obviously a very moving experience. I can remember vividly the families of the victims coming in. There had been this murmuring and noise, and then, all of a sudden, it was almost like someone shut the volume off on a television. It was just absolutely quiet. It was just amazing to hear that many people immediately become quiet.

These families walked in, and my wife and I were both crying. We felt so bad for them, and yet we knew there wasn't much we could do, other than be there and at least show how we cared about what happened to their family members. It was really an emotional moment. It was almost like being at a funeral for a close relative or a close friend. It was one of the more emotional times I can remember. I can remember the sadness I felt when my dad passed away. It was a similar sort of feeling. You felt so bad for these people that you just wanted to go out and hug them.

The people in the crowd were saying nice things to them. The Steelers were there. I could tell they were really moved, too. That was a really classy thing for them to do, to come in, sit there and participate, and then leave.

I can remember how nice it was for our local clergy to participate, and what a great address Governor Ridge gave. I have always really respected him, but I respected him even more after that.

After it was all over and I had felt all of that sadness and sympathy, I felt proud of our community. Even though it was a terrible occurrence, it really showed how people here care about other people and how they care about our country. This is a very patriotic area.

Later, the anger developed. But that night, I felt so sad for those family members that I couldn't feel anger.

County employee John Peters attended the ceremony.

Peters: The service was nice. It was sad. We were standing there. We had candles and all of this stuff. When I thought about why I was there, I mean, we were there because forty innocent people died. They did a great thing, and they should be commended for it. That was a hell of a decision to make. They died for the country. But, in some ways, it was so pointless. All because some crazy bastard sits over there in a cave, hiding and dictating this hatred toward us because we are not living by his standards.

I was standing there; it was really sad. I felt really bad for the families, especially the kids. But I still felt really angry. At one point, I was thinking, "It would really be good if each one of these people here, in some way, could get a hold of one of the terrorists."

So there I was, standing there with this anger, hate, and sadness thing going on. I was in a state of shock. Yet, I was awed because I have never seen anything like this in Somerset before.

Things like this never happen here.

Terressa Walker returned from vacation in time for the ceremony. She had partnered with Tom Bender for several years as a Family-Based Mental Health Services treatment team at MH/MR.

Walker: My son was really intrigued. The grand old flag. It was the biggest flag he had ever seen. That is his favorite song, the Grand Old Flag. So he asked his father if he could go up there. He is three. He didn't know why everybody was there. The reports he saw on TV, he didn't pay a whole lot of attention to. He didn't ask me a whole lot of questions about it. He just remarked about the smoke and the firemen going in to take care of the fire and the smoke. So he really didn't understand why everyone was coming to the courthouse, but yet he wanted to go and see that enormous flag. That is what he called it, the Grand Old Flag.

It was really overwhelming, the number of people that were there. I was shocked by it. It felt good. It felt good to pray with everybody, sing, and listen to what everybody had to say. I was pretty far back. I couldn't see a whole lot. But just being there helped me feel a part of it, a part of what was going on here in my own community. Being away in Virginia, I think I had a sense of feeling removed from it.

I wanted to show the people who came, family members and visitors, what a neat place this is and that there are a bunch of good people here. And that the lives that were lost here were not only important to them but were important to us. Our way to show the country, the world, that there is good here.

In the past, I would listen to reports on the radio about summits and presidents and heads of state and prime ministers and all of these different people sitting around a table. I didn't really check the next day to see what happened, if hands were shaken, if treaties were signed.

But after September 11, 2001, that all ended. I remember thinking that Friday at the memorial service that those things are important and I need to pay attention to them. Right here in our backyard, we were touched by all of that.

We will forever be touched by what happens around those tables, by what all of those men, those prime ministers and presidents and heads of state sit around and talk about. They will talk about this; they will talk about Somerset. That is pretty awesome to think about. We are not invisible.

Bill Cowher, head coach of the Pittsburgh Steelers, attended the service with his team.

Cowher: We practiced on Wednesday. There was still no decision yet whether we were going to play. Later, we found out that they were going to cancel the weekend.

We were actually on the practice field, and I went up to Mr. Rooney and talked with him about what we could do. Everyone wanted to know what they could do. We discussed giving blood. We made some monetary gifts. Then we found out that there was going to be a memorial for the victims of Flight 93, so we decided to get a bus and go up.

I discussed it with all of the players. I told them that we were going to go up to Somerset County for a memorial service for the victims and families of Flight 93. It was all voluntary. If they wanted to be with their families, they could. I understood that. The players talked about it, and I would guess that about ninety-five percent of them decided that they wanted to go up.

So we all got together Friday and went up. My wife and I drove up in our car, following the bus. We parked near the other buses for the families.

We stood there as a group and watched as the service went on. It was just tremendously moving. Probably one of the most moving experiences I can remember. Even to this day, just thinking and talking about it brings tears to my eyes.

It was an unbelievable experience. Afterwards, we met some of the families. They all seemed so innocent to be involved in this. It was just coincidental, and they were helpless victims of circumstance. It really brought home the idea of not taking anything in life for granted and making sure we appreciate the loved ones we have.

It was amazing because you looked out at the people who were there on the street. You saw people in three-piece suits; you saw farmers who came in with their blue jeans on. You had blacks and whites and all ethnic groups. You had all of the different socioeconomic levels of people, all pulled together, united at that one time. It was such a feeling of pain and sympathy and also of being proud to be an American.

I thought Governor Ridge gave a very moving talk. It was a very, very special evening altogether. I don't think there was a player who was there who didn't come away with a lot of the same feelings that I am expressing to you now.

We hoped that being there would, in some way, help. We all had such a feeling of helplessness. Being able to show those families the grief we felt for them at least made us feel like we were able to fill a little bit of that void that we all had in our hearts. Hopefully, it helped the families.

We are in the public eye, and we may get a lot more attention than other people. But that was a time for all of us to realize where our roots really are. That day put a lot of things into perspective. I think that day showed a lot of people across our country that family, friends and faith are three things that mean so much.

It created strength and a bond between people. It made us feel that it is not the notoriety that we receive, but it is the country that we live in and the people that make it up that are important. It was great to see how we could all pull together and unite at a time like that. We were all no different than those farmers in coveralls.

Sharon Griffith was a MH/MR counselor who provided support at the crash site and the morgue. She thought about going to the service after finishing her shift at the site for that day.

Griffith: I remember driving up the night of that memorial service, thinking that I didn't want to go and then thinking that I should go. Everybody was going. I drove up to town and I saw people as far as a block away. I guess the crowd had gotten that big. I turned back down another street and I went home, which is right outside of town. There was not a car on the road then.

I got my dog and I went to the baseball field out by my house. There wasn't a neighbor around. I just couldn't be around the people and the noise in town. I sat down on the baseball field and watched the sun go down.

I prayed for all of those people who had lost so much.

Barry Kister finished his shift after observing the family visit that triggered his own memories of family tragedy. He then attended the Courthouse service.

Kister: I waited for the night shift to come in and then I left. I wanted to hear Ridge speak at the memorial service.

I parked in a parking lot a few blocks from the Courthouse. I was walking up, still in uniform, with all of my ID tags on. The site was on a strip job, so I was dirty. I got up to about a block away and stopped because the crowd extended that far back from the Courthouse. I was looking to see if I knew anybody and where I was going to go. I was just standing there, and this lady turned and looked at me and said, "Were you at the crash site?"

I said, "Yes, ma'am."

She came over, hugged me, and said, "God bless you."

Nobody had ever said anything like that to me before in all the times I've been in a fire or ambulance uniform.

That is when the realization of what was happening really set in.

Ken Nacke and some of his family arrived in Somerset County in time to attend the Courthouse Memorial Service.

Nacke: We went through Somerset to get to Seven Springs. We drove past the Courthouse, but there was hardly anyone there yet. They were just setting up.

When we came back down on the bus that United provided for us, people were lined up for blocks. It was heartwarming and breathtaking. It took away the pain for a minute to see this small town coming together for people they didn't even know. Such a small town and there were so many people there. It looked like people came for miles around.

I got off the bus and noticed these two large buses pull in behind us. I started recognizing the faces coming off the buses. I saw Dan Rooney, Coach Cowher, Jerome Bettis, Kordell Stewart and Mark Bruener.

I said to Dad, "Can you believe this?"

Not that they wouldn't be there, but my brother was a huge Steeler fan.

It seemed they wanted no fanfare. Bettis came around, and I started talking to him. What a really nice guy. I think he was already briefed as to who we were.

As soon as we took our seat, the vigil kicked off. The Courthouse was beautiful. People were everywhere and there was a color guard. They read the forty names and a child lit a candle luminary for each one. Gov. Ridge and a couple of other people made speeches that were moving and heartfelt. I can't remember what they said. I was too worried about Mom and Dad sitting next to us. I felt like I was in the role of the parent, their caretaker, their protector.

The vigil brought tears to my eyes.

We went back to our bus. I saw my mom and dad talking to Dan Rooney, Coach Cowher, Stewart and Bettis. Then I saw them get on their bus. My dad says you can never say thank you enough. I'm pretty sure he was telling them this was more special than they could imagine, because Joey was such a Steeler fan. Really of all the Pittsburgh sports teams. That was because they were the first professional teams we ever saw play. We lived in the Penn Hills area for a couple of years.

I had to get on their bus to retrieve mom and dad. Mark Bruener and the Cowhers were embracing Mom and Dad, crying along with them. Joey's son, Louis, couldn't make it, and he was as big a fan as his Dad. I thought we could take one of the programs from the service and have a few Steelers sign it for him. They overheard us, and the next thing I knew, the players were coming up and signing the program, without even being asked.

When we got off the bus, a female reporter from Pittsburgh and her cameraman snuck around the bus and approached Kordell. He was talking to my mom at the time. Immediately, they started filming and asking him questions. He put his hands up and told her that this was not the time or place for an interview. He said he would talk to her when he could, but it wouldn't be back there at that time.

He was respectful to the lady, but very protective of my mom, who he was shielding from the camera.

As the Courthouse ceremony concluded, those toiling at the brightly lit hot zone six miles away noticed a change.

Tom Brown, along with Dan Buck Sr., had been in charge of setting up the DECON line. Tom worked at the site Friday evening.

Brown: It was after dark. I could tell that something was up by the mood of the agents, their demeanor, how they were handling themselves. It was significant. They went from a mechanical mode to an air of excitement.

I wandered over to the safety officer and said, "What's up?"

He said, "We just found the Cockpit Voice Recorder."

It is the black box as they call it, which is actually orange. The device is about the size of a breadbox, to be specific.

It went off the site pretty quickly.

Finding the second black box completed the initial phase of the FBI recovery operations. On 4:20 p.m. Thursday, investigators had unearthed the Flight Data Recorder (FDR).

Wells Morrison manned the FBI headquarters at the crash site command center when agents recovered the FDR.

Morrison: We recovered one on one day and the other the next day. We recovered the Flight Data Recorder first. It was strange. The black boxes are right next to each other on the aircraft, yet one was found thirteen feet deeper into the crater than the other. One of our agents flew it down to the NTSB to start downloading the data.

You are always thinking that is one of your goals. You get the Flight Data Recorder and the Cockpit Voice Recorder. They are not black boxes. They are more like orange cubes. If it had gone in water, there is a transponder that would have gone off. But that didn't help us find it in the crater because it only activates if it is in the water.

We were surprised, quite honestly, that we didn't find them sooner. But we did find both of them. They both worked. We may be the only crash site that has recovered both of the black boxes.

The agent who was in charge of the Evidence Response Team is a good friend of mine, Bob Craig. He knows that I am a great fan of Theodore Roosevelt. So he calls me on the radio and says, "We found it."

Well, I have been around long enough to always clarify what you are talking about. Don't assume. So I said, "Found what?"

He says, "Who is your favorite President?"

I said, "Theodore Roosevelt."

He said, "OK, his cousin, FDR."

Black Boxes

The black boxes are usually orange cylindrical containers that the FAA requires for commercial planes. Two black boxes are generally placed next to each other in the airplane's tail section. Each is equipped with an Underwater Locator Beacon (ULB), which activates when immersed in water. The black boxes are water pressure resistant to 20,000 feet and fire resistant to 1100 Celsius for 30 minutes.

Older units use magnetic tape, newer units are digital. The Flight Data Recorder (FDR) records 25 continuous hours of many operating variables, such as air speed, heading and altitude. The FDR is used to generate an animated video of the flight. The Cockpit Voice Recorder (CVR) records 30 continuous minutes from the cockpit microphones.

A CVR committee is created to study recordings and develop a transcript. The committee has representatives from NTSB, FAA, airline, aircraft manufacturer, engine manufacturer and pilots' union. CVR transcript release is regulated by federal law and usually not made public until the complete crash report is made public.

That is how I got the message that we had recovered the Flight Data Recorder. I got a little bit of a kick out of that. He didn't want to say it over the radio, even though the radios are coded. No one should be able to pick it up, but we didn't want to risk getting that out into the public before we were ready to announce it.

I waited at the command post because they were going to bring it up. They photographed it where they found it. They brought it up to the Evidence Response Team trailer and photographed it again. They logged it there and then brought it up to the command post. I designated one agent as the custodian of it, and he was on the plane shortly thereafter en route to Washington. The next day, I think it was thirteen feet further down, we found the cockpit voice recorder.

We also recovered, and I will speak generically, significant documents related to the hijackers. Also, we recovered some things that we believed were used as weapons by the hijackers.

Tom Brown manned the DECON line during other important discoveries of evidence.

Brown: One of the most chilling moments I can remember also involved one of the FBI agents. He was a great guy and would talk to us on a regular basis when he was coming in and out of DECON and throughout the day.

We could tell by the level of activity when something important was happening. If there was more activity, I would pay attention and try to see what was going on. It was happening the one day, and I was looking toward where all of the activity was.

He motioned for me. When I walked over, he showed me what they had found. It was the passport from one of the hijackers. There was the guy's photograph and his signature. That really struck me.

It struck me again a few weeks later when I was watching a TV story about the suspected terrorists. Their pictures were flashed on the screen. I recognized the guy that I saw on the passport.

The *9/11 Commission Report* verified that the Shanksville site provided a trove of evidence. Investigators found Flight 93's CVR and FDR to be in perfect working order. All four black boxes of Flights 11 and 175 were never recovered and the CVR of Flight 77 was so badly burned it was non-functional. In addition to identifying information of the hijackers, investigators recovered 14 pieces of knives used by the hijackers as weapons.

The 9/11 Plot

According to the 9/11 Commission, Kahalid Sheikh Mohammed (KSM) was the principal architect of the 9/11 attacks. He grew up in Kuwait and earned a degree in mechanical engineering at North Carolina A&T in 1986. He pursued terrorist training and activities immediately after graduation. The US pursued him as early as 1996 for his involvement in other terror plots.

In 1996, at a camp in the Tora Bora region of Afghanistan, KSM presented Bin Laden and al Qaeda's chief of operations, Mohammed Atef, with the idea of using airliners as weapons against the US. Nearly three years later, Bin Laden gave his blessing for further planning of such an attack, which became known as the "Planes Operation."

The 9/11 plot cost al Qaeda approximately $500,000. Al Qaeda raised $30 million yearly from donations. It received little from Bin Laden directly, as much of his fortune was frozen or divested from him by Saudi authorities. The donations supporting al Qaeda came directly from individuals or were corruptly channeled from legitimate charities. Half of al Qaeda's yearly income went to the Taliban regime to pay for safe haven in Afghanistan.

Mohamed Atta, terrorist pilot on AA11, was selected by Bin Laden to organize the operation within the US. Bin Laden hoped to have the attacks carried out on May 12, 2001, seven months after the bombing of the USS *Cole*. However, Atta needed more time to plan the operation. The exact date was not selected until mid-August. Tickets on the doomed flights were purchased between August 25 and September 5.

Taliban officials were aware of al Qaeda's plan for a spectacular attack against US interests. Many did not support the idea but were overruled or swayed by Bin Laden in a plan to help assassinate Afghan Northern Alliance Leader Ahmed Shah Massoud.

On September 9, terrorists disguised as journalists killed Massoud.

A Taliban/al Qaeda offensive against the Northern Alliance began September 10.

Terrorist Team Members

The four known terrorist teams consisted of 19 young Middle Eastern men who trained in Afghan al Qaeda camps and lived openly in the US prior to the attacks. The teams consisted of a pilot and 4 "muscle" hijackers who would gain control of the cockpit.

The four pilots received flight training in the US, generally financed with al Qaeda funds. They had been in the US for several years. The "muscle" hijackers were approximately 5'6" and relied on surprise, sharp weapons and a thorough knowledge of the legitimate flight crew's routine.

The pilots were generally higher-level al Qaeda operatives, while the hijackers were generally poorly educated and unemployed. They spoke poor English, had limited involvement in the planning, and arrived in the US no more than six months before the attacks.

Most of the team members were selected for the operation by Usama bin Laden during terrorist training in Afghanistan. As many as ten other potential hijackers had been selected for the teams but did not take part due to quitting the operation, travel problems or other reasons.

Zacarias Moussaoui was frequently and erroneously referred to as "the 20th hijacker." He received flight training and may have been a back-up 9/11 pilot or a pilot for a second wave of attacks. INS arrested Moussaoui on immigration charges on August 16, 2001 after a tip from a suspicious flight instructor in Minnesota. He pled guilty to multiple terrorism charges in 2005 and received a life sentence in 2006.

All 19 known terrorist team members were killed in the attacks. Federal authorities deported or took into custody 539 persons residing inside the US after 9/11.

Pakistani forces captured Khalik Sheikh Mohammed in 2003. The 9/11 Commission frequently cites information from his aggresive interrogation.

Mohammed Atef was killed by a US air strike in Afghanistan in 2001.

Usama bin Laden remains in hiding at press time.

Chapter 18

'So he would be remembered'

The Family Assistance Act passed by Congress in 1996 mandates a standard procedure in the aftermath of a civil air disaster. The air carrier involved and the American Red Cross coordinate to help victims' families visit the crash site. They also work with other agencies to facilitate the identification and return of remains and personal effects.

This process for the Flight 93 crash was complicated by several factors. Being a case of air piracy, the FBI led the investigation instead of the NTSB. Secondly, a national emergency significantly reduced air travel and complicated United's efforts to bring family members to the site. Third, the nature of the terrorist attack caused some family members to refuse flight arrangements to the site, and UAL had to coordinate lengthy ground travel arrangements.

United had been in contact with the families as soon as they could positively identify the flight and certify the passenger list. Then, UAL notified the American Red Cross, who set up command posts at both the Newark and San Francisco airports to help the families in any way they could.

UAL's Special Assistance Team (SAT) began to assemble at their world headquarters in Chicago when it was confirmed that United flights had crashed. The FAA granted special permission for UAL to fly an airliner from Chicago to the airport in Johnstown on the afternoon of September 11, 2001.

Kisa Valenti and John Mates of Seven Springs Mountain Resort helped United personnel prepare for the arrival of the families.

Valenti: John and I decided that Willi's Ski Shop would be a good location for their family center. That took a little communication with Willi's since they were going to be moving into that space in four or five days.

Mates: That worked out well because Willi's was flexible with us. They delayed moving in for the winter season by a few weeks. The other room that we had downstairs for the agencies' headquarters was our area for kids' camps. It was full of kids' toys and equipment, which had to go somewhere. We were looking at 12,000 square feet, so there was a lot of stuff for kids that we had to store.

Valenti: The people from United who came in that first night were only going to work with the families. That was the only group that came here. The rest of them had gone to Johnstown. By Wednesday, they said the rest of the staff wanted to move down here. It made more sense having one area.

Mates: As time went by, they just kept adding things. They wanted to do this, and they wanted to do that. We tried to accommodate them the best we could. They pretty much filled the hotel.

After it was determined that the families would stay at Seven Springs Mountain Resort, United began to develop travel plans to the resort for each family. Loved ones began to arrive by car, bus and airplane as early as Friday, September 14. As a result, some of the family members attended the Courthouse memorial service in Somerset.

Plans were also being made at the crash site for the families. Although the bulk of the families came to the crash site in two organized bus caravans the next week, there were a few family visits as early as Friday.

Ken Nacke was able to visit the site for the first time on Saturday.

Nacke: I wanted to get out to the crash site as soon as I could. I was working whatever angle I could with the State Police to get it to happen.

I went out by State Police car with Tim Lewis, a trooper from the Greensburg Barracks. He took me through the service route, where the family buses went through the next week.

There were troopers along the route. They were all saluting Lewis's car as we were driving by. At every checkpoint, every guy was at attention. That was Captain Monaco's idea. It worked so well, that he decided to do it for the family buses when they came through the next week.

I was out there for about two hours. I met a bunch of the troopers, an FBI agent and someone from the NTSB. They told me what they thought they knew so far.

All of us knelt down and said a prayer. It was right where they had just finished paving and where the hay bales were going to be set up.

136

Rick Lohr and Bill Baker of Somerset EMA helped with preparations for the families at the site.

Lohr: One of the head NTSB people came to us the first night and told us what was going to happen when the families visited. We went up to the command center and looked around. He wanted it cleaned up a bit. We coordinated with PBS Coal Company to get it cleaned up. Then we built an altar out of straw. We expanded it, maybe, three times?

Baker: At least. We started out, I think, with a dozen bales of straw and it just kept on going.

I called my Fire Chief in Berlin, Gerry Parry. He works very closely with the dairy farmers. I told Gerry that I needed a dozen bales of straw. He took them to my house, loaded them on my trailer, and hauled them out there the next day. They were donated from Calvin Will's Northview Farm outside Berlin.

We took them up whenever the paving was done and set them up like an altar. We stepped them up and tried to make it look nice and neat. There were already some stuffed animals and candles and things that people had left there, so we set those things up on the straw. After that, it just expanded. We had to keep finding more straw. We found some out by the media center and hauled that in. Pretty soon this thing was about thirty feet long, and it was just packed full of straw. You couldn't tell that there was any straw underneath with all the things left behind.

Lohr: The first family came in and had that first isolated visit. It was the family of one of the stewardesses. They left pictures that evening, and we covered those pictures with plastic so that the weather and dampness wouldn't harm them. I will remember that evening for as long as I live.

The straw memorial served as the focal point of reflection for many family members and site workers. Jill Miller coordinated the Somerset Ambulance's First Aid station at the crash site.

Miller: I had to go past Friedens Elementary School every day. That was where my twins were in third grade. It's only one mile from the morgue. I would cry passing through there every day.

Toward the end of the week, the whole school sent us cards. Very touching. My three girls gave me Beanie Babies to put on the straw memorial. They all picked one out, knowing that it wasn't coming home, and asked me to take it and put it as close as I could. They did that on their own.

Every day, before I got started and again before I left, I would spend a few minutes at the memorial. I never realized how difficult it would be for me to see those three Beanie Babies there.

Pennsylvania's Senators Arlen Spector and Rick Santorum flew into the heliport, bringing the American flag that flew over the Capitol Building on September 11. This symbol of gratitude toward the heroes and their families soon waved atop a flagpole to the left of the straw memorial.

Another inspirational structure was erected with considerable controversy. Pastor James Vandervort was the pastor of the large Christian Missionary Alliance Church in Somerset.

Vandervort: Our youth pastor, Ben DeStefano, was thinking of things we could do to help. So he got some of the young people together Tuesday night and went around town buying up all of the bottled water they could find. I think they bought all that Wal-Mart had, and Wal-Mart then, in turn, donated half of it. Then they went wherever else they could find some and eventually took it out to the site.

While they were there, the Salvation Army leader mentioned something about a cross. Ben came back and asked whether we had one we could take out there. We had one we used for a Passion play last Easter. Wednesday night they took the cross out and set it up. They put it where the media was. Either Thursday or Friday the Salvation Army fellow called and asked if we could install a larger cross somewhere near the area where the families would be. So some of the men in our church got together and bought four by fours and built another cross. Jonas Scheffel and Bob Gohn were two of the men that worked on it. They did a great job.

Then our ladies got some white cloth to wrap around like they did on the smaller one. They put it on one of the trucks from Scheffel's John Deere dealership to take it out. I went along with them. I think there were about six men and three ladies who went.

When we got out to the site, they were macadamizing the road up through there. So we had to stop and wait for a while. Then they decided they would let us go part way. We went up near where the Salvation Army had a canteen with coffee for the fellows who were working. We got up there and waited to see who would give us some instruction about where we could put this cross.

The State Police escorted us, but they didn't know where to have us put it. Someone thought that since there was a flagpole near the steel building already, we might be able to put it somewhere near that. Then they decided they didn't want it right next to the flagpole. We said okay, and we started digging.

It wasn't long before someone came up and said, "Is the pastor here?"

Someone pointed to me. If I remember correctly, that first gentleman who asked us about the cross was a State Policeman. He was really all for us putting it up. There was no problem with that. He just wanted to make sure they followed procedure. He said he would try to check it out.

It wasn't too long when a fellow from the FBI came up. I think he kind of assumed that we were doing this without anyone having invited us to bring it. So he began to ask questions about it. Then he told us to stop digging.

We got into some conversation about the cross and why we wanted to put it there. I explained to him that we wanted to put it there as a symbol of faith and courage and hope for people who would go by it at any time.

A reminder that, even in the midst of tragedy, God is with us and he loves us and somehow he will work this out for good. God didn't cause it, but He can make good come out of it. I told him we weren't going to put a church sign on it. We weren't interested in advertising the church. We just wanted to put it there. Nothing else would be on it but the white cloth.

He didn't think we should do it. His reason was that there might be people who would be offended by it. He wanted to check with somebody else. He said there might be people of other faiths and they may be offended.

I said, "All right, we will wait."

So he left.

We were waiting, and this big guy from the State Police came driving up in a hurry. He jumped out of his car and asked if the pastor was here.

I went over to him, and he said, "I want you to know that I don't have any problem at all with you putting this up. As far as I am concerned, you do what you want to do. I am not telling you to do it; I am not telling you not to do it. You just do what you want to do."

He was very encouraging and very supportive. While I was talking with him, the others with me were praying that somehow this would work out.

So I went back down to them and said, "Keep digging."

So they kept digging. We almost had it deep enough, but not quite. About that time, another FBI guy came along with the other fellow who came the first time. They both wanted to talk to me.

I walked up from where we were digging and began to talk to them. He reiterated that he didn't think this was a good idea, that maybe we ought to wait until after the families had come and gone and then do it. He thought that there may be people who would be offended by it, so he would really like to see us wait.

I tried to express to him that, for the families who felt this more than anybody else, this symbol could be encouraging, it could help them. This could remind them of faith and hope and courage and that God loves them and he will help them through this time. We would like to put it up for the families, as well as anybody else who comes here.

So he said, "Well, there may be people offended. How would you feel as a Christian if you came up and there was a Star of David there?"

I said, "I wouldn't have any problem with that at all. That wouldn't bother me. That is what this country is about."

He said, "Do you know who the Jewish Rabbi is here in Somerset?"

I said, "To my knowledge, there is not one in Somerset. There may be one in Johnstown, but I haven't been around here long, and if there is one, I haven't met him."

So he said, "Would you be willing to contact him?"

I said, "Well, first of all, I wouldn't know who to call. I have no idea who he is. And second of all, I really don't think that is my responsibility. If he wants to bring a Star of David up, I support him. I have no objections to that. But I think it is his responsibility to take the initiative. Not mine. If an atheist wants to come and put some kind of symbol that represents what he thinks, let him. I have no idea what he would put that he thinks might help people, but if he has something, let him put it there. That is fine. If I understand this nation, it is not about freedom from religion. It is about freedom of religion. So if an atheist wants to do that, fine. The Rabbi wants to do that, that is fine."

So he and the other FBI fellow walked away for a few minutes and chatted by themselves and then came back and said, "Well, I guess you can go ahead and do what you want to do."

I thanked him and then said, "You know, I am not interested in getting you in trouble. If someone above you tells you tomorrow that this cross has to come down, I will bring the crew back out and we will take it down."

I went back to the cross and said, "Keep digging."

After we got it up and expressed our thanks to the Lord, I said to our group, "When we leave here, I don't want you talking about this to anybody. I don't want you to say a word because I don't know what the results are going to be. I don't want to get the FBI fellow or the State Trooper fellow into any difficulty."

The next day, Sunday morning, a local news report said, "Last night someone came and put up a cross. We have no idea who it was."

I said, "Yes!"

The staff at Seven Springs Mountain Resort transformed the entertainment complex into a center of mourning and comfort. The family members stayed in the hotel but were free to utilize the facilities of the resort. Many of them chose to remove their identification badges so that they could accompany their children to the pool and game room or eat in the restaurants apart from the meals organized for families.

The media was forced to accept limitations on access to the families. The family center, agency headquarters and certain areas of the hotel were off limits to the press or anyone who did not receive credentials through United. State Troopers, Seven Springs Borough Police and Seven Springs Resort Security staff enforced the access restrictions.

All media interviews took place in the Exhibit Hall. For hours, press personnel gathered inside, drinking coffee, eating and talking while waiting to use the dozens of satellite trucks parked just outside.

Seven Springs staff arranged for Willi's Ski Shop to be transformed into the family assistance center. This was the focal point of the families' activities. Directly below Willi's, an area previously utilized for a children's day camp became the headquarters for UAL, FBI, Red Cross, DMORT and any of the agencies working at Seven Springs.

The family assistance center provided a secure area for the families to become acquainted, eat and talk informally with the staff of the Red Cross and other agencies. Children could be found watching TV, while adults read the yards of banners from local schools and communities wishing the families well.

Helen Thompson, R.N., spent over a week as a volunteer Red Cross nurse working with the heroes' families.

Thompson: A lot of the family members who came forgot to bring things. On Friday, we had an elderly man who forgot all of his medications. He was diabetic and had a heart condition. We called a Red Cross physician for prescriptions.

The physical part was easy because if someone had a headache, you could give them ibuprofen or Tylenol. I got attached to a lot of people, so they would come over and say, "Helen, you know I need this."

The one adorable little lady whose son was killed said to me, "Honey, I'm low on potassium."

I said, "Let's go over here and eat a banana. Let's just sit down at this table and I will fix you a cup of hot tea."

United Airlines and Seven Springs had food all of the time for these people. There were tables in the middle, but then there were little lounge areas where families could just sit and regroup. She sat down and was eating her banana and sipping her tea. She started telling me about her son when he was an infant. She told me his entire life story. She went through his first day of school, his prom, who his date was, everything.

When you looked out of the window where we were sitting, you could see clear to the top of the ski slope. After she told me all about him, she looked out the window and said, "Honey, the only thing I can say is that I feel a sort of peace now. Look at this place. It is beautiful."

She wept... She just wept.

Sue A. Opp was a bartender at Seven Springs. Her parents had a vacation home there while she was growing up. She started working there during college and has done so ever since. She and her husband, who also worked at Seven Springs, have two sons.

Opp: I worked that Friday night, the night of the memorial at the Courthouse. I was working a convention in the ski lodge at the Foggy Goggle.

It was very somber. Instead of eating at their tables and talking, people were sitting at the bar with their plates, staring up at the TV's.

Later, I went to the Bavarian. The Bavarian is the cornerstone bar in the main entrance of the resort; it opens at 10:00 a.m. and stays open until 2:00 a.m. That is where I met some of the families. There were four men I talked to, in particular, and then a few people that would come up for a while and then leave.

I didn't say much to anybody. I noticed that people had on different ID's. Some had United tags; some had this color ribbon or that color ribbon. I didn't know which was which. I just knew who the media people were because they would talk and ask questions. "Where are the families staying? What floors are they on? How long will the FBI be here?"

The four men I talked to for a while sat at the side of the bar where the sinks are. They were very nice. There were three of them in their fifties, and the other one said he was twenty-four or twenty-five. They said they had lost two people. It was just those men until the one wife came down.

Her husband introduced her to me and said that it was her brother who was killed on Flight 93. The gentleman beside him told me that their relative's name was David Cashman.

I remember that because he kept telling me, "Remember Cash Man. Please just remember that name."

I know there was another name given to me. I think it was the person David was traveling with, but I am not sure. I just remember David Cashman.

I talked to them most of the night. They talked to me about their family members, what they were like and all of that. At that time, there was still the question of how the flight went down. Did it go down because somebody wrestled it down? Did it go down because we shot our own plane out of the air?

I was thinking, if we shot our own plane down, we had to do it; and if it went down by the passengers and crew, then we were lucky. It surprised me that they had the same viewpoint. I thought they would feel differently. It is so awful to think of our own forces shooting down your family member.

They said that going to the crash site was emotional for them, but it wasn't like coming through the town. They said that all of the ribbons, people waving and saluting, and the signs and stuff was what got to them. They were really impressed with Somerset.

That was the reason that man kept saying, "David Cashman. David Cashman's family says…" So they wanted me to tell his name to somebody important so that he would be remembered. I don't really know anybody important.

They told me to quote them. I was thinking, "Who would I quote you to?"

THE AFTERMATH

Chapter 19

DMORT

The site recovery operation required a temporary morgue for processing the human remains. After several sites were investigated and rejected, the Pennsylvania National Guard Armory in Friedens was designated as the temporary morgue. The National Guard staff removed equipment. County residents who would later become part of the Disaster Mortuary Operational Response Team (DMORT) transformed the structure into a facility to store and identify human remains.

Due to the restrictions on air travel and the tremendous demand for DMORT services in New York City and Washington, many county residents were drafted to work at the morgue. Somerset Hospital's radiology department contributed seven technicians who established and manned the x-ray facility. The county coroner deputized local funeral directors as deputy coroners to help with the gruesome work at the morgue. Local contractors provided whatever assistance was necessary.

Greg Menser worked at his family's plumbing and heating business in Somerset.

Menser: They called my Uncle Todd to see if we could hook up some temporary water lines at the morgue. My uncle had to get himself, my dad and me cleared to go in there.

It was really weird.

They had the whole place fenced off and guarded by State Police. We had to show ID to get in. Once we were in, we had to have a State Policeman with us at all times.

There were human remains lying on the tables. It was still pretty warm in September, and the smell was just unreal. It was a different world.

They had two refrigerated tractor-trailer trucks there, one for identified remains and one for remains that they didn't identify yet. They had the Armory sectioned off into different parts. One section was a photo lab that was used for taking pictures of everything, one was for DNA, one was for cleaning, those kinds of things.

They brought in Rubbermaid containers full of Ziplock bags. There were a lot of the undertakers from around town out there helping. Some people who we knew from the hospital were out there helping, too. They were the gophers; they even had "gopher" written right on their aprons. Then there were a lot of people there from the FBI and other agencies.

They needed four wash sinks with cold water only. We ran temporary water lines in the ceiling and dropped them down to each one of the wash sinks. Then we hooked the faucets up so they could properly, you know, do their thing. We did that and got out of there.

We knew that we were going to see stuff that we didn't want to see. Uncle Todd kind of warned us about that, but until we got there…

DMORT
Disaster Mortuary Operational Response Team

In the early 1980's, the National Funeral Directors Association formed DMORT, a committee created to address mass fatality disasters. Eventually it grew to be a multi-disciplinary, non-profit organization for forensic practitioners capable of responding quickly to mass fatality incidents. Its mission expanded when Congress passed the Family Assistance Act in 1996 and created the NTSB's Family Affairs Division to assist local authorities in victim identification.

DMORT has two highly specialized Disaster Portable Morgue Units (DPMU) stationed at the Federal Emergency Management Agency (FEMA) Logistics Centers in Rockville, MD and San Jose, CA. The DPMU's contain all equipment necessary for a mass fatality disaster.

The DMORT team includes medical examiners, forensic pathologists, forensic anthropologists, fingerprint specialists, forensic odontologists, DNA specialists, mental health specialists, and multiple additional scientific, administrative and security personnel.

I mean there were things that I never saw anywhere. It was the worst job I was ever on, for sure.

Morgue workers processed each piece of human remains that had been collected and bagged at the site. Each was catalogued and assigned a number, photographed, x-rayed and examined. This information was compared against a database of identifying characteristics such as birthmarks, dental records and tattoos. Families gave blood for DNA analysis. They also provided personal items, such as hairbrushes, for DNA testing. This allowed precise identification of the remains.

The initial goal was to have a positive DNA match for each person reported to be on the plane. For the families, this provided direct confirmation of the fate of their loved one. Additionally, site workers and DMORT strived to recover as much of the human remains as possible and to keep the remains from commingling.

Penny Reiman supervised radiology efforts at the morgue.

Reiman: On Wednesday, I heard that our radiology department might be needed. About 7:30 p.m. Wednesday, I received a call from Mark Miller. He is a manager at the hospital who was very involved in helping the coroner at the site. Mark said they needed our help.

The first thing I did was to call Greg Lowry. He is a biomedical engineer at the hospital. He is my right hand man as far as equipment. He and I went to the Armory and assessed the situation. We knew that we would need a processor. It would have to be in an area with a water source and a drain.

As far as the x-ray machine, I wasn't as concerned about that because they are pretty mobile. We found a janitor's closet that was piled full. The National Guard helped us clean out the closet so we could make a dark room. Around 9:00 p.m., we came back to the hospital and started making calls.

My original thought was to get a new processor or get one of our small processors from the hospital and take it out there. Greg's idea, which proved to be much better, was to call one of the companies that we deal with and see if they had an extra processor that they could loan to us. We made calls to three companies and had three responses. We decided to go with the Baldwin Corporation from Pittsburgh. They said they would be there at 9:30 a.m. Thursday. We went out and got everything hooked up and were ready to go by about noon on Thursday.

We had a portable x-ray machine that we took out to the Armory. It was on bicycle tires and could fit in the back of a Jeep.

After DMORT came, they said that often their dark room was just made out of black plastic. That wouldn't have been as good as what we had. We had to move from room to room to process the film, but it worked very well.

I think we did do a little work Thursday afternoon. Then Friday was the day that everybody got there. They said we could be there from two to six weeks and that we would be running twelve-hour shifts. We needed two people per shift. That concerned me because I didn't have a lot of extra staff.

I asked Linda Ellis, one of the other supervisors in the department, if she would coordinate the staffing for me. Whoever wanted to help was to let me know. I only asked that they were experienced technologists. There were seven people who ended up working, including me. I could have had more volunteers if we needed them, but we had to keep the hospital's radiology department running, too.

Normally, DMORT has its own radiology people. They didn't in this case. I think it was Sunday that they pulled a technologist from the Pittsburgh Veteran's Hospital in to help. Then they got somebody in there mid-week from the West Coast. The gentleman from the V.A. Hospital then left.

We worked steadily until the following Tuesday, about five or six days. Then, after that, they asked if I would stop in and make sure everything was going okay. They didn't really need any more staff after that.

First everything was categorized and numbered. We were the next station. We x-rayed whatever they brought us, any remain that they felt was large enough to number as specific recovered remain. We categorized the films in jackets. We dated everything.

It was emotionally draining and tense.

The first night was bad. I closed my eyes and I would see whatever I saw that day.

While working at the morgue as a counselor for MH/MR, Justin Beal was drafted to help DMORT with the identification of human remains.

Beal: If you walked into the front of the Armory, it was pretty much like a school entrance, a couple of doors with bars on them. They were propped open at the time, with fans running. There wasn't a lot of air movement. It was hot and there was no air-conditioning.

It was guarded. A State Police Officer checked your identification. They had already checked once when you pulled into the parking lot.

You entered into the building and to the right was where the remains were. That was tarped off. The forensic anthropologists would come out from time to time to give something to a runner. I did some running. I also did some data entry for the FBI's ante mortem and post mortem database. I was in an office with about six people doing the data entry. There was a Critical Incident Stress Management (CISM) person, who was a computer geek, who networked all of the computers. I didn't know anything about that, but I could keypunch. I was entering evidence: luggage, personal items, identifiable remains, things like that.

There were posters on the walls. They had each passenger's name there. When you found an identifying item, it was put next to that person's name.

The ante mortem is the family doing a long form about identifying information: body marks, birthmarks, dental items, bridges, anything like that. We would log in any evidence. It would go into that database and it would match somewhere. Then they would do the DNA, and they could identify anything that matched.

What was especially disturbing to me was when the families started coming to the crash site. I was up there right after a couple of the families had been there. I went to look at some of the things that were left at the memorial and realized that I had entered data on some of these people. That was a shock. Remembering, connecting, giving it that personal connection was overwhelming. That was disturbing stuff to witness, to feel, to process. Just sitting and talking about it now... [Stops.]

That was some heavy-duty stuff.

Everything was signed in and out at each stage. You actually had to sign something saying that you had this item. That way they could track who had it, when they had it, who took it where, who received it. If anything was altered or suspicious, they could go back through and identify at which point it was different and why.

It was pretty quiet. It was tense. There was a sense of urgency to process all this. I think everybody was so focused on trying to get this done for the families.

Outside, I think people relaxed a little bit. Some of the emotions started to come out in a quiet, sullen way. Trying to make small talk. Also the workers were really grateful. They thanked the Red Cross for the food and everything else.

No family members came forward with identifying information or DNA samples of the hijackers. Remains which didn't match the 40 DNA samples obtained from heroes' families were identified as Hijacker A, B, C, and D and kept separately. The remains of the passengers and crew were eventually returned to the families for cremation or interment.

As the families began to arrive in Somerset County, the county coroner and the coroner's special counsel prepared a variety of options that would allow families to determine how they would like their loved one's remains to be handled.

Dan Rullo is the Somerset County Solicitor who served as special counsel to the county coroner for Flight 93 issues.

Rullo: Instead of having us dictate to the families what was going to happen, we gave them certain options.

We knew the remains were going to be fragmented and there were going to be multiple times in which remains would be identified. Some of the victims would be identified quickly because of dental records, birthmarks, or something like that. Others would take a significant period of time until the DNA testing came back.

We were told it could take four to five months because the same DNA testing laboratory we would use in D.C. was also being used for the Pentagon victims. There also may have been the need to use that DNA testing laboratory for some of the people who were killed in New York.

I developed a form that we gave to the families to let them select an option. Essentially, there were four choices.

With the first option, as soon as we received a positive ID, we would let the families know and return those remains to them. Then they had the option of not being contacted again, so they could put some closure to it and not have multiple times when remains were being shipped to them. Then, in a very dignified manner, the county would take care of disposing of the balance of the remains.

The second option was that each and every time we received a notification of positive identification, we would make sure that the families were told and allow that remain to be delivered to them.

A third option was to be notified of a positive ID and then wait until all of the remains had been completely identified, gather them all together, and ship them out at one time. That way they could have their memorial service and put a close to it at that point.

The last option was that the family didn't want any of the remains, just to be notified when there was a positive ID, and again the county would dispose of the remains in a dignified way.

Part of the meeting that we had with each family was going through and explaining what the options were. We had to have that form translated into Japanese, Spanish, and German.

United was starting to bring families to Seven Springs. We felt it was important to let those families have as much information as we could, as quickly as possible, and outside of the media. There were essentially two waves of families that came. We went out, along with a couple members of the FBI, and let the families know that we were available to meet to discuss any aspects of this recovery and identification process.

United was very cooperative in anything we asked them to do. They provided us two hotel rooms, one floor apart. While we were meeting with the first family, the other family would be in the hotel room upstairs. When we would be done with one family, we would go upstairs to meet with the second family.

Our timetable became messed up because we couldn't just spend five minutes with these people. They were remarkable people. That is one of the things I found, that they were very remarkable people. You couldn't spend just a few minutes talking to them. They wanted to tell you about their loved one. They wanted to tell you about phone calls that they might have had with them from the plane. Some of them wanted a lot of information.

As we started to receive the remains, we started to get some IDs based upon field records, like fingerprints, birthmarks and dental records. The first family to get notification of a positive ID was the Spanish-speaking family. I had met with them one of the evenings at Seven Springs. I also saw them at the Indian Lake memorial service. They had a lawyer with them who was from Philadelphia. He was a very nice man who was bilingual and was able to help translate some of the discussions we had. When the coroner and I would meet with that family, there was a grief counselor who sat in with us. His name was Henry Lopez. He was military. He had a very calming personality.

When the positive identification came, they were still at Seven Springs, but they were ready to go back to the Philadelphia area. The coroner was unable to meet with them before they left. He asked if I would go out and tell that family that we had a positive ID.

There were about ten family members present. Some of them could speak English, some could not. Mr. Lopez was bilingual. I had to tell this family that we had made a positive identification of their daughter. The hardest part about doing that was the delayed reaction, waiting for the translation to see the reaction in their faces.

It was tough. I would much rather have dealt with the legal aspects of those things.

We had a lot of people from the West Coast and Hawaii who weren't able to make it here. We made calls late into the evening, talking to those people, because of the time zone difference. We had a lot of those conversations in my conference room here. We would go on the speakerphone and discuss the options available to them and whatever else they needed.

We met with some families more than once. In a situation like this, you have a wide spectrum of people's responses. Some are very matter of fact and want to just know the facts; they don't want to get into more than that. Others, you can tell, you are talking to them and nothing is sinking in because of their grief. So on a couple of those, we actually needed to meet with them a second time when they wanted to clarify some things.

The Red Cross and Salvation Army maintained the same food and care services for the morgue workers as they did at the crash site. Although many of these volunteers did not feel they contributed much to the overall operation, most of the workers who received or observed their kindness felt differently.

Sharon Griffith of MH/MR observed the effects of the volunteers' kindness on DMORT staff.

Griffith: What impressed me was there was so much compassion from so many people just doing their little biddy parts, trying to make this less tragic. I worked with a couple of Red Cross servers. They were there all day, all night, in the rain, in the hot sun. I watched these women and this man who were the servers connect with all of these very, very intelligent, schooled, scientific people. They provided the human element in a job that was so hard. I didn't want to imagine what the DMORT people were doing in there.

Those servers were there every day. The one woman drove from Uniontown every morning and drove home every night. Every single day, they were out there for what, almost three weeks?

The nicest, sweetest people that wanted to do something to make it better for all of the people that came in to work those difficult jobs. Those servers exemplified to me what so many people in this area tried to do. Just make it a little bit of home for all of these people that were here for so long.

Everyone with the different agencies had to do their specific jobs. They were all focused on that. But I feel like the people that drove there every day to hand out coffee and water, they wove us all together. They brought food in and they broke the boxes down. They did all of this stuff so that the workers would have hot meals.

The workers would go through the line, and they would feel like someone knew them. The Red Cross people would say, "Did you talk to your wife last night?" or "Did you get a chance to watch any of that game?"

They knew those people as individuals. They were the thread. They helped to make sense of this incomprehensible thing that happened in Small Town, America.

THE AFTERMATH

Chapter 20

Families Visit

The two large excursions of heroes' relatives to the crash site took place on Monday, September 17 and Thursday, September 20. Those trips began in the family center, where over three hundred family members gathered for breakfast. Dennis Kashurba, the psychologist from the Children's Aid Home, circulated among the tables, wearing a new Red Cross Disaster Team vest.

Dennis Kashurba: I was with the family members at breakfast before the site visit. I felt as if I didn't know what I could say that would help or even make sense. I also had the fear of saying the wrong thing to make things worse for them. So I tried to shut up, listen, and be there.

The family center was much like a conference room with round tables in the center, a breakfast buffet at one end and a podium at the other. The family members came in as small groups at different times. They weren't escorted in as a large group.

Some folks had a very hearty breakfast, and some stared at a cup of coffee or a Danish. You could feel their pain and helplessness.

After some period of time, United and the American Red Cross made their presentation regarding arrangements. They told them who was going on which bus, where they would go and what they would see. Then the families walked downstairs to board the buses for the crash site, hopefully to get some degree of closure.

In the family center, families received briefings from the agencies headquartered one floor below. The FBI updated them on the most recent information regarding the crash. The Red Cross and UAL explained the schedule and tried to describe what they might see that day. Behind privacy screens, relatives gave blood samples for DNA testing to help identify their loved ones.

After the briefings, the families that chose to go to the crash site were led to a bus caravan. Those that chose to stay at Seven Springs remained at the family center, returned to their rooms or wandered about the resort.

In addition to forty or more family members, each bus carried a Red Cross spiritual aid, a United representative and one or more Red Cross mental health workers. The Monday trip required six motor coaches to transport the family members to the crash site. The buses departed Seven Springs in tight formation, protected by a State Police escort.

As the caravan descended the forested mountain and began to pass scattered houses, the families expressed surprise and gratitude at seeing signs of support and American flags. The feeling grew even stronger as the caravan approached the more populated areas on the edge of Somerset. Businesses had changed their signs to read "God Bless America," "Thank You, Flight 93 Heroes" or other inspirational messages. As the buses approached the edge of Somerset, individuals and groups of people lined the route and waved.

The coaches rounded a sharp turn and apparently surprised a knot of well-wishers who were waiting for the buses. An elderly man, realizing that the families had arrived, turned toward them and came to attention with a crisp salute.

When the buses entered Somerset, the Borough Police and State Police had already blocked traffic and allowed the buses to go unimpeded through the traffic lights. As the caravan approached each set of officers, they would come to attention and salute until all the coaches had passed. Family members cried, waved, blew kisses and saluted in return.

Corporal Craig Bowman, who coordinated communications for the Pennsylvania State Police on 9/11, helped the buses get through town.

Bowman: What really got to me were the busloads of families. I knew that there were forty innocent people who lost their lives there. But where it really hit home is when I was told to come down to Somerset Borough and arrange with the Borough Police to get these buses a clear passage through town. We didn't want them sitting at stoplights.

Out of respect, we saluted the family members. I was down at a big intersection. I had another guy with me. We had all of the traffic stopped, and I saluted the buses.

To see the number of buses...

I was thinking how many people were so much more directly affected than those of us here in Somerset County. I got choked up standing there at attention, saluting the buses.

The outpouring of support towards the families continued during the slow trip through Somerset. Although still apprehensive, family members appeared somewhat more at ease after having seen this display of caring from the local population.

The buses lumbered out of town and traveled through the less populated areas on Route 31 east of Somerset. Some family members began to converse with local volunteers about the newly erected windmills or the Amish farms that they saw through the windows. These discussions temporarily distracted the families and their caretakers until they approached the hamlet of Shanksville.

In Shanksville, several dozen residents congregated in the yards between houses. A large piece of plywood painted white announced "God Bless the Heroes." It had already been signed by hundreds of well-wishers. Flowers surrounded Shanksville's makeshift memorial. The townspeople waved, cried and said, "God bless you." From inside the buses the family members pressed their faces and hands against the windows and mouthed, "Thank you." The heroes' grateful relatives asked to stop to meet the townspeople, but the caravan continued slowly through town.

Marge Montgomery was a certified nurse midwife and worked as a Red Cross volunteer. Marge and her husband had four children of their own and two from his first marriage, from which he is widowed.

Montgomery: The buses were finally loaded. I was sitting in the very back with a minister from the Shanksville area. There was one other nurse on the bus who was very vivacious and handed out the goodies, snacks and drinks.

I was on the bus with the Spanish-speaking folks and Mark Bingham's family. I happened to be sitting right behind the Bingham family. They were just such gracious, warm and loving people. Just to be in contact with them was a real gift. They were sharing childhood pictures.

The mood was somber and there were tears, but there was also some laughter. People were sharing some stories about the funny things their loved ones had done. Very appropriate grieving in a very loving way. They were talking about the beautiful rolling hills of Somerset County. We talked about how this is called the Roof Garden of Pennsylvania. Some of the folks said what a beautiful description that was for where their loved ones were resting. They felt great irony that here they were, out in the middle of nowhere.

There was a lot of pride. That was very apparent from many different people. The people on this flight were very special heroes, and their lives made a difference. At the time, there was less specific information available, but we generally knew what had happened on the plane.

Coming through Shanksville, there were all of those displays by the residents. How grateful the families were that people had done that and were feeling a part of their loss and the tragedy. I talked with some of them about my own feelings.

We think we live here in this nice, secluded, safe spot. My own children go to the Valley School in Ligonier. My little seven-year-old daughter was out playing in the playground when this plane flew overhead very, very low. My son was inside the school and heard the plane going overhead, too. They thought it was really strange. These maintenance guys were watching, and they didn't think it was going to clear the mountain. Anywhere along the plane's path, there could have been another tragedy. It seemed to have been chosen that they landed in the middle of nothing. In a spot where no one else was hurt except for those whose lives were already in jeopardy.

Just beyond Shanksville, the buses began to pass the State Police guarding the site. The intersection of Buckstown Road and Lambertsville Road marked the extent of the outer perimeter. Troopers posted the road every fifty yards the rest of the way. Alongside some of the marked police cars, troopers built small fires to ward off the morning chill. As the buses came into sight, they all came to attention and then saluted as the buses passed.

The waves of saluting police officers carried the buses to the intersection of Little Prairie Lane, where a right turn put them in front of the media village. Hundreds of media personnel, Salvation Army and Red Cross volunteers as well as local residents wedged themselves between groups of standing and mounted State Troopers. This human wall lined the road to the point where the media village stopped. The caravan continued to creep toward its stop at the command center.

There, Joe Marotta, the United representative in charge of the operation, began to help the families disembark. Looking up the asphalt toward the command center, families could see troopers, ambulance workers and other plainclothes personnel standing around vehicles, campers, and tents.

As the families started up the newly laid slope of road, the site workers came to attention and saluted on both sides of the road.

The families walked toward the flag that flew over the US Capitol on September 11 and the cross, erected after much debate. To the right of that lay the straw memorial already lovingly adorned with mementos from site workers and the families who visited the preceding weekend. But most of the heroes' relatives walked beyond all of that to the end of the newly laid asphalt and onto the bed of supporting shale. They continued walking up to the fluorescent orange mesh fence that separated the command center from the field that sloped down to the crater.

The impact point looked like a construction project with the workers on break. Large piles of dirt and heavy equipment stood around a large hole. Charred trees at the edge of a forest provided the background. No debris was visible. Stillness and silence radiated from the crater. The families replied with muffled sobs and louder cries of grief.

The Red Cross counselors backed away and allowed the families to do whatever they needed to do with their time at the site. Some helped the elderly move from the fence back to the area of the straw memorial. Others fetched bottled water from the Salvation Army.

For the next ninety minutes, FBI, State Police and NTSB officials circulated among the families, answering questions. Clergy prayed with small groups of mourners. Some families took pictures. Others just stared at the crater.

Tom Bender worked at the site when the families arrived.

Bender: Monday there were several handicapped vans that came before the buses did. They were there for probably an hour and a half, two hours. We had heard reports of Laura Bush coming up to the memorial service at Indian Lake and also Governor Ridge. But we didn't know if they were coming to the site, as well. We weren't sure what to do. People would give us all of this information, and we wondered what were we supposed to do.

When the buses were coming, we were told that they were on their way and that they were probably at the media center or something like that. We just kind of waited. Jamie Svonavec was one of the local guys excavating in the crater for the FBI. He had come up with a pickup to get fuel for some of the heavy equipment down at the crater. When the buses finally came up, his fuel truck was there and I was talking with him. We saw the buses come and the State Police line up. They all came to attention. He said, "I didn't want to be up here for this; I don't want to see this."

The State Police stood at attention, the buses stopped. Everybody just kind of stopped whatever they were doing and took their hats off. I had tears running down my face. It was really sobering for me to see. I wasn't very far from you guys when you got off the bus. Seeing little kids, little girls, wives, nieces… [Stops.]

That is when it became real on a different level. That was tough, one bus after the other. I think there were six. That was tough to be so close, to watch all of the expressions and to see this line of State Police that were at attention, just completely stiff.

The silence.

There was usually a lot of hubbub up there and it was complete silence except for the families talking. We didn't know if we should go up there and be

155

with them. Initially we had been told United doesn't want CISM people around. We didn't know who to believe. Then somebody told us to go anyhow. So we did. We were kind of off to the side. The families were near the memorial or looking at the site and leaving notes, flowers, and personal items.

There were a number of people who were dignitaries or heads of something that didn't actually have a lot of contact with the families but needed to be there to show themselves. They seemed helpless. It seemed like they wanted somebody to talk to. They kind of came around, and we were just making small talk. I remember the head of the Red Cross, Bernadette Heeley. I remember shaking hands with her and I said something like, "You must have been really busy lately."

She said, "Yeah, I just came from New York City."

Then she talked about the devastation. We agreed that it was good that we could stay busy.

There was a guy who worked as an aide to the Secretary of Transportation. I talked to him for a while. I talked to some of the family members, but not a lot, mostly other people.

There was some laughter. It is good at funerals to have laughter with the crying. Then everybody left and went to the memorial service at Indian Lake.

That was really odd for me. I felt like I wanted to go up to the straw memorial. So I went over to the straw bales that were set up there overlooking the crash site. The machines all started up again. I talked to some of the guys working the machines, and they said, "Why did they make us stop when all the families came? I would have wanted to see people digging and working, trying to find my uncle's body."

I was looking at the memorial, just reading some of the notes. One of the guys from Pittsburgh CISM said, "You shouldn't go up there and look at that stuff. It is not good for you."

But I felt like I needed to do that. It was so real and personal, reading the notes to people's brothers and sons.

Bill Baker of Somerset EMA continued his work at the site as the families arrived.

Baker: I preferred to work there at nighttime. It was quieter. The first couple of nights, it was as busy as it was during the day. But after the first few days, things would settle down at about 10 or 11 p.m.

In the wee hours of the morning, I would walk around and go up to the memorial and have some time to myself there. Looking down toward the site and then looking at everything that people left for the memorial was very humbling.

On the Monday when the families came, I had been there from Sunday at 6 or 7 p.m. It was about 9 a.m. Monday morning, and Rick had come in to relieve me. We had a dispatcher whose dad drove his camper the whole way back from an RV show in Harrisburg so we could use it. I told Rick that I was going to go into the camper and lie down for a little bit before I went home. I was so tired I was afraid to drive. As soon as I lay down, I was out.

Sometime later, I woke up and I heard these engines running. I couldn't figure out what it was. I looked out the window and saw all of these charter buses lined up from one end of the road to the other. I couldn't go home because I was parked in. I was awake then, so I just stayed up and worked. I didn't get home until after 3 p.m. My wife was having a fit because I hadn't showed up at home, and I hadn't called her because I had been sleeping and then was busy.

It was tough and very humbling. I couldn't imagine the amount of pain that they must have been going through. I was running on pure adrenaline. I was so tired that every day on the way home I would break down and cry the whole way. Before I got home, I would get myself back together and cleaned up so my wife didn't have to deal with me being like that. Then, whenever the families came, I would go through that all over again, except worse.

I could see the pain in their faces. It really bothered me because we were working so hard and everybody was putting in so many hours but it wasn't going to change the results of what had happened. I sometimes wondered if the families, as they looked down over the site, felt that maybe somebody was going to be able to pull out a survivor.

Also, to be honest with you, on a couple of the days, it kind of made me mad because we would have to stop working when they would come to visit and we couldn't get anything done. All I wanted to do was to get done with that recovery and get home to my family. I didn't have a problem with stopping out of respect. It was just the stress level and that I was so tired.

Lieutenant Governor Mark Schweiker spent many days at the crash site.

Schweiker: If anyone wanted to know the nature of overwhelming grief, then they only needed to spend a few days on that hillside.

There was the recovery work that was proceeding in a mechanical sense, and, yet, the site had become a shrine. The sense of pain and overwhelming grief was even worse when the family members were there.

The blackness of the point of impact was spread through the field, because the ground was charred. This added to the feeling of starkness at the staging area, which was probably 300 yards up the hill from the crater, almost like it had been prepared to be a viewing area.

Overlaying the whole scene was the notion that America had been attacked, and these brave people aboard Flight 93 had started the fight back.

They were lost and nothing was going to change that. Rescue wasn't possible. It left us despondent. We worked every day to affect a complete response and support the arriving family members. But through it all, there was an empty feeling because there was nothing we could do to bring them back.

I hit a point, after I don't know how many days of going morning, noon and night without sufficient sleep, when I had my one public loss of composure. I had just spent time with a circle of reporters, and I don't know what hit me. I don't remember the question. It just hit me in the gut and words were not going to do it. It was overwhelming emotion that took over.

It's hard to experience violent endings and abject grief and keep your composure constantly.

Sharon Griffith, of MH/MR, watched as the families visited the crash site.

Griffith: It was a day different than all of the other days. We weren't told anything about what to do. People just did what they did that day naturally. People started lining up along that road. I was up at the very top where the straw memorial was. Now maybe the State Police were told to line up and come to attention, but we weren't. There was a group of us up right where you guys walked. We just came to attention, too. It was like paying homage.

We heard earlier that the families were coming. Half an hour later, nobody was there. People were still standing there lined up. Then the handicapped buses came. That was probably a good hour. Then they left and the big buses came. I remember watching, thinking, "My God, they just keep coming."

There were so many people. I was hoping that they could take some sense of serenity from here, that this would give them some small comfort.

There are some things I remember. It was quiet. You could have heard a pin drop. Then this little boy comes off with his nice suit on and his bow tie all screwed up. He yells, "Is this where the plane went down? Where is the plane? Is that the plane up there?" He points to the helicopter. He was verbalizing what we, as adults, were screaming in our heads.

There was that red and white tent. That is where I met an aunt. She was by herself. She was just sitting there looking out. It was hot that day. I think that is why she went over and sat in there. I just started talking to her and she said to me, "I know my nephew was one of those ones that fought back because I know my nephew and he don't take no shit off anybody."

I thought, "Damn, you go, girl."

At another point, one of the families was in the tent after a while because it was very hot that day. It was the grandma, and it must have been her son that was killed. Her two grandsons were teenagers. They were standing there at the edge, looking out over the field. She had her arms around both of them, and she

158

was shorter than both of them. She said, "Isn't this a beautiful place where your daddy is? Isn't this a beautiful place to be?"

The serenity of that day is what I think of. I hope that other family members got some sense of that tranquility.

But the sons, it was different for them. The one I was watching from very much afar. Later on, everyone was out of the tent again. There was a chair there, and the one son was looking through some things he was holding. I kind of gathered they were pictures. He was looking through them for a long, long time. Just sitting alone, looking through these pictures with the field behind him. Just looking.

After the families had gone and there was nobody up at the straw memorials, I went up there by myself for a little bit. These pictures were lying there of him and his dad and his brother. That is when I knew that was what he was looking at. I think of him often. He was angry. I would be angry, too, if I was a teenager and lost my dad.

I remember there was a man carrying a flight attendant's jacket over his shoulder... [Is quiet and tearful.]

You know, those things are hard for me to not see when I close my eyes at night.

PART 2

THE AFTERMATH

Chapter 21

'A week of loss and heartache'

The heroes' families spent about 90 minutes at the crash site. Marge Montgomery continued to provide what support she could during that time.

Montgomery: I just stayed back to see if there was anybody who needed anything. There was a lady who was very upset and hot. We found an umbrella to hold over her.

After we had been there for quite a while, we were starting to get instructions to move them back. It was very difficult to ask them to leave. I tried to be gentle, saying, "The folks are asking for us to move back to the buses."

I remember the Japanese mom who cried so hard. I was thinking that she might never have an opportunity to come back here. How can we ask her to hurry?

Eventually, the families reboarded the buses to travel a few miles to the memorial service at Indian Lake Lodge. Once again, they passed the media village and well-wishers in Shanksville. The caravan then turned to the left to pass the Shanksville-Stonycreek School on the way to Indian Lake. The heroes' relatives appreciated the sight of the building housing 500 children located only seconds from the crash site.

The coaches continued toward the lake and turned onto the long lane to the resort. Those in the first bus caught sight of an Honor Guard on both sides of the road. Attired in their dress uniforms, the fire and ambulance companies who walked the debris field on 9/11 stood at attention.

Jill Miller of Somerset Ambulance and Mike Sube of Somerset Volunteer Fire Department stood in that line.

Miller: We had an ambulance that followed the buses with the families. We picked them up in Somerset coming from Seven Springs and dropped them off there on the way back. A crew stayed with them the whole way through the service at Indian Lake. We had extra people out there because we were in that lineup of first responders for the buses to drive through.

I think it went remarkably well. The pressure and the stress the families were under was awful. The ironic thing was that some of the family members came up to thank us. One woman that really sticks out in my mind said to one of our members, "We are so sorry for you that, when you got there, you couldn't do what you came to do."

There they were with this great loss, and they were worried about us. They are a bunch of amazing people.

When the buses were coming, a couple of our members said to me, "What are we supposed to do?"

I said, "Just stand there and look straight ahead."

They didn't. I did because I had been a mess and I knew I would be a mess. I had a really long week by then and was on the edge. I just stood and looked straight ahead. A lot of the family members were saying thank you through the windows or waving. We lost it. We did pretty well until they all got through but... [Tears up.]

Everybody really felt strongly that the people on that plane were about the greatest Americans we have had for a long time. We were able to hold it together until they got through, but it was very somber right after that. The only good thing was when they drove up and walked out to the tent, they were literally right above us on the hill. So we couldn't really be bawling and sobbing like two-year-olds because they were right there. They could have turned around and seen that.

Sube: We were asked to come to the memorial service because the families wanted to meet the first responders. We shined our shoes, our trucks and everything else. We got out there and were waiting and waiting and waiting. We saw the tent at the golf course. That was where we thought we were going. We thought we would wait where we were until a certain time when we would go up to the service. Then we were told that we weren't going to be able to attend the service or meet the families. There were several different stories, but the bottom line was that we weren't going to be able to go.

So we waited. Finally, Mrs. Bush came, and everything happened there. We met Congressman Bill Shuster, who came through first and shook everybody's hand. Then Representative Bastian came and shook everybody's hand, both sides, up and down. He personally thanked everybody. Mrs. Bush,

Governor Ridge, and Mrs. Ridge actually drove up to the lodge and then walked back down to shake hands with everybody.

Mrs. Bush, then Governor Ridge, then Mrs. Ridge went right down the line, shaking hands with every single person and thanking them. The fact that they took the time to personally shake everybody's hand put into perspective for us the magnitude of this incident.

Then the buses came through and we all stood at attention. It was very moving, seeing the people in the buses with their hands against the windows. We saw their mouths say, "Thank you."

They were crying and very emotional. I felt very proud to be standing there with fellow firefighters. That was probably one of the best feelings I have ever had being a firefighter. I didn't do a whole lot, but what I did do meant something to these people.

After passing the first responders, the buses made a sharp left turn at the Indian Lake Lodge parking lot. They started past the Pro Shop onto a fairway of the golf course. Suddenly, the coaches jerked to a halt. The scene changed abruptly as men in black suits with German Shepherds and earpieces surrounded the buses. Secret Service dogs sniffed under and around the motor coaches. Family members stared. After a brief inspection, the convoy restarted and eventually parked in a line that stretched over the length of a par four fairway.

The first bus unloaded. Joey Nacke's father led the way to a massive white tent overlooking Indian Lake. On such a beautiful, late-summer day, it looked more like a scene for pending nuptials than a memorial service.

An enormous amount of preparation was necessary to create an appropriate personal, and national, tribute to the fallen heroes. Indian Lake Mayor Barry Lichty, Georgia Lehman and Janice Yingling of the Red Cross and UAL's Fenna Queer all helped with the memorial services.

Lichty: I was told by the Red Cross that this all had to be done in secrecy. At that point, there was still the chance that the President might come. They didn't want this to get out to the media, and they didn't want the general public to be here for the service. It was to be strictly for the families. The Red Cross, the lodge management and I all discussed the various options. We decided that the best thing to do would be to put it over in a secluded area away from the lodge if we could. So we got into golf carts and drove all over the golf course. We decided on an area where they could drive the buses up over the fairways and put everything under a tent. After that, it all fell together pretty quickly.

On Sunday, I believe, I was told that Laura Bush was going to be there. Shortly thereafter, I found out that Lynne Cheney would be coming in on Thursday. The Secret Service came and pretty much closed off the whole area on Sunday. Somehow the word did get out about the memorial service. I was getting calls from television stations to confirm it, but I just pleaded ignorance to all of their questions.

The Red Cross did a really great job of putting together those services in a short period of time.

I thought it was very moving. The Red Cross and the United people were very sympathetic and seemed to be willing to do anything to help the families get through this. Watching how sad those family members were was very difficult.

Lehman: On this crash, Margaret Peppy was the disaster mental health officer. She was the one who organized a lot of the transportation. Our mass care officer, Dan Boils, who is my counterpart in Blair County, coordinated with the Salvation Army about food issues. When there were leftovers, we tried to make arrangements to donate to a charitable organization that could use them immediately.

Also, our responsibility in air crashes is to hold the memorial services. This time there were two. Janis had to help find an appropriate location, flowers and memorial cards, all very quickly.

Yingling: We provided each family member with vials of soil from Somerset County. We had to get the vials and the little jewel boxes to put them in.

We met with Barry Lichty, the Mayor of Indian Lake, several times about arrangements for the memorials. Of course, we had to have the FBI and the State Troopers come in and secure the site and give us instructions on where Mrs. Bush was to sit if she decided to stay for the memorial or for the dinner afterwards.

It was a very solemn affair. The only individuals that were permitted to stay for the dinner with the family members were the mental health people or the dignitaries, none of which included any of the other Red Cross volunteers.

Normally, we only have to deal with one memorial service. But in that instance, we had to do two. Plan, prepare, execute. Of course, the second time it rained, so we had to do some reworking of the original plans to accommodate everyone. We actually had a speakerphone for some family members from Hawaii. They were unable to attend, but they were able to listen.

There was a gentleman in charge of the clergy. He is a Red Cross volunteer from the Virginia area, I believe. His name is Claude DeEscue, and he was the person in charge of the service. He designed and coordinated that service. He made sure that it was non-denominational.

The Red Cross person who was the event planner spent a lot of time with that particular function. Her name is Amy Gabriel. She is Georgia's counterpart from the Red Cross in Wilkes-Barre. Unfortunately for her, she has experience. They had an air crash very close to their chapter. She did a phenomenal job.

Queer: The Monday morning of the first memorial, I started at Seven Springs and then drove to Confluence to pick up the programs for the service. My friend Barb Herald helped me with them. We realized on Sunday that we needed a printer to make programs by early Monday morning.

Barb got that set up for us. They printed the programs that day, let them dry overnight, and we picked them up on Monday. Then we stopped at Laurel Quick Print in Somerset and picked up some other things.

We went up and made sure that everything was set up at Indian Lake. They brought in these beautiful little vials with Somerset County earth for the families. I made sure that all of that was ready to go up at the tent.

I have been to Indian Lake many times, but I have never been on the golf course. I looked down from the tent at that beautiful lake, and I was in awe.

When the people started arriving, we went over by the golf snack shop. I just stood there and watched everybody come by. The Secret Service brought First Lady Laura Bush up after she met the first responders. She said to us, "Thank you all for all of your help throughout this."

She is such a beautiful person. The Secret Service took her straight up to the memorial site, and then the buses came. I helped some of the family members off of the buses. After that, I went down and stayed in the lodge until the memorial service was over. They had dinner set up for them. I had my Blazer there in case somebody needed to leave. Once they were seated, I left.

State Troopers formed an Honor Guard at the entrance to the tent. Joey Nacke's father led the way off the first bus, but halted before the Honor Guard. He insisted that his teenage grandsons, Joey's boys, enter first. They accepted the invitation and responsibility with shoulders back and heads upright.

Inside the tent, a semicircle of chairs faced a podium and overlooked the lake. Red Cross volunteers seated the families around the stage and then helped as needed as the service commenced. Helen Thompson and Marge Montgomery continued to help their charges at the service.

Montgomery: I was sitting in the far back on the right. I passed out programs to the families, and then at the end, I was helping pass out the little packages with soil. I thought that was very, very perceptive that someone would think to do that. The families were very appreciative and kept coming back for more, for other family members who weren't able to come.

The First Lady did a very nice job also. She was very warm and comforting. I can't remember what she said now, all these months later, but her presence recognized how important the loss of those lives was to the whole country. That was very valuable to the families.

We went to the lodge afterwards. I was one of the last to come in because we let the families find their places first. It was a very nice meal. I sat at a table with nurses who had been on the buses. There was a table right next to us with a gentleman in a loud Hawaiian shirt. He was a riot. He needed a cell phone, and I had one. He had to make a call to somebody in Ohio or somewhere. He was joking about how I might never see my cell phone again, and he went off with it. That family had left some Hawaiian shirts up at the site. He said that his sister was a party person and she would have wanted us to laugh with our tears. That was a nice, helpful ending to the day. That helped relieve some of the tension.

I was feeling considerable tension throughout it all, as I think most people were. I was also grieving over the recent diagnosis my brother had received of terminal cancer. I have never felt more physically tense than I did in the days after that. That man in the Hawaiian shirt provided some insight into healing in a healthy way.

I was on one of the last buses coming out, helping some of the folks who were having difficulty moving around. On the way back, I finally got to do a little nursing. Folks were having problems with headaches and not feeling well. I was getting ginger ale or pain medication, or tissues. It had been such a long day for them, and they were wiped out. I didn't get home until 9 or 10 p.m.

Thompson: When we got off at Indian Lake, I made sure that all of my people got seated. I think we had forty-six or forty-seven people on our bus.

The rumble that morning was that President Bush or Laura Bush was coming, and we were like, "Yeah, right."

To be honest, I wasn't thinking about that. I just wanted to get my people seated. The head of the Red Cross spoke, and Governor Ridge spoke. When he finished, he addressed the First Lady, and I was shocked. I looked, and there in that front row was Laura Bush.

She was so sincere. She was specific in her comments to each of the families. She was much more petite than she looks in pictures. She is this tiny little lady. The preacher who closed the ceremony while we all lit candles said, "Grab the person next to you and give them a hug and thank God for every day you have."

A secret service guy was near me. I said something like, "Peace be with you."

He grabbed a hold of me and in the emotion he said, "I love you."

It was just so emotional. Everybody hugged each other.

We had little tables set up over at the end of the tent. United or the Red Cross had provided each family member with soil. One of my responsibilities was to help hand those out. They had a little card. It was like a memorial for the families, something that they could take home. I was passing them out, and at the end of the service, they made the announcement that Mrs. Bush would like to meet the families.

I went up and talked to one guy who was really having a rough time. He went up to Laura Bush and said, "This is my sister."

166

He had a picture of his sister. She said, "I'd like to take that home to my husband and show him."

This guy was just so impressed by her sincerity.

Michele Ridge came over and was talking to us. The way that people could identify us was that we all had on Red Cross vests.

The Ridges were wonderful through the whole thing. She was very tearful and very emotional.

Laura Bush walked out from the tent and came over to talk to Michele Ridge. She came over and took my hand. She thanked me for being a volunteer and helping. My husband asked later, "What did you say?"

I said, "I don't know what I said. I know she hugged me, and I think I mumbled something like, 'Thank you for all you have done.'"

She was very hands-on with the families. I think that was really needed.

We walked to the lodge. It seemed like everybody's spirits lifted. They were talking a lot. The rugby player's mom that I had gotten to know was a very classy lady. She shared with me that she felt some closure.

I could finally eat. I had no appetite up to that point because I was very apprehensive about the whole thing. One bus left early because it had the small children. But a lot of the people just lingered, and it was 10 p.m. or 10:15 p.m. until we got back that night.

It was a long day, but it was a good day in that what United Airlines and the Red Cross set out to accomplish happened. I feel honored that I was a part of that, even though it was just a little part.

With her speech at the memorial service, First Lady Laura Bush helped the families to understand that the whole nation felt their sacrifice.

Bush: Thank you, Governor Ridge, for those words of encouragement and for your leadership during this time of sadness for your commonwealth and our country.

This has been a week of loss and heartache of a kind none of us could have imagined. What happened in New York City, in Washington, and here in Pennsylvania, caused deep suffering across the nation.

We are still grieving as details become known – and especially as we learn the names of the lost, the story of their deaths, and the story of each life. All of us, as Americans, share in this grief.

The burden is greatest, however, for the families – like those of you who are with us today. America is learning the names, but you know the people. And you are the ones they thought of in the last moments of life. You are the ones they called, and prayed to see again. You are the ones they loved.

A poet wrote, "Love knows not its own depths until the hour of parting."

The loved ones we remember today knew ~ even in those horrible moments ~ that they were not truly alone, because your love was with them.

And I want each of you to know today that you are not alone. We cannot ease the pain, but this country stands by you. We will always remember what happened that day, and to whom it happened.

I know many of you have felt very directly the compassion of America, both in the communities where you live and in this community where we meet. And on behalf of my husband and the nation, I want to thank every person who has reached out to you with words of sympathy and acts of kindness.

In hours like this, we learn that our faith is an active faith … that we are called to serve and care for one another … and to bring hope and comfort where there is despair and sorrow.

All of this is the work of the living. And as it begins, however long it lasts, we will always hold close the memory of those who have been taken from you and from us.

One of last Tuesday's victims, in his final message to his family, said that he loved them and would see them again. That brave man was a witness for the greatest hope of all … and the hope that unites us now. You grieve today, and the hurt will not soon go away. But that hope is real, and it is forever, just as the love you share with your loved ones is forever.

Gordon Felt visited the crash site with his family on Monday, September 17, 2001.

Felt: I'll never forget the streets lined with State Troopers. Time stopped as they brought those buses out to the crash site.

That was the start of a new journey for all of us. We had all suffered a deeply personal loss. That first trip out to the crash site made us realize that our personal loss was going to be shared with the world.

It was also the first opportunity for us to begin to bond with our new family, the other family members and the community in Shanksville who have been so wonderful to us over the years.

At the end of the day, after we got back to Seven Springs, the media wanted interviews with the families. We were asked if anyone wanted to make a statement. I felt very strongly that some family member had to step forward and say something about one of the heroes as an individual.

We want to make sure that our loved ones are remembered as unique individuals. That's the great fear that we have. Our country lost thousands of people that day, and I don't think any of the families want those thousands of people just to be lumped together with, "Oh, those are the people who died on 9/11."

I remember making a statement first and then the questions afterward. There were rows of media people in the hall. It was a very numbing experience, but important. We had to start putting individual stories with the names of the forty people on that plane. We had to share our pain and give up some of our privacy to memorialize the loss of our loved ones.

Chapter 22

Families Come and Go

Tuesday and Wednesday were transition days at Seven Springs. Many of the families who visited the crash site on Monday departed for home, as those going on Thursday arrived at the resort. John Mates and Kisa Valenti of Seven Springs continued to provide UAL with whatever they needed for the families.

Mates: As time went by, they just kept adding things. They wanted to do this, and they wanted to do that. We tried to accommodate them the best we could. They pretty much filled the hotel. We still had some convention services going on, but some groups had cancelled because of what just happened and because there were no flights. That is how all of these rooms became available.

Valenti: We lost three conferences at that point, one of which rescheduled. So as the rooms were being released, that gave us more rooms to help them.

Joe Marotta could never tell us when they were going to leave. That was becoming a little bit of a problem. We still had reservations scheduled, and I didn't know when or if I had free rooms.

United was really in a difficult situation. They didn't feel that they had the right to limit it to immediate family. Also, some people stayed for both memorial services or needed to go out to the site more than once. The families themselves didn't know, from day to day, how long they would stay. Each one of the thirty or forty United people staying here was assigned to a family. So each one was trying to coordinate with the family members that were coming in.

There was a tremendous amount of organization necessary. These people were from all over this country and from other countries. United needed to get flights for all of them, and there weren't even that many flights yet.

God bless poor Joe, every day I would say, "Well, what do you think, Joe?"

Of course, he couldn't tell me. What were we going to do? We had to just go with the flow, and it was changing daily. Joe and I just kept trying to figure it out. Not every day, it was every hour. It truly was.

When it started to become overwhelming, we kept one person at the desk, and Joe kept calling that same person at the desk. If we had three rooms for Smith, he would say he needed four rooms for Smith and only two rooms for Jones. By the end of that week, even the desk was confused. We were starting to lose control.

I started doing room checks myself. I went and knocked on every door that I thought somebody should be in. That was the only way we could keep track.

The one day, we were thirty rooms short. I got it down to about twenty-two by knocking on eight empty rooms that United thought somebody had occupied. At that point, we knew we were still short. So we had the front desk staff say to new guests arriving that we were trying to accommodate some of the family members from the crash. Then they would ask if the guests would mind upgrading to a condo at the top of the slopes versus the hotel. So we upgraded them to the condos, and it all worked out.

Every morning I would check, and nobody was sleeping in a car. We did end up having to double up a few Red Cross people and some of the United people.

They started to leave that second Friday. I knew that weekend was critical.

Mates: We didn't need the agency control area as much as we needed the family center upstairs and hotel rooms. It worked out that they were still able to work in the control area, and we could take back that top room where Willi's was located. We still had functions that had to go on over at the ski lodge. Once the family center was down, we were able to direct the people who had functions at the ski lodge down the normal way instead of shuttling them around the restricted areas. The conventions all understood, though.

Valenti: Absolutely. We had many people offering whatever they could do to help. Once everyone realized the families were here, people were dropping things off for them. Our PR Department was the headquarters for people coming in, like the schools making cards and signs.

Mates: Joe and the other organizers left. They were so patient, so nice to work with. It wasn't, "I need this, this, and this." They were very polite.

Valenti: It is amazing because I think Joe is an accountant and this is not his regular job. So he literally got up from his desk and had to do this. They all had other responsibilities at United but had been trained in the event of a crash. Some had been to another crash, but nothing of this magnitude.

We were truly impressed with how the United people who were here to work with the families really tried to accommodate them and make them comfortable.

I think one of the biggest things that we did was to make them understand that there would be people here. This is a resort, and guests and staff were going to be in and out. They were really big on ID's and security, but that was going to draw attention to the families if they were walking through the halls. Eventually, they realized that they needed their ID's to get into the restricted areas, but it was really in the families' best interests to just blend in with the crowd in the rest of the resort. Some of these families had small children, and that way they could more easily take them to the pool or bowling or to the game room.

Mates: I think we ended up putting in seventy or eighty phone lines and TV lines to all of those areas.

On Wednesday, the media found out that the families were coming here. We ended up using Festival Hall as a media room. The media were able to stay there and do anything they wanted, but not at the ski lodge area. So they parked their satellite trucks outside Festival Hall and broadcast from there. They even used the stage in there for news conferences.

Our Seven Springs Police Department, assisted by our resort security, did a great job keeping the media away from the restricted areas. We also made a chapel in the lodge.

Valenti: It was in one of the meeting rooms. We put in flowers and seats and lowered the lights. There was a chaplain that was available to be with any of the family members if they desired. It was open continuously, and we kept a security guard there so that they would have some quiet.

Mates: I remember how quiet it was.

Valenti: I remember going into breakfast at the family center before the trip to the site. I was apprehensive because I wasn't sure what I was walking into. All of the families would be in there, and I didn't know what the mood would be.

As I walked in, there was a lot of conversation. There were a lot of people moving to and from the buffet table and sitting down and talking to other people. I was just watching this whole bonding thing going on between the people. I realized that they really needed that time to share with the other families.

I think for all of us to have been able to do something like we did for them made our jobs a little more worthwhile and rewarding. A lot of people you talk to say, "If I could have only done something."

I am glad we were able to do something.

The beautiful late summer weather that had continued since September 11 changed abruptly in the early hours of Thursday morning. A cold rainstorm forced the Red Cross to alter plans for the Thursday trip. The memorial service at Indian Lake had to be moved into the lodge. At the site, they covered the area around the straw memorial with a large tent. At Seven Springs, UAL stocked the buses with ponchos and umbrellas.

Fortunately, the rain began to dissipate as families boarded that morning at Seven Springs. The second excursion moved along much as the first.

At Indian Lake Lodge, the Red Cross changed plans again when Governor Ridge had to cancel.

Pennsylvania Attorney General Mike Fisher attended both memorial services and substituted for Governor Ridge as the speaker before Lynne Cheney on Thursday.

Fisher: On Thursday, I got to the Somerset County Airport and was waiting for the Governor. The Governor did not show. His press person said that the Governor had asked if I would greet Attorney General Ashcroft and FBI Director Mueller and take them over to the site. I did so and introduced them at the news conference and made some comments on behalf of Governor Ridge.

After the news conference, the Governor's staff asked if I could stay for the memorial service, deliver some remarks, and introduce Lynne Cheney. I told them that I would cancel my plans and do so but that I didn't have any remarks prepared. They had a general outline of what the Governor was going to speak about at the memorial service. I edited those remarks further and delivered that as my speech.

It was another very sad day. It had rained a lot the night before and that morning, so this service had to be held indoors. They had everything set up for the memorial service at Indian Lake Lodge. It was a similar service to the one on Monday, and Mrs. Cheney presented a lovely speech.

I stayed and talked to virtually all of the family members that day. There were some very tragic stories. I have a lot more specific memories from that day because I spoke with so many more of the families.

I spoke with the woman whose husband was an environmental attorney from California. He had three children sitting there in the front row. It was heartbreaking.

I remember talking to another fellow who was from New York City. His father had been killed while traveling to California for a funeral.

Many of those families talked about being so saddened by their loss but being so proud that their loved one was an American hero and may have saved thousands of lives. Hopefully, that source of pride, at least partially, softened the blow of this tragedy.

I was reflecting on all of that on the way home that night when Leslie Gramas, who worked for the Governor, called at about 8:45. She said, "Mike, I am just calling to let you know that at 9 p.m. the Governor is going to be named by the President as the Director of Homeland Security. That is why they kept him in Washington."

Lynne Cheney provided the keynote address at the Thursday memorial service.

Cheney: Thank you, Attorney General Fisher. Thank you for your kind words and for your strength during this difficult time.

On September 11, the Vice President and I, like all of you, listened and watched in horror as the terrible news came in from New York, Washington and here in Pennsylvania. Words simply cannot describe the anguish that washed over our nation during those first hours and days.

With each new report, we began more fully to understand the enormity of the events that were unfolding, and what those events would mean to so many Americans; to mothers and fathers, to brothers and sisters, and, most heartbreakingly, to children.

The Vice President and I want those of you who have lost loved ones to know that you are in our thoughts and prayers. The President and Mrs. Bush want you to know that, too. The journey you face is unique in many ways, but you are not alone. All of America is with you.

Your loved ones' lives were cut short, and we mourn with you. We are so sorry. But all of America is trying to turn that sorrow into something good. We are talking to those we don't hear from often enough. We are putting aside our problems and trying to help others. We are stopping to think about what really matters during the time we have on this earth.

The men and women of Flight 93 were brave in a way few of us will ever be called on to be, and they have inspired us. One proud citizen observed, "In the past, the words of our anthem seemed abstract, referring to bravery in battles long over. But last week's bravery, stemming from care and concern for others, was happening over and over before our eyes."

I hope it is of some comfort to you that your loved ones have made us better. They have made this country better, spurring us to think anew of why we love this land. Every tear that is shed when we sing "America the Beautiful" or "God Bless America" is a tribute to those you have loved and lost.

A poet once tried to find comfort with these words. The dead, he wrote, are "made one with Nature."

We hear their voices "in all her music, from the moan of thunder, to the song of night's sweet bird." They are "a presence to be felt and known in darkness and in light." They are "a portion of the loveliness which once [they] made more lovely."

Someday we shall all join our dear ones who have gone before, but for now, whenever we see beauty, we will think of their beautiful souls. When we witness kindness, when we hear of heroism, we will remember them. And when we try ourselves to show regard for others and when we try ourselves to be brave, we will be creating the truest memorial for those who died on Flight 93.

Ken Nacke rode the bus caravan to the site on both Monday and Thursday.

Nacke: On Monday, I was worried about my mom and dad, who sat in the front of the bus. I think what I remember most of that trip was all of our cousins and aunts and uncles that made the trip to the memorial service. Safety in numbers.

I don't think I had started grieving yet. I was more driven to figure out what had happened. I think that was my defense mechanism, and also what I do for a living. I was very sad, and I couldn't sleep. My oldest brother was gone, and I couldn't put those feelings into words, and I was worrying about my mom and dad.

Captain Monaco told me something profound when I went up by myself on Saturday. He said, "Get your grieving done now; shed your tears now so you can be strong for your mom and dad and your family."

Good words and good advice. I let my emotions go when I was out there by myself so it wouldn't put added stress on my mom and dad.

I tried to take on as much of the responsibility as I could while we were out there, so they wouldn't have to do it. I talked to the DMORT people. I gave them a blood sample for the DNA comparison. I provided as much identifying information as I could, like what clothes he was wearing, what he was carrying with him.

Those are questions I didn't think my parents had to answer. Let them get on with their grieving.

My dad and I went for a walk around Seven Springs one night when neither of us could sleep. We were just reminiscing. My dad was very guarded with his emotions. I said, "This is going to sound stupid, Dad, but you should feel proud of yourself."

He looked at me, and I could only imagine what was going on in his mind. He just lost his oldest son, and his second son is telling him he ought to be proud.

I said, "You raised us to be the people that we are. You gave us the fundamentals. You taught us to stand up, defend and protect ourselves and what is important to us.

"Granted, Joey is not here, and we all miss and love him, but take pride that your son reacted in the way of his upbringing. That's a true reflection on you as a parent and as an individual.

"When the hurt is gone one day, you are going to realize that you did a great job as a parent."

He looked at me and said, "My job here is done. I can't teach you any more."

We knew about both services on Monday and Thursday. My mom wanted a family representative at both for Joey. My wife and I talked to our kids and asked if they wanted to come up for Thursday's service. They wanted to be a part of it and have an opportunity to pay their respects.

I thought they should see it for themselves. He treated my children as if they were his own.

My kids loved Uncle Joey. They loved the time they spent with him. He lived with us for a while when he got promoted and took a job close to where we lived. He lived in our basement.

Being a parent, I thought they needed to say their goodbyes in the area where his spirit is.

That evening, from the Capitol, President Bush addressed Congress and the nation. He identified heroes' relatives in the audience. President Bush then named Pennsylvania Gov. Tom Ridge as the man in charge of homeland security. Julia Owen, Tyler Rogers and the rest of the pages watched that speech in person. •

Owen: I stood on the floor of the House on September 20 when President Bush gave that speech. You didn't see this on TV, but after he walked out of the Chamber, everyone in the room spontaneously started singing "God Bless America."

To be in the House Chamber, even when it's empty, is an inspiring experience. To be in there, with the entire Congress, the Cabinet, the Supreme Court and the President after 9/11… and, then to have everyone in that room spontaneously break into, "God Bless America."

I was so choked up.

Rogers: It must have been the same feeling they had in the Chamber after Pearl Harbor.

Flight 93 Crew

Captain Jason M. Dahl, 43

Dahl was a 16-year UAL veteran who began flight lessons at age 13. He was not originally scheduled for Flight 93, but changed plans to be home the following week to see his son.

First Officer LeRoy Homer, 36

Homer was an Air Force Academy graduate who flew cargo planes during the Persian Gulf War. He was married and had a 10-month-old daughter.

Lorraine G. Bay, 58

Bay was a flight attendant with UAL for 37 years and ranked fourth in seniority among Newark attendants. She chose to work Flight 93 over another flight because it was nonstop.

Sandra Bradshaw, 38

Bradshaw requested a minimum number of flights (two 2-day trips per month) after becoming a parent. Flight 93 was her last scheduled trip for September.

Wanda Anita Green, 49

Green was a flight attendant with United for 28 years. She changed her schedule to work Flight 93 to have time off two days later.

CeeCee Lyles, 33

Lyles previously worked for 6 years as a police officer in Ft. Pierce, FL. She had only been a flight attendant since January 2001.

Deborah Welsh, 49

Welsh was the purser for Flight 93 (liaison between Captain and staff). She was not originally scheduled for Flight 93, but changed her plans at the request of a co-worker.

Flight 93 Passengers

Christian Adams, 37

A Biebelsheim, Germany native, Adams was employed by the German Wine Institute. He was traveling on business to attend wine-tastings in San Francisco.

Todd Beamer, 32

Beamer's wife was pregnant with their third child, due in January 2002. Traveling on business to California, he had reservations for his return flight that same day.

Alan Anthony Beaven, 48

Beaven was born in New Zealand and practiced environmental law in the US. He had one last case in California before he was to take a sabbatical to India. He had three children.

Mark Bingham, 30

Bingham's mother and aunt were both flight attendants with United. He ran a PR firm with offices in both New York and San Francisco and was a frequent cross-country flyer.

Deora Frances Bodley, 20

Bodley was a junior at Santa Clara University. She had been visiting friends in New Jersey and Connecticut.

Thomas E. Burnett Jr., 38

Burnett was returning home after attending a business meeting in New Jersey. He was originally scheduled to fly on a different flight that left later in the day.

Georgine Rose Corrigan, 55

Corrigan was an antiques dealer from Honolulu, Hawaii, where she lived with her only daughter, Laura. She was returning home after attending an antique show in Massachusetts with her brother.

Edward P. Felt, 41

Felt lived in New Jersey with his wife and two daughters. He was head engineer for a software firm, flying to California for a business meeting.

Colleen Fraser, 51

Both Fraser and her sister, Christine, were disabled and living together in New Jersey. Vice Chairwoman of the NJ Developmental Disabilities Council, Fraser was at the White House when President George Bush signed the ADA into law in 1990.

Andrew Garcia, 62

Garcia and his wife, Dorothy, lived in Carmel, California. Founder of a company that sold and distributed industrial parts, with a significant number of pieces related to the airline industry, Garcia was traveling east for business.

Jeremy Glick, 31

Glick and his wife, Lyzabeth, lived in Hewitt, NJ, with their 12-week-old baby girl, Emerson. He was traveling to San Francisco on business.

Kristin White Gould, 65

Gould lived in New York City and was a medical journalist. She was traveling to San Francisco to vacation with friends.

Lauren Catuzzi Grandcolas, 38

Grandcolas and her husband, Jack, were expecting their first child. She had attended her grandmother's funeral in New Jersey and was returning home.

Donald Freeman Greene, 52

Greene was Executive Vice President of Safe Flight and had his piloting license. He was traveling west to meet his three brothers for a hiking trip near Lake Tahoe, Nevada and then to New Orleans for business.

Richard Guadagno, 38

Guadagno was a federal law enforcement officer, trained on how to respond to a hijacking. He was returning home after attending his grandmother's 100th birthday celebration.

Toshiya Kuge, 20

Kuge was a sophomore at the School of Science and Engineering at Waseda University, Tokyo. He played American football and was a huge Pittsburgh Steeler fan.

Hilda Marcin, 79

Marcin was born in Germany and immigrated to the US when she was eight. She was flying to California to live with her younger daughter.

Nicole Carol Miller, 21

Miller was a senior at West Valley College, San Jose, CA. She was returning home after vacationing with her boyfriend.

Louis J. Nacke II, 42
>Nacke was planning on celebrating his first wedding anniversary in five days. He had two teenage boys from his first marriage. He was traveling to San Francisco on business.

Mark Rothenberg, 52
>Rothenberg was owner of MDR Global Resources, an import business, and had flown over one million miles. He was en route to Taiwan for business.

Christine Snyder, 32
>Snyder was a certified arborist and returning from a conference in Washington, D.C. She was married in June near the water at her home in Honolulu.

John Talignani, 74
>Talignani was a retired Manhattan bartender. He was traveling to California where his stepson had just died in a motor vehicle accident while on his honeymoon.

Honor Elizabeth Wainio, 27
>Wainio lived in New Jersey and was a district manager of the Discovery Channel stores. She was traveling on business.

Marion R. Britton, 53, traveling with Waleska Martinez, 37
>Britton and Martinez were both employed by the US Census Bureau in NYC. They were traveling together to attend a conference in San Francisco.

William Joseph Cashman, 60, traveling with Patrick Joseph Driscoll, 70
>Cashman and Driscoll were close friends who were flying together to meet another friend in California for their annual hiking trip in Yosemite. Both men were devout Catholics who attended Mass daily.

Patricia Cushing, 69, traveling with Jane Folger, 73
>Cushing and Folger were sisters-in-law who became close friends. They were traveling on vacation together to San Francisco.

Joseph DeLuca, 52, traveling with Linda Gronlund, 46
>DeLuca and Gronlund had known each other for 15 years and had started dating 6 months earlier. They were traveling to visit Napa Valley together.

Donald Peterson, 66, traveling with Jean Hoadley Peterson, 55
>The Petersons were traveling to attend a family reunion in Yosemite. They were the only married couple on board Flight 93. They were not originally scheduled to be on the flight.

PART 2

THE AFTERMATH

Chapter 23

Operation Accomplished

By Friday, September 21, the heroes' families had departed for home. As the agencies began to disassemble their headquarters, the staff transformed Seven Springs back into a mountain resort.

Fenna Queer with United Airlines helped some of the families depart.

Queer: After the first memorial, I went back to Pittsburgh to help. We would arrange transportation to get the families to the airport. Then somebody would take them to their gate, get them checked in, get their seat assignments and sit with them until they left. USAir helped a lot by giving us a quiet place for the families to wait, instead of having to sit in the boarding area.

At first, I didn't know what to say while I was sitting there with the families. But they made that easy. They were so grateful and so thankful. They were very open about everything. My biggest fear was that I was going to cry in front of these people. But they were strong. They needed to talk about other things. Basically, that is what I tried to do.

They loved Somerset County. They just could not believe that the people here were so friendly. I remember coming to the memorial service on Friday night. I sat with the families and the United representatives. When I went back to Seven Springs the next day, everybody was commenting on how the town was decorated with red, white and blue.

They were astounded by the memorial service. That was so wonderful and put together so quickly. Our area got a lot of praise from the families. I would be sitting with some of them, waiting to depart, and they would say, "Wow, that town was just something else."

Psychologist Dennis Kashurba experienced some of the same reactions from the families.

Dennis Kashurba: I had family members actually go so far as to say that they would consider relocating to this area as a result of the warmth and caring which they perceived from the local people. One wife was telling her husband that he could telecommute from here.

It reminded me of why I have always cherished living in this area. The level of pretense is so much lower than other places that I have been. I think there was a revelation for some people from metropolitan areas that the people who live out here in fly-over land are real people with the same feelings, emotions and desires that they have.

That was also clearly reflected at the memorials, where the handwritten notes by local people connected them to the heroes and their families.

No matter how different we are, there is that common humanity that unites us, the desire to do something for a person in need.

The week after leaving Somerset County, some of the heroes' families were invited to visit the White House. Gordon Felt was among those who met with President and Mrs. Bush.

Felt: Another reinforcement that this was much bigger than just the loss of a brother was getting asked to the White House the following week. It was so overwhelming to be with this large group of family members who didn't really know each other but had just gone through this incredibly traumatic experience and were thrust into the venue of the White House.

We were standing in one of the waiting rooms and beginning to meet other family members. I was standing next to Hamilton Peterson. We struck up a conversation about our kids. We started to get to know each other. We were brought into the East Room where there were some speakers. Then, the President came out and spoke to us.

Following that, the President went into one of the side rooms, and each family was brought to him. It was such an overwhelming experience. It might have been three minutes or four minutes, but it seemed to be quite a long time to be holding the attention of the President of the United States and for him to talk with us about my brother.

I was there with my wife and kids, Ed's wife and daughters and my mom. The President was gracious and concerned. The First Lady was there as well and was just wonderful.

We moved on and then the next family came in. They had a reception for us, and they allowed us to wander around the first floor of the White House and into the State Dining Room.

Aside from meeting the President, the other aspect of that day that stood out in my mind was when we were leaving. There was a corridor that we walked down, and it was lined on both sides with staff members, interns and people employed in the White House. They applauded as we walked through. They seemed to be saying, we could have died, and your loss may have saved our lives.

That tribute and the one that we got from the State Troopers in Pennsylvania who were lining the road, saluting, as our buses were heading out to the crash site the first time, are two images that I am so proud to have experienced and will vividly stay with me for the rest of my life.

As the operation at Seven Springs closed down, the work at the site and morgue continued through the weekend. However, the original FBI estimate of a 6-week investigation proved to be a gross overestimation. Two weeks after the attacks, the FBI finished its investigation and recovery work.

Even Wells Morrison of the FBI was surprised at how efficiently the investigation progressed.

Morrison: A lot of individuals took the initiative to get things organized and get things done. But how this happened in two weeks? We were looking at four to six weeks. I think that is what most of us thought. But it just went faster than we imagined. We could still be there today if we only had a half a dozen people. There are only so many people that can work in the crater at one time. So you had to be careful about overloading, as well. We brought in just enough people, and we worked long days.

We had a lot of people working the crater. They got it down to a pretty smooth-running machine. The first couple of days are usually your toughest. Getting organized. Getting set up. They just got it organized and set up and running smoothly out there.

I will reiterate that the people of Somerset County are great. You can be proud to live in Somerset County. The people really did what you expect Americans to do.

Penny Reiman continued to supervise radiology services at the temporary morgue, while Roger Bailey maintained his responsibilities of working the DECON line until the end of the operation.

Reiman: Toward the end it was very wearing. I didn't want to go out there again, but I needed to do it. The second Sunday, I got a call from Bob

Mulcahy. He is the Funeral Director in Central City. Bob said, "We miss you in here. We haven't seen you for a while. What's wrong?"

I said, "Oh, I just didn't think you needed anything. I thought if you needed me you would call me."

"There is somebody that wants to talk to you."

"Who?"

"The FBI needs to talk to you."

"Oh great."

My daughter was making cookies for 4-H, and I thought we would make some cookies and take them in. I went in, and my first comment to Bob was, "Well, if they needed to talk to me, they knew where to find me."

Ken Dunn is an FBI agent. He said, "I just wanted you to have this. I appreciated working with you."

He gave me an FBI hat. He wanted to give it to me personally. That was touching.

Bailey: The FBI talked to Tommy Brown a lot. They talked about how tense and tight they were. So Tommy came up with an idea. He came back to the fire department and said, "I would like to host a night where we get everybody from the crash site and have something for them to drink and eat because they can't go out in public and discuss and relieve the stress of the day."

We had a thing at the fire hall for the site workers on the Saturday night before they left. The NTSB, the FBI, the ATF, the State Police and the United people. We got some beer and some hotdogs. It wasn't a party. We called it stress relief, some place where you could go and sit down together and just unwind and let it out. It started about 8:00 and went until about 11:30 p.m. That place was packed. I bet there were 300 people there. The site workers thought it was great.

The first couple guys came in and said, "You don't have a boot out for donations? Get a boot out!"

Just unbelievable.

The next day, I was out there working. That was the day when they were cleaning up and leaving. One of the agents, Ken, I got to know well. He said, "I'm traveling today and tomorrow and have Tuesday off. I've got to go to New York on Wednesday. We would love to pack you guys up and take you with us."

Jon Meyer of WJAC-TV expressed a reaction to the shutdown of the operation that was common among site workers.

Meyer: The day after the FBI shut down, I tried to get up for work in the morning and couldn't get out of bed.

I had absolutely no energy left after working eighteen-hour days for nearly two weeks. I called the station and told them I was sick and couldn't get out of bed.

I think I slept for twenty-eight hours. I had been going on adrenaline, and after the FBI wrapped up, the adrenaline was all gone and I just crashed.

County Solicitor Dan Rullo watched as the site jurisdiction officially changed from the FBI to the Somerset County Coroner.

Rullo: The day when the FBI turned the site over to us, there was a press conference at the media center. There was a hellish rain with heavy winds. The FBI announced they were turning the site over to the coroner. The next day, after that heavy rain, a lot of the stuff that was hidden in the trees was down on the ground.

We realized very quickly that we had to send another group of people to canvass through the area again. We couldn't leave it that way.

When we first said we were going to go back in, the FBI wanted to send a team back in, too, although it was the coroner's site at that point. The FBI decided not to go back in.

The Emergency Management people have this special response group that is comprised of emergency personnel from throughout Pennsylvania. There were a couple hundred of these people who came in from various fire companies from all over western Pennsylvania to finish the recovery. These people were essentially shoulder-to-shoulder, some of them on their hands and knees, going through the site.

Rick Lohr and Somerset EMA organized the second recovery effort.

Lohr: We coordinated what was called "Operation Clean Sweep." We brought over 300 volunteer fire and ambulance personnel in from western Pennsylvania. They were all members of the Southwestern Pennsylvania Emergency Response Group. It is a task force that is comprised of thirteen counties in western Pennsylvania, including Somerset County. It is two or three years old.

Originally, a resource request was submitted to PEMA for 150 to 200 Pennsylvania National Guardsmen. That was not going to happen because of the high state of alert at that point. When it was determined that the National Guard wasn't going to be available, somebody from PEMA came up with the idea of using this group.

We did not want to take volunteers from Somerset County because if you pull one hundred fifty to two hundred volunteer firemen and something happens in the county, you have real problems.

The last weekend of September they came out and worked. They stayed here in Somerset at the county's expense. The Red Cross and Salvation Army fed them up at the site.

They picked up plane parts and flagged body parts. The area was divided up into ten grids. There were ten teams. Each team had approximately ten to fifteen people in it. They worked shoulder to shoulder, knee to knee sometimes.

Each group was assigned an undertaker. When they would find what they believed was a body part, they would flag it. Then they would have an undertaker pick it up.

As the site work ended in Shanksville, recovery operations continued at the World Trade Center site in New York. In Washington, recovery work at the Pentagon proceeded as the military prepared for war in Afghanistan.

The government also issued a warning on another potential attack on the US homeland.

The *New York Times* reported this story on the front page on Sunday, September 30, 2001 under the prophetic headline, "Some Experts Say US Vulnerable to a Germ Attack."

After September 11, 2001 ...

	9/11
	9/12
	9/13
Thousands attend memorial service at Somerset County Courthouse on 9/14	9/14
	9/15
	9/16
Stock Exchange reopens with 7% drop but no panic on 9/17	9/17 — Caravan of family members visits crash site. PA Gov. Ridge and First Lady Laura Bush speak at service on 9/17
	9/18
	9/19
President Bush makes first formal address to Congress and the nation since 9/11 on 9/20	9/20 — Second caravan of family members visits crash site. PA Attorney General Mike Fisher and Lynne Cheney speak at service on 9/20
Families leave Seven Springs; agencies disassemble HQ there on 9/21	9/21

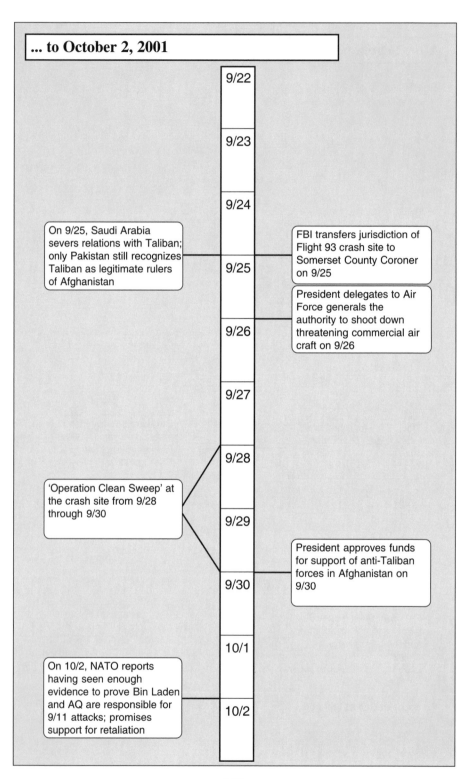

... to October 2, 2001

9/22

9/23

9/24

On 9/25, Saudi Arabia severs relations with Taliban; only Pakistan still recognizes Taliban as legitimate rulers of Afghanistan

9/25

FBI transfers jurisdiction of Flight 93 crash site to Somerset County Coroner on 9/25

President delegates to Air Force generals the authority to shoot down threatening commercial air craft on 9/26

9/26

9/27

9/28

'Operation Clean Sweep' at the crash site from 9/28 through 9/30

9/29

President approves funds for support of anti-Taliban forces in Afghanistan on 9/30

9/30

10/1

On 10/2, NATO reports having seen enough evidence to prove Bin Laden and AQ are responsible for 9/11 attacks; promises support for retaliation

10/2

PART 2

THE AFTERMATH

Chapter 24

Anthrax

On Tuesday, September 18, 2001, one week after the terrorist attacks, an undetermined number of letters, each containing a threatening note and anthrax spores, received Trenton, New Jersey postmarks. Investigators would later suggest that five letters were actually mailed but only two were found.

The first suggestion of a bioterrorism attack was the hospitalization of Robert Stevens on October 2. Stevens was a photo editor for the *Sun* tabloid in Boca Raton, Florida. Investigators postulate that a contaminated letter reached the offices of American Media, Inc. (AMI), which publishes both the *Star* and the *National Enquirer*. The letter was never found.

Government officials initially downplayed the likelihood of bioterrorism as the cause of Stevens' illness. His death on October 5 marked the first fatal case of inhalation anthrax in the United States since 1976. Two days later, investigators detected anthrax spores on Stevens' computer keyboard at work. This led to the closure of the American Media, Inc. building.

At least two more letters with threatening messages and even more potent anthrax received Trenton, New Jersey postmarks on Tuesday, October 9. Investigators examined the United States Postal Service (USPS) mailboxes that fed the Hamilton, New Jersey mail processing facility responsible for the postmarks. They found traces of anthrax in only one drop box. It sat across the street from Princeton University.

Any doubt that a bioterrorism attack was underway vanished when a letter from the first mailing was found, already opened, at NBC News in New York City on October 12. The photocopied and hand trimmed note read:

09-11-01
THIS IS NEXT
TAKE PENACILIN
NOW
DEATH TO AMERICA
DEATH TO ISRAEL
ALLAH IS GREAT

A nervous nation watched that night as the NBC News anchor finished his broadcast by displaying his bottle of the antibiotic Cipro.

Three days later, on October 15, staffers in the office of Senator Tom Daschle opened a letter from the second wave of bioterroristic attacks. The enclosed note read:

09-11-01
YOU CAN NOT STOP US.
WE HAVE THIS ANTHRAX.
YOU DIE NOW.
ARE YOU AFRAID?
DEATH TO AMERICA
DEATH TO ISRAEL
ALLAH IS GREAT.

Government mail service was shut down and Congress adjourned.

Once again, Tyler Rogers, Julia Owen and the other House pages were forced to deal with the unexpected.

Rogers: After 9/11, we started cracking jokes about disasters coming, but anthrax certainly changed our daily lives. They closed the Library of Congress, so we held school in our dorm. We went to the Capitol for our job, but that changed, too, when the House adjourned.

Owen: For two days, they forced us to go. They took everyone to Ocean City. I got to go home. That was weird, getting kicked out of the places where we were going to school, working and living because of possible anthrax contamination.

We hardly ever got mail after that.

Rogers: My friend sent me a package right after I left to be a page, and it didn't get to me until two weeks before I was going home at the end of the school year.

Across the country, hundreds of anthrax scares and hoaxes strained law enforcement and emergency services already on alert from the 9/11 attacks. Many jittery Americans were afraid to handle their mail, and thousands took antibiotics to ensure their safety from an unseen enemy.

Somerset Borough Manager Ben Vinzani, Pennsylvania State Police Corporal Bill Link and volunteer firefighter Roger Bailey were kept busy in Somerset County by the anthrax hoaxes and scares.

Vinzani: After 9/11 we had some concerns regarding our infrastructure. We were especially concerned about our water supply. We were not necessarily worried about a terrorist attack, but some type of copycat incident.

We initially placed the water supply under 24-hour coverage and progressively downgraded the degree of alert over the next few weeks. Our borough police were very busy during this period of time, as were most of our borough employees.

We didn't have any copycat incidents until the anthrax attacks occurred. That ended up being a very scary time that kept Somerset Volunteer Fire Department very busy.

Anthrax Facts

The human form of the disease is caused by contact with spores produced by Bacillus anthracis bacteria. Anthrax is not spread by human-to-human contact. Rather, it is largely a disease of livestock. Human transmission requires exposure to infected animals and/or their meat or hides.

Anthrax has been very rare in the US over the last 50 years, due to livestock vaccinations and more modern animal husbandry practices. It is more common in some Middle Eastern, Asian and African countries.

In the US, an average of less than one case per year was reported through the years 1970 to 2000. Prior to 2001, the most serious outbreak led to nine cases and five deaths in 1957 at a New Hampshire textile mill, where workers unknowingly processed infected Asian goat hair.

Cutaneous anthrax results from spores infecting skin and hatching new bacteria, which produce a potentially deadly toxin. The death rate is 20 to 25%, without treatment. With common antibiotics such as penicillin or doxycycline, the death rate is less than 1%.

Inhalation anthrax results from spores being inhaled into the lungs. Hatching bacteria cause an infection and produce toxin. The death rate in pre-2001 outbreaks was 80 to 100%, even with treatment.

Anthrax spores can survive for years in soil or packaged as biological weapons. A contaminated building must be fumigated with chlorine dioxide to kill spores.

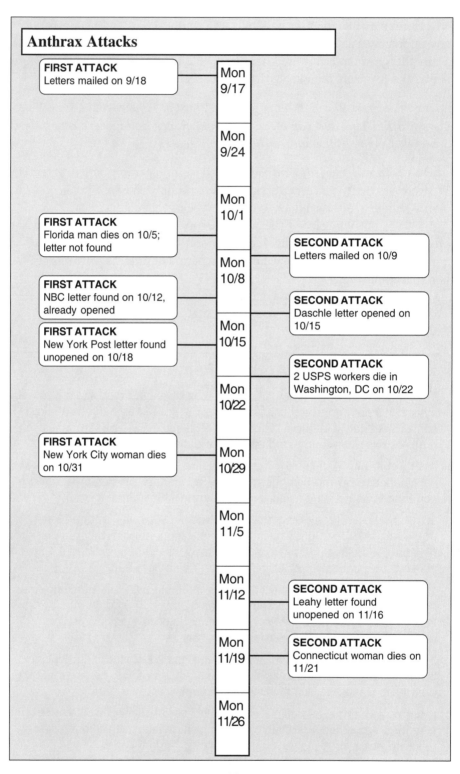

Anthrax Attacks

FIRST ATTACK
Letters mailed on 9/18

Mon 9/17

Mon 9/24

Mon 10/1

FIRST ATTACK
Florida man dies on 10/5;
letter not found

Mon 10/8

SECOND ATTACK
Letters mailed on 10/9

FIRST ATTACK
NBC letter found on 10/12,
already opened

SECOND ATTACK
Daschle letter opened on
10/15

FIRST ATTACK
New York Post letter found
unopened on 10/18

Mon 10/15

SECOND ATTACK
2 USPS workers die in
Washington, DC on 10/22

Mon 10/22

FIRST ATTACK
New York City woman dies
on 10/31

Mon 10/29

Mon 11/5

Mon 11/12

SECOND ATTACK
Leahy letter found
unopened on 11/16

Mon 11/19

SECOND ATTACK
Connecticut woman dies on
11/21

Mon 11/26

Link: I can't even remember how many different people we talked to who thought they had stuff. There was a lady in Shanksville that had something in her mail. People all over started thinking they had it. We had to start shuffling stuff to the labs. You want to talk about tying up people for some time! Fortunately, all of it turned out to be nothing.

The one I remember the best was Planned Parenthood. Jimmy MacKenzie and I went out, and the mail was actually over in a car at a grocery store. A female employee had taken the mail with her on her lunch break. She opened it up and read this threatening note with white powder on it.

We didn't know what the proper procedure was with anthrax or even if it really was anthrax. Since we didn't go by proper procedures, we had to get decontaminated there and then go to the hospital. That was just a mess. We had to take Cipro.

I was thinking, this is just crazy. I could have been a painter or something… whatever job instead of doing this stuff.

It was a couple days, maybe a week, until we were notified that everything was fine. You kind of worried about it but you almost had to laugh it off, you know, just another incident in this crazy world.

Bailey: With an unknown substance, you always go in full protective gear. You go to the best level of protection you can have.

When we got a call, normally County Control would say "HAZMAT Incident," and we would call them. They don't really want to put it over the air. When we'd call, they'd say, "We have so-and-so who was opening a package with a suspicious substance inside. This is where it is."

We'd take our HAZMAT truck. The number of firemen who would go out depended on what time of day it was. If it was in the evening, we could get ten, twelve. In the daytime, there were six, maybe. We had a procedure we developed with the State Police where we had to bag it in one of their bags, and then bag it again.

Two of our guys would suit up in sealed Tyvek suits with air packs. Once we had everything bagged and we cleaned the contaminated site with disinfectant, they would decon us. We went to the staging area where they would hose us down, wash us and then undress us.

We would take it out and then the State Police would transport the stuff to their crime lab. We'd know the results in a couple of days.

On October 18, the second, and last, letter found from the first attack was discovered at the *New York Post*. It contained the same note as the NBC letter. Four days later, the government reported the inhalation anthrax deaths of Thomas Morris Jr. and Joseph Curseen, postal workers at the Brentwood USPS Center that served Washington, D.C.

October 2001 closed with the fourth documented anthrax death. Kathy Nguyen, a New York City hospital worker, died on October 31 from inhalation anthrax, despite no clear exposure to the dangerous spores. The most likely source, cross-contamination of her mail, further terrorized the American people.

The second unopened letter from the second attack was eventually found on November 16. It was addressed to Senator Patrick Leahy, but due to a misread zip code, it had been sent to the State Department mail facility. By the time it reached that facility, government mail was being impounded. The letter remained unopened until being discovered by investigators. The presence of the anthrax was suspected when a USPS employee at the facility developed inhalation anthrax. He survived.

The letter intended for Senator Leahy was the same as the Daschle letter. However, the anthrax preparation had been more highly refined, making it more easily inhaled. Subsequent testing determined that both preparations of anthrax used in the attacks were of the Ames strain. That strain of anthrax was originally researched by the US government before being sent to over twenty research labs around the world.

The anthrax episode ended as bizarrely as it began. On November 21, Ottilie Lundgren of Oxford, Connecticut, died at age 94, one day after being hospitalized with inhalation anthrax. Her only connection to the attacks was that one piece of mail delivered to a neighbor a mile away in early October tested positive for tiny amounts of anthrax.

Investigators traced that letter back to the Hamilton, New Jersey USPS facility that processed the contaminated letters. They concluded that the letter sent to Ms. Lundgren's neighbor passed through a mail machine at the facility within 15 seconds of the letters to Daschle and Leahy. Hundreds of other pieces of mail received by Americans also had similar brushes with an unknown number of envelopes sent in the attacks.

The FBI named one "person of interest" in the case. However, at press time, no one has been charged with a crime in connection with the anthrax attacks.

Anthrax Attack Tolls

- Eleven people diagnosed with inhalation anthrax and 5 died.

- Eleven people diagnosed with cutaneous anthrax and none died.

- Scores of workers at the US Capitol, the USPS and targeted media companies tested positive for anthrax exposure.

- Over $250,000,000 was spent to decontaminate buildings after the attacks.

- Thousands received weeks to months of antibiotic treatment for exposure or prophalaxis.

Chapter 25

War in Afghanistan

At the same time that the government and the people of the United States were struggling to recover from the 9/11 attacks and fearing anthrax in their mail, they were also preparing for America's first war in a decade.

By early October, US diplomatic efforts had totally isolated the Taliban and provided the US military with bases for launching an attack on Afghanistan.

In total darkness, on the night of October 7, 2001, fully armed American jets roared off the deck of the aircraft carrier USS *Carl Vinson*. These aircraft were joined by other US and British planes on the first military mission of the war in Afghanistan. Cruise missiles added to the barrage of airpower aimed at key Taliban and al Qaeda targets. At the same time, CIA and military special operations units initiated ground action.

Explosions were reported in the Afghan capital of Kabul at approximately 12:30 a.m. eastern standard time. President Bush announced the commencement of military operations as jittery Americans tried to settle down to eat dinner or watch Sunday sporting events.

Pittsburgh Steeler Head Coach Bill Cowher was leading his team in its inaugural regular season game at newly constructed Heinz Field.

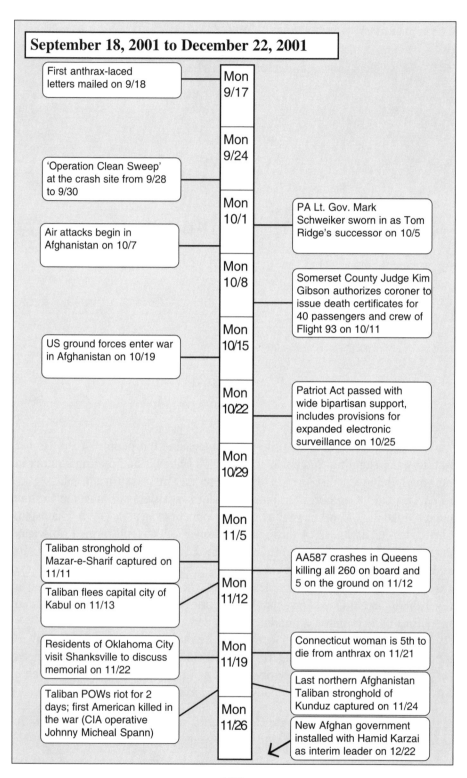

September 18, 2001 to December 22, 2001

First anthrax-laced letters mailed on 9/18

Mon 9/17

Mon 9/24

'Operation Clean Sweep' at the crash site from 9/28 to 9/30

Mon 10/1

PA Lt. Gov. Mark Schweiker sworn in as Tom Ridge's successor on 10/5

Air attacks begin in Afghanistan on 10/7

Mon 10/8

Somerset County Judge Kim Gibson authorizes coroner to issue death certificates for 40 passengers and crew of Flight 93 on 10/11

Mon 10/15

US ground forces enter war in Afghanistan on 10/19

Mon 10/22

Patriot Act passed with wide bipartisan support, includes provisions for expanded electronic surveillance on 10/25

Mon 10/29

Mon 11/5

Taliban stronghold of Mazar-e-Sharif captured on 11/11

AA587 crashes in Queens killing all 260 on board and 5 on the ground on 11/12

Mon 11/12

Taliban flees capital city of Kabul on 11/13

Residents of Oklahoma City visit Shanksville to discuss memorial on 11/22

Mon 11/19

Connecticut woman is 5th to die from anthrax on 11/21

Last northern Afghanistan Taliban stronghold of Kunduz captured on 11/24

Taliban POWs riot for 2 days; first American killed in the war (CIA operative Johnny Micheal Spann)

Mon 11/26

New Afghan government installed with Hamid Karzai as interim leader on 12/22

196

Cowher: We played in Buffalo the week before. Then we came back to Pittsburgh for our home opener. That was the day we started the retaliation in Afghanistan.

It was a bit somber sitting in our new stadium to begin with. I don't think anybody really knew what was going on in the first half.

I actually found out on the sideline from an official who said halftime was going to be a little bit longer than normal because the President was to address the nation.

I looked at him and asked, "Why is he addressing the nation?"

He said, "Oh, you didn't hear? We just started bombing Afghanistan."

I said, "Oh, okay..."

So I had to talk to the players about that at halftime.

The next phase of military operations consisted of a ground assault by joint coalition and Afghan forces opposed to the Taliban government. The stronghold of Mazar-e-Sharif fell on November 11, 2001.

Rapid progress in Afghanistan created some cautious optimism in the US following the 9/11 and anthrax attacks. However, waves of terror swept across the country again on November 12. American Airlines Flight 587 crashed into a Queens neighborhood only three minutes after takeoff from JFK airport. All 260 people on board and five on the ground died.

American Airlines pilot Gregg MacKenzie, like many Americans, feared terrorism was the cause.

MacKenzie: I was working out at the gym and it came on the news. My first instincts were that it was another terrorist thing. I went into the computer, and they had all of the information blocked out. It was about 48 hours before I learned who the crewmembers were.

That one was actually a little closer to home for me because I knew those guys. I didn't know anyone from September 11, 2001, personally. I may have run into them or flown with them one time, but no one that I can actually remember. But Stan, a fellow from that trip, I had flown with before.

The Airbus is the airplane I fly, and my home base is New York. That one really hit home and affected me a lot more.

After terrorism was ruled out at the Queens disaster, the nation refocused on Afghanistan. Taliban forces abandoned Kabul less than a week after the American Airlines 587 crash.

US forces did not suffer a fatality until a CIA agent died during an uprising of Taliban and al Qaeda prisoners in late November. The relatives of Johnny Micheal Spann became the first US military family in the new war to see its worst fears realized.

By early December, the US-led coalition controlled all major cities in Afghanistan. The remnants of Taliban and al Qaeda forces fled to rural mountainous areas. In one such area, the Tora Bora caves complex, Afghan forces, allied with the US led coalition, engaged in a pitched battle with the enemy that lasted for days.

Usama bin Laden may have escaped capture in this engagement; however, during the war, coalition forces killed or captured a quarter of al Qaeda's hierarchy. Included in the body count was Mohammed Atef, Director of al Qaeda's military operations and a planner of the 9/11 attacks.

On December 22, 2001, a new government led by Hamid Karzai ruled Afghanistan. In Somerset County, one military family watched as its loved one could be seen with the new Afghan leader.

Mary Piatt-Bruner helped coordinate MH/MR's response to the Flight 93 crash. Her brother, Lieutenant Colonel Walter Piatt, was Deputy Chief of Staff for the Army's 10th Mountain Division. On September 11, he was stationed at Fort Drum, New York.

Piatt-Bruner: My brother was working on September 11, 2001, and was getting intelligence briefings. An officer came in and said another plane was down in a place called Somerset, Pennsylvania. Obviously, my brother was shocked.

Later I said to him, "Did he know where you are from?"

He said, "No. I never said anything. I just took the information and did with it what I was supposed to do. I just prayed that it just landed in a field somewhere. What else could I do?"

He shipped out for Afghanistan the weekend after Thanksgiving. He had previously been in Bosnia for a while. At first we didn't know where he was going, but we assumed it was Afghanistan.

Eventually, people started to see pictures of him. A friend of mine said a friend of hers was on the Fox News website. There was an article there from the Associated Press that had a quote from my brother.

Then later, there was a *TIME* magazine article out on the 10th Mountain Division. There was a picture of the commander. My brother is standing in that picture, although they don't identify him.

Since then a friend of my dad's found a picture of him on the internet getting off a transport plane with the interim head of Afghanistan. I think there was also a picture of him with Defense Secretary Rumsfeld. So we do see him around.

He and I get to email each other about once a week.

While some Somerset County residents fought in Afghanistan, many more continued the ongoing recovery related to Flight 93. Eric Haglund continued his counseling at the site during the late recovery efforts.

Haglund: Over a month after the crash, we did a debriefing with some of the guys who were involved in finding the last of the remains.

They really had a sense of duty. They admitted it was very difficult. They had found some significant human remains and a lot of personal items. They said that the personal items were even harder to find than the remains. The remains were mostly not identifiable. But the personal stuff, clothing, or someone's hat, things like that, put names and faces on it all.

During that debriefing, I caught myself thinking, "Isn't this bizarre? I am sitting here at this table talking about a terrorist attack and human remains, and I'm here in Shanksville."

I caught myself in another surreal moment. If somebody had told me that I was going to be doing this a year ago, I would have just shaken my head.

Later, I walked around, not realizing until I was standing there, that I was actually standing on the site of impact. There were all of these markers of different colors around, where remains and debris had been found.

I stood there and said a prayer.

It was tough to take in.

The county coroner and his special counsel, Dan Rullo, continued to work with the heroes' families concerning identification of remains as well as other legal issues.

Rullo: One of the things that became very obvious was that the process was going to take months in order to get all of the positive identifications. In many cases, the families were expressing concern about how to get on with their affairs. They wondered how they could start to get some of the assets and bank accounts changed, or life insurance payments applied for, or whatever. Those kinds of legal questions were coming to me.

A coroner in Pennsylvania does not have the authority to issue a death certificate unless there has been a positive identification. So in order for the families to get on with handling their affairs, they were required to go to their individual jurisdictions and try to get a Declaration of Death.

We realized, in the meantime, that there was some kind of procedure that New York was attempting, some kind of an affidavit process that would expedite the death certificate. Mr. Pinkerton, who is a funeral director from Pittsburgh and part of the DMORT team, put me in touch with a fellow in Ventura County, California. He had been involved in the Alaska Air disaster. He was an assistant county solicitor and was very helpful in getting me information about how they expedited the death certificates. Their statute was different from Pennsylvania's, but it gave me some idea as to how to proceed.

I talked to the coroner, and in order to assist these families, we filed a lawsuit. Actually, it is called an Action for Declaratory Judgment. We asked the Court to declare, in light of the circumstances, that no one survived this crash and to immediately issue death certificates.

By that time, my guess is that we had some ten or fifteen positive ID's. There were actually forty-four people on this plane. For four of those people, the FBI said there was no reliable documentation about their identity. Those were the terrorists. So I filed this Action for Declaratory Judgment, asking the Court to authorize the coroner to issue death certificates and have them disbursed by the Bureau of Vital Records of Pennsylvania.

The case laid out the fact that United Airlines had a certified passenger manifest list that identified who these people were. That list identified one extra person on the flight. Originally, there was a concern that a child might have been on the plane. But as it turned out, one passenger actually bought two seats, side by side, for more comfort. We had to get that certified passenger manifest.

The next thing I needed was the cooperation of the FBI. They would have to testify that this plane left Newark at such and such a time, that the plane never stopped, that nobody had the opportunity to get off, and that there were no survivors. Then we had the coroner talk about the excessive time that would be needed to get all of the positive identifications.

I met with Judge Gibson, and we had a date certain scheduled. I had to send out notices to all of the next of kin because we had to get the families to consent to the jurisdiction of Somerset County. We had the hearing and were able to have the Court declare these people deceased in the crash and issue death certificates. This all occurred within thirty days from the day of the crash.

I have been told such promptness is essentially unheard of in a crash of this magnitude. I remember the judge concluded the hearing on October 11, 2001, at about 10:10 a.m., one month exactly to the time that ... [Stops.]

It was ironic.

After the crash site area had been thoroughly searched again during "Operation Clean Sweep" for personal effects and remains, arrangements were made to return the site back to a peaceful mountain meadow.

Rullo: United Airlines engaged a company from Monroeville, Pennsylvania, called Environmental Resource Management (ERM). We met with them at Indian Lake and talked about what was necessary to reclaim this site and follow Department of Environmental Protection (DEP) regulations. We decided about security, how to reclaim the site, where to put new topsoil, where to remove the existing soil, etc. There were a lot of legal issues that were still involved once the recovery was complete. For about six weeks, I spent my practice time almost exclusively dealing with the crash.

They fenced part of the area and put four to six inches of topsoil across the entire heavily graded area and through the wooded area. They cut down a lot of trees. When they cut the trees, they chopped them into bits and buried them in the pit. So if there were any remains embedded in the trees, they were still going to be interred with everything else there.

ERM came in with United and told us what their plans were. They took core samples to determine whether the soil was contaminated with jet fuel. Once they got a clearance from DEP, they actually drained the pond to determine if there were any more parts of the plane or anything in there. They also tested water samples.

Once that was all done, then the area was graded with new topsoil and seeded. They wanted to get that done before the snow fell. We had to go back and redo some things in the spring.

What we didn't want was having souvenir hunters going through there with a metal detector looking for things. That is why we wanted to get the work done quickly and keep the site secured.

Responsibility for site security changed initially from the State Police to a private security firm hired by UAL. Later, Somerset County took control and hired additional sheriff's deputies to patrol the site in vehicles around the clock.

Hundreds of people continued to visit the site daily to pay homage. A makeshift memorial of straw bales stacked at the media village became a site of reverence. Mourners left mementos and prayed at this memorial or at either end of Skyline Drive. As the number of visitors grew, Stonycreek Township supervisors created a temporary memorial off Skyline Drive.

Barbara Black was the curator for Somerset County Historical Society. She lived in Shanksville.

Black: A few weeks after the crash, the county wasn't sure what to do with all the tributes being left. People were coming from all over, getting as close as they possibly could and leaving objects, messages, signing rocks. The county wasn't sure what to do, so they gathered together local officials, the National Park Service and our Congressional Representatives.

On October 10, they came to the decision that the messages and objects that people were leaving meant something. We weren't sure how long this was going to go on. We didn't know if, once the bad weather started, people would come anymore.

So the county asked if I could take care of these tributes because of my training in taking care of objects. I'd never really taken care of objects that have been taped together with duct tape with plastic put over them and made of materials that normally a museum curator wouldn't deal with.

So this was a whole new realm for me. How do I take care of things that were being left on the ground with candles placed on top of them, with the wax dripped all over them?

201

It's incredible what people left. It's incredible what their messages were, so strong, so heartfelt. They were very much a part of this event. These were messages left by people who had made the journey to come and pay their respects, and left incredible things that may have a meaning to them that you or I may never know. We can try and guess.

Baby shoes... what does that mean? No children were on the plane. Does that mean that it was a symbol of these heroic people, that they saved the future for their children? Could be. We don't know.

Anything made out of red, white and blue, whether it was an air freshener for the car or a child's toy that happened to be those colors. If they didn't have something red, white and blue, then they took out some crayons and they drew something and would leave it.

The next largest group of items were religious items of all types, some in languages I don't even know. We tried to have those translated.

At the Historical Society, we had a vacant building where we took the objects, dried them, cleaned them using conservation methods, catalogued them and assigned them each a number. Each item has a unique number so we can track it. They were put into acid-free storage boxes. Everything was catalogued, described, measured, photographed and put into a storage facility.

Discussions began regarding the possibility of a permanent memorial. Just before Thanksgiving, a delegation of Oklahoma City residents visited Shanksville to offer advice regarding the development of a permanent memorial.

State Representative Dr. Robert Bastian attended the meeting with the Oklahoma City contingent. Prior to his political career, Dr. Bastian was a well-known Somerset County veterinarian. Perhaps due to his background, he speaks of politics and politicians with surprising insight and candor.

Bastian: The people from Oklahoma City made two key comments. Number one was that they started with a committee of 360 people. Nobody gets anything done with 360 people. They cut it down to a bare minimum.

The second point, which I thought was the most important and critical thing, was that they got every politician to agree to keep his damn nose out of it. Because there are always innuendoes from politicians: We need to get this guy to do the groundwork because he is my buddy and he needs work. You need to get this guy to do something. This one needs to make the movie and this guy needs to get the flagpole.

Keep them the hell out of it. It will run a lot smoother after that.

I hope that whatever happens out there is solemn, dignified and simple.

Many Somerset County residents who had been involved immediately after the crash found it difficult to visit the temporary memorial.

202

Counselor Sharon Griffith begrudgingly visited the site with some of her family.

Griffith: I didn't want to go back out there. I had no desire to. I had heard there were a lot of people going.

I felt almost protective. I didn't want the families thinking all of these people were coming to look. I saw it as almost like gawking. So I didn't want to go out there.

But my niece and nephew, who are ten and eleven, came in from Pittsburgh. They wanted to go. So I took them out Thanksgiving Day.

Then I saw what that site is to all of the people that didn't experience this as we did living here. It was so different.

They wanted to write something to those families: "We are praying for you," or "God Bless the United States." They wanted to do what we have been doing here. They wanted to connect with those families. I didn't see it the way it probably is for so many people until I saw it through the eyes of my niece and nephew.

My nephew spent the rest of Thanksgiving Day working on this huge poster. He wrote to all of the families on this poster. He drew the outline of the plane in the ground. He drew all of these weapons. "Usama bin Laden, we are going to get you," and "God Bless the USA." Intricate details.

He probably worked for four hours on this. He was so purposeful in what he did. That was his way of working out this thing that was so incomprehensible.

It was healing for him. I never imagined when we were taking him that day that it would ever be like that.

PART 3

MOVING FORWARD

Chapter 26

America's County™

Somerset Daily American reporter Vicky Rock, WJAC-TV reporter Jon Meyer and video journalist Keith Hoffer continued to follow the Flight 93 story throughout the next year.

Rock: What I remember the most about covering this story is the families. From the first days when families came to the crash site until now, nine months later, the families have been remarkable in their courage.

Those who have wished to speak to the press usually first tell us about their loved one who died on the flight and then, without exception, talk about the local people who helped in the recovery or who are in contact with them. One mother said that the people here responded "like a herd of angels."

The passengers and crew of Flight 93 will always be remembered here. I think people here are honored to be entrusted with that memory. We have come to think of the families as our friends and neighbors and hope they feel the same way about the people of Somerset County.

Hoffer: One of the things that is really great now is being able to talk to some of the family members when they come into the area. I feel it is such a privilege to talk to them. We always like to tell them that we were some of the first on the scene and that we felt so much pain for them. Every time we do a story on one of the memorials, it brings all of those feelings back up again.

Meyer: When I meet the families, I tell them that it has been an honor covering this story. I like to thank them for what their family members did for all of us around here.

It was such an incredible story in many ways. Had this happened at any other time, this would have been the biggest national story you could imagine. However, it happened on the worst day in American history. So it ended up being overshadowed by the events in New York and Washington.

Hoffer: I would like to shake the hands of all of the family members and thank them. What their relatives did was so heroic, even if they just sat in their seats while the other people retook the plane. It was just so heroic.

Meyer: Another interesting part of the story that has been incredible to cover is how the people of this area have bonded with all of the families from throughout the country. Some of the family members have become so familiar with people here that it's like they live here now.

The people around here are so compassionate that they would let the families sleep in their houses if they needed to. They really would. They would open up their bedrooms and let them sleep there. That is a really interesting story to cover.

Also, it's interesting how the family members are always thanking the people here. After their loved ones had stopped this plane from hitting the Capitol or hitting something else, what they thought of first was to thank the people of Somerset County for treating them so nicely. That is incredible.

The temporary memorial off Skyline Drive continued to grow with mementos left by the steady stream of daily visitors. Barbara Black continued with her daily rounds of collecting.

Black: Donna Glessner was a friend of mine before the plane went down and is still a close friend. She experienced what I had experienced with all these things being left behind at the memorial. Every day when I would go collecting, I would tell my family, "I'll be out there for half an hour. I've just got to check on things and pick some things up."

Five hours later, I would return because people were coming and there was no one there. They wanted to know the story. They wanted to know where the plane came down. They wanted to talk to somebody. They wanted to tell their story. It was extremely important to them to tell their story.

Donna said, "Barbara, we just can't have people coming to our community and not be taken care of. They leave and they've had no contact with anyone here. This isn't right."

She stood up in church one day and said, "Would anyone volunteer to help me take shifts out at the memorial just to talk to people, to have a human presence there?"

She got twenty people to stand up, right then and there, who said they would help. That group has grown to over forty people who are out there seven days a week, all day long. They take two-hour shifts and provide a human presence.

She asked me, as a trained museum person, to help her develop some guidelines and show her how to train people to talk with other people. I asked the county commissioners, who were responsible for the site at the time, if it was okay. They said, "We think it is wonderful. We don't have any money to give you to help support this, but go ahead and do it."

Since February 2002, the Flight 93 Ambassadors have been helping visitors at the temporary memorial. Mary Jane Kiehl, a Flight 93 Ambassador, talked about her work on a cold day in early 2002.

Kiehl: We're out for two hours at a time. Two hours today and we're Popsicles by the time we are done.

It was originally just on Saturdays and Sundays, but then a few of us said that we could give some time during the week.

It is really an interesting experience to be out here. I look at this as something I can do out of respect for the victims' families. We have gotten to meet a number of them, and they are really very lovely people.

We found out through the back door when Katie Couric was coming, and we met Lisa Beamer, Liz Glick, Alice Hoglan and Deena Burnett.

Then there were the Japanese people who came with an interpreter. They were really nice and asked a lot of questions.

People come locally and from all over the United States. We have a guest book that people sign. We just had someone from France. We have had people from Chile, Norway, Czechoslovakia, Canada, Germany, and all over the United States.

They usually go through and read the comments that are on the boards. A lot of them sign the boards. They ask some questions.

Probably the most common question asked is, "Where did the plane crash?"

I tell them if they look at the front of the flag and go straight back to the woods where the trees are bare, that is the crash site. You can't see much there because it is all filled in.

They take a lot of pictures, and sometimes we help them by taking pictures of them at the memorial.

We have to explain to some of the children what that giant dragline is across the road there. If they are not from the area, they don't have any idea that they use those to dig coal out of the ground.

Some of the ambassadors help collect things that are left here and take them over to the Historical Center. The perishable stuff goes pretty often.

Sometimes, on a day like today, we have to chase things down because of the wind.

Sometimes it takes people a while to realize that we are ambassadors here. Then they will ask us more questions. Sometimes they will shake our hands or give us a hug and tell us they are glad we are here. I explain that I am doing this for the families. They can't be here, but I can be.

John Peters of the Somerset County Planning Commission helped install the bronze plaque bearing the names of the forty heroes at the temporary memorial. The plaque was originally displayed near the straw memorial during the family visits in September 2001.

Peters: The bronze plaque was on display at the county office building after it was removed from the crash site. It was then mounted on a two and a half-ton slab of black granite. The commissioners asked me to escort the truck hauling the monument out to the new temporary memorial site.

Our problem was that guardrails surrounded the parking area on three sides. It was only about four feet in between each set of guardrails. I didn't know quite what to do. About the time we started taking the guardrail apart, a county sheriff's deputy showed up and wanted to know what the hell we were doing. He thought we were tourists, but then he looked at the truck and realized we were working there.

We took out six of the guardrails. The guy used my twenty-foot towing chain that I have never used in my life to pull out the guardrail posts. So he backed the truck in. I thought I was pretty well done by then, but I was the only one with a cell phone, so they asked me if I would stick around.

Then we got into the technical matters. They asked, "How do you want it to face?"

I said, "Well, I'm just a peon. I was just supposed to get you guys here."

There really wasn't much of a choice, maybe fifteen or twenty degrees of parallel with those flagpoles out there. We decided to put it parallel to the flagpoles.

Then I did the womanly thing, "It is a little crooked. Guys, we need to kick this corner back, no that corner."

It is really neat now looking at the monument. If you position yourself to make a diamond shape: the monument, the flagpoles, and you. Then look at the monument and raise your eyes, you are looking right at the crash site.

The Stonycreek Township Supervisors came, and we put the guardrail back. While we were doing that, a lady came to the site. She asked me where the point of impact was. I had just found out from the supervisors, who had gone to get a wrench. So I explained it to her, and she started crying and was really emotional.

A little while later, the supervisors came back, and another woman and her husband showed up. She was on a bridge crossing the Potomac and saw the plane that went into the Pentagon. Her emotions were very similar to mine. She was very angry at the whole thing.

It was interesting because you could see both ends of the spectrum there in a matter of fifteen minutes.

The temporary memorial became center stage for the six-month commemoration of 9/11. Ben Vinzani, Somerset Borough Manager, was honored to be a part of that ceremony.

Vinzani: We became involved because Somerset Borough received a flag from the USS *Carl Vinson*. It was the aircraft carrier that had the distinction of being the first to respond in the war on terrorism. They flew the flag during their first response, and after that, took it down and sent it to us because of our area's involvement with the start of the war.

We decided that it would be an appropriate gesture to present the flag to the families of the victims at the six-month commemoration.

There was a church service in Shanksville prior to the ceremony at the temporary memorial. It was very busy with media all around. I was asked to go into the basement of the church and spend some time with the family members. I felt very privileged, honored, and somewhat numbed by the whole experience.

We were eventually escorted up to the main floor of the church and sat together as the service progressed. Everything was handled very tastefully in the church itself. The media was allowed to have one camera, and the rest of the stations were allowed to use that footage. It was very quiet and solemn throughout the whole service.

We were escorted out of the church and drove over to the crash site. When we got to the crash site, every protocol that was adhered to in the church was thrown out. As soon as I got out of the car, there were at least five microphones and cameras in my face with people asking questions. How do you spell your name? What is your position? What do you do? Where did you get the flag? What does the flag mean?

This was all before I even got to the podium and before anyone made any remarks. Some of the reporters actually were beyond being assertive. They were aggressive. There was no way that it could have been controlled unless we had fifty State Troopers there to provide security.

I had prepared a speech but decided that it was better if I spoke about what I felt at the time. I explained about the meaning of this flag and the letter and basically presented the flag to the families. They passed it around and touched it; eventually it came back to me. We still have it in the borough building lobby on display.

I was very honored to be able to be a part of any of this. Sometimes, when I look back on what has happened, I don't think we realize the magnitude of the events that we were a part of. Decades from now, we are going to look back on this and it will be just as significant as Pearl Harbor.

Firefighter Roger Bailey took part in the White House six-month commemoration before ending the day at a service in Somerset.

Bailey: Somerset EMA had been contacted about sending a busload of first responders to the White House. They asked for three firefighters from each of the departments, some of the Somerset Ambulance people, and the State Police.

Jim Clark, Dan Buck Sr. and I went from Somerset. We boarded a bus at 3:45 a.m. for Washington. We walked right up on the White House lawn. It was cold that day. Some of the policemen from Arlington were sitting right in front of us.

The President gave his address. Then he came down and shook hands with some of the people out front and left. Ridge stuck around, and we walked down, shook his hand, and told him where we were from. We just milled around there a little bit, took some pictures, got on the bus, and came home.

I went to the memorial service out at the Alliance Church that night. Afterwards, I talked to a woman there from United. I told her about being a first responder, working DECON, and how tough it was to deal with. I can still see the first crate that I picked up with those wallet pictures of a child.

As a mild winter dissolved into the spring of 2002, more 9/11 memorials appeared in and around Somerset County. On September 11, 2001, Shanksville-Stonycreek's superintendent was attending the funeral of a relative in Johnstown. Monsignor Raymond Balta of St. Mary's Byzantine Catholic Church officiated at the service. Both presided over the development of what would become popular 9/11 memorials.

Singel: Our kids received all sorts of support from throughout the country. They received letters, cards, teddy bears, and all sorts of things. One of our second grade teachers, Karen Miller, came up with a great idea for us to thank everyone. She suggested that we make a huge thank you photograph.

One of our problems was that we didn't know if we would have enough kids. So I started counting people and drawing it up on a piece of paper. Each of the letters was forty-two feet high, twenty-five feet wide, and there were seventeen feet between letters.

Moe Duppstadt, who is our maintenance man, got a chalk line, and we laid it out. I was still not sure what it was going to look like from the air, so I went up on top of the building. It still looked okay from up there.

We started testing it out by getting a couple of classes and seeing what it would look like when they made the letter T. It still looked pretty good.

We decided to call Jim Will from Berlin who does aerial photography. We scheduled several dates but had to cancel them because of the weather. I believe we finally got a go for it on October 16, 2001.

It was a beautiful, clear day, and there wasn't a cloud in the sky. We started with the T and the H being made by the smallest children. I went up on the roof with a radio. As the classes came out from the school, they would fill up the other letters. I would radio down that we needed more bodies in the H, the K or whatever. A couple of parents happened to be dropping kids off at the school, and we grabbed them to fill in some of the letters.

About that time, Jim called on a cell phone from his airplane. He flew over and snapped a few pictures of it. We never realized what a big deal it was going to be. I wrote a letter to go along with it, and we sent it out to a number of places as a thank you.

After that, it got a lot of attention. We had a call from Oklahoma. They wanted our permission to put a copy in their memorial at Oklahoma City.

That was one of the nicest things that happened from this event. It was really fun for those kids, teachers and parents.

Another thing that happened about a month after the crash was a call from a man named Paul Doucette. He is with the Cornell Companies from Texas.

Mr. Doucette said that they would like to do something for our school, but they weren't exactly sure what that should be. I met with our principals, and we discussed a variety of options and talked back and forth with Mr. Doucette. I kept explaining to him that we really didn't feel like victims with what happened.

Whatever we did, we wanted it to represent something that would somehow honor the community and the school for what everyone did following the tragedy.

Mr. Doucette certainly agreed with that and wanted us to continue working on some ideas. We kept trying to focus on the idea of something that would offer inspiration to others.

Eventually, the idea developed of commissioning some type of a sculpture as the centerpiece of some type of a garden. We discussed the garden more and eventually settled on the idea of putting stones in the garden with quotes on them. Then the question came up as to where we would get the quotes. We decided to get the children to be the ones who would come up with those.

Jan Loney was the sculptor. She came in and meshed very well with our art teacher, Joy Knepp. For weeks they let the kids come up with a variety of ideas of how the sculpture should look and what it was to represent.

Throughout this whole process, the teachers could see this recurring theme of a helping hand. They eventually came up with the idea of imprinting everyone's hands from the school into the design of this plant with pods that is growing skyward. It took about six months from start to finish.

Jim Glessner, one of our teachers, recently retired early to spend more time with his landscaping business. Jim employs some of our students from time to time. Lauren Zimmerman was one of the students who happened to be working with him at the time. Jim and Lauren decided to draw up some ideas for a design of the garden. They eventually refined it and presented it to Mr. Doucette.

I notice a lot of people out there taking pictures in the middle of the school day. It happens all of the time now since the memorial sculpture was publicized in the newspapers.

Msgr. Balta: I was sitting on Main Street in Johnstown looking at the Morley's Dog statue. I was thinking, "Here's a lawn ornament that has become immortalized as a piece of art. Something should be done to remember the people that perished in the terrorist attacks."

We have a parishioner that mentioned that his trucking company, MC Trucking, was transporting debris out of Manhattan from the World Trade Center. So I called and asked him about that.

He said that once investigators cleared the debris, it was just being released. Nobody had really thought about what to do with it, so it was being sold as scrap. It was being sent to China, Argentina, India, wherever.

I thought rather than having it being sent to other countries, melted down and returned here as bicycle parts, why not get some piece of it for a memorial.

I talked to some architects about the feasibility of it. They said we would have to enclose it and fence it off.

I had a totally different idea. I wanted something people could go up to and touch. I thought it was important for people to feel this thing. How big and strong it was. That piece of steel weighs about 12 thousand pounds. When you touch it, you realize what a horrific force it took to distort it like that.

We called a man in Manhattan who said there was one significant piece of structural steel left. The rest was being embargoed because there had been a lot of negative reaction to the metal being sold as scrap. This was on a Thursday afternoon. He added, "You have to get it out of here by tomorrow morning."

I called MC Trucking, and at 8 a.m. they loaded the piece of steel onto a truck and brought it in that Friday night. Saturday morning I went up to look at it.

It was heart stopping.

Then the question was what to do with it? Do we get a designer and get all that complicated? I had thoughts of an artist staring at it for days and then saying, "It's just not talking to me."

I thought that would not be the right approach. On Monday morning, I took it to a fabricator. I didn't want it to be gruesome. I wanted it to shine. I had them clean it and paint it. Two weeks later, it was being set in the ground.

Everyone wanted to be a part of it. Everybody did anything they could, and they all donated their own part of it. The only glitch was that the city cited me $12 for not having a permit. (Laughs)

I didn't have a permit to put up a World Trade Center memorial. They threatened to stop construction when I had a crane and some trucks here. I can remember going down to the city office and saying, "Do you realize what this is? It's a piece of the World Trade Center. Twelve dollars. How significant is that, compared to this?"

I got the building permit.

What's been so impressive is that so many people have come down to see it. They just stand there and touch it and talk about it. It certainly has had more of an impact than a piece of scrap metal.

Singel: Our school got a lot more attention again with Mayor Giuliani coming as graduation speaker in May 2002.

The senior class decided to write to some people and ask them if they would consider speaking at out graduation. I was down at an assembly program one day and my secretary came down and said, "Rudy Giuliani's office is on the phone for you."

I said, "Bonnie, this is not a time for jokes."

At times, one of my board members will call and say that it is the President or somebody like that.

But then she said to me, "No, this really is one of his secretaries."

So I came up, and it was Kate Ansen calling for Mr. Giuliani. She said, "Mr. Singel, we have this letter from your seniors inviting Mr. Giuliani to speak at their commencement. Are you aware of this?"

I said, "Well, not really. But it wouldn't surprise me. We encouraged the kids to write for guest speakers. They could write to whomever they wanted."

She said, "Well, would this have your blessing if he could come?"

I said, "Well, yeah. Certainly. I wouldn't have any problem with that."

I was thinking at that point that the next thing out of her mouth would be something like, "He appreciated the offer but is unable to appear."

Instead, she said, "He really wants to do this."

She went on to say that he had read the letter and that, if he could work out the logistics, he would be very much interested in coming to speak at the graduation.

I said, "We will work with you and do whatever it is that you need us to do so that he can appear."

"The one thing we don't want is to have this leak out to the press right away."

So we met with the seniors and told them and tried to sit on it as long as we could. Eventually, the story did leak out, and we got a call from his office. They wanted us to continue to downplay it because they weren't sure they would be able to make all of the arrangements to get him to appear.

213

We waited for a long time to officially announce it, until his public relations director called and said, "It is a go. You can start releasing the information, and we are going to put it on the AP wire."

On May 31, New York City Mayor Rudy Giuliani addressed the 36 graduates of the Shanksville-Stonycreek Class of 2002. He brought greetings from the city of New York and expressed the idea that the residents of that city and the residents of Somerset County had been tied together by 9/11. Mayor Giuliani went on to say that the United States was attacked because of its belief in freedom and justice. Those beliefs are what give strength and unity to Americans.

The graduation created the opportunity for Shanksville to be invaded again by the national media. Many residents, already media weary and wary, hoped the departure of Mayor Giuliani would commence a quieter future for the area. No one knew that Somerset County would soon be the stage for another dramatic disaster ten miles from Shanksville.

In late July, eighteen coal miners were working the same vein of coal that had been mined at the Flight 93 crash site. The two mining crews were inundated with 70 million gallons of underground water from an abandoned neighboring mine. One crew was able to fight their way to the mine entrance. The other nine miners remained trapped underground.

A Herculean effort by hundreds of local miners, emergency personnel, state mining engineers and Governor Mark Schweiker freed the men after 72 hours of entombment.

Schweiker: It was a godsend. We were able to bring up all nine and those families were reunited.

It was also a godsend for a lot of us to be able to balance the emotional ledger. We lost all on 9/11, and in the summer of 2002, all lived.

I was happy for the people in Somerset that they could rally and affect a rescue since on 9/11 that opportunity was denied them.

The rescue created friendships and bonds that will exist forever. Somerset County is a holy place for me.

Many Somerset County residents who helped in the aftermath of the Flight 93 crash also helped with the Quecreek Mine rescue. The media covered the entire story in real time. The rescue of the miners helped lift the weary spirits of county residents and the aching nation as a whole.

The Quecreek rescue also reinforced Somerset County's nickname of *America's County*™. Somerset County Chamber of Commerce later trademarked the name.

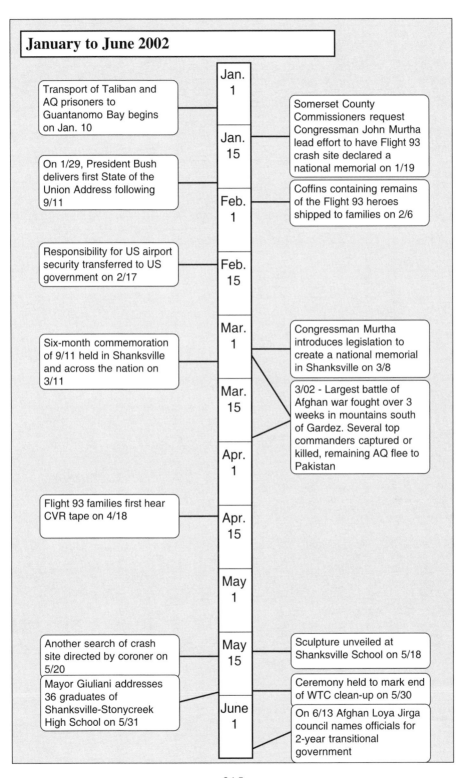

January to June 2002

Transport of Taliban and AQ prisoners to Guantanomo Bay begins on Jan. 10

On 1/29, President Bush delivers first State of the Union Address following 9/11

Responsibility for US airport security transferred to US government on 2/17

Six-month commemoration of 9/11 held in Shanksville and across the nation on 3/11

Flight 93 families first hear CVR tape on 4/18

Another search of crash site directed by coroner on 5/20

Mayor Giuliani addresses 36 graduates of Shanksville-Stonycreek High School on 5/31

Jan. 1
Jan. 15
Feb. 1
Feb. 15
Mar. 1
Mar. 15
Apr. 1
Apr. 15
May 1
May 15
June 1

Somerset County Commissioners request Congressman John Murtha lead effort to have Flight 93 crash site declared a national memorial on 1/19

Coffins containing remains of the Flight 93 heroes shipped to families on 2/6

Congressman Murtha introduces legislation to create a national memorial in Shanksville on 3/8

3/02 - Largest battle of Afghan war fought over 3 weeks in mountains south of Gardez. Several top commanders captured or killed, remaining AQ flee to Pakistan

Sculpture unveiled at Shanksville School on 5/18

Ceremony held to mark end of WTC clean-up on 5/30

On 6/13 Afghan Loya Jirga council names officials for 2-year transitional government

215

PART 3

MOVING FORWARD

Chapter 27

Preparation

The attention of the national media paused only for a short commercial break before refocusing on Somerset County. By late August, reporters were visiting Shanksville daily in preparation for the first anniversary of 9/11.

The temporary memorial had expanded with gifts from around the world. Somerset County officials continued to hold jurisdiction over the crash site area and worked throughout the summer to improve the dirt road that led to the temporary memorial.

By early September, a gravel parking lot had been added, and further improvements were made to prepare for the large number of visitors expected to attend the first anniversary commemoration. However, with no basis for predicting how many people would attend, estimates ran from two thousand to fifty thousand.

Beyond the immediate area of the site, little could be done to prepare for an onslaught of visitors. Shanksville still had no stoplights, one store and six roads to enter and exit. While much of Somerset County buzzed with excitement over the anniversary, many Shanksville residents anticipated the approaching day with anxiety or dread.

Residents sitting on Rick and Tricia King's porch on a Sunday afternoon after Labor Day watched the steady parade of visitors, workers and reporters passing through town to the site. Neighbors would stop by to relate their media story of the day. One described being chased through her yard by a journalist, only narrowly escaping into her garage as she ducked under the closing door. Undeterred, the reporter sprang to the porch and began to pound on the front door.

Some residents expressed genuine fear that the anniversary service would be a target for terrorists. One theme was that since Usama bin Laden frequently returned to the sites of previous attacks, he might find the tens of thousands of people in Shanksville on September 11, 2002, a very attractive target. Also, the ceremony was to be attended by hundreds of family members of the heroes and Director of Homeland Security Tom Ridge. Further, rumors persisted that President Bush was to visit sometime during the course of the day.

Tension increased when a suspicious container was found at the temporary memorial and the State Police called in Somerset County HAZMAT. Roger Bailey was among the HAZMAT team members that responded.

Bailey: I remember it was dark when they found a cooler out there. That was right before the first anniversary, a night or two before. There was a canister inside of it, or something that was kind of goofy. They eventually found out whose it was, and we didn't have to do much. I guess everyone was on edge.

We had already been out to the National Guard Armory to meet with the Secret Service, Emergency Mangement Services, State Police and FBI. We got their code names and procedures for emergencies.

The day of the anniversary, we were staged at the Shanksville fire hall. We set up far enough away so that we weren't going to be part of the problem. We would be part of the solution.

Our role was to be prepared for a chemical or biological incident or if someone blew something up with conventional explosives. We were there to take care of the situation as far as HAZMAT. If there was contamination, we would suit up, go in and set up a DECON. If anybody was hurt, we would get the DECON station going so that they could get medical treatment.

The day before the anniversary, the temporary memorial was closed to the public and access to the surrounding area restricted by the State Police. The heroes' families returned to the county in the days prior to September 11 and stayed at Hidden Valley Resort on Laurel Mountain. A bus caravan carried them to the crash site for some private time on the afternoon of September 10. Mental health workers Terressa Walker and Tom Bender rode on those buses.

Walker: It was a gorgeous, beautiful day. While they were loading the buses, they were giving out these little bracelets for the family members. That was weird because some families wanted them and some didn't.

They were silver bracelets that said "Let's Roll" on them and a date. Some asked, "What is written on that?"

When I showed them the bracelet, they decided if they wanted it or not. I wasn't prepared for that.

What we were told before we went was just to go and be with the families. Support them. That is how it happened in New Jersey when they heard the voice recordings. They asked for local mental health workers to be there. No one talked about the other stuff that each of these families had been through or how they were in such different places at the first anniversary.

We got on the buses. I sat with this little boy dressed up in a suit, the cutest little boy. He said, "Do you like my tie?"

I said, "You look so sharp!"

He was probably the best-dressed person there. I couldn't imagine what he was going to wear for the actual memorial service because he looked so good that day.

His aunt, his dad's sister, was killed in the plane crash. We talked about Harley-Davidson motorcycles. He was there with his father, his mother, his grandparents and other family members and friends.

He was really willing to talk. All you could hear on the bus was the two of us talking about the town and Harleys. The first time that he actually talked about going to the site was when we got to Shanksville and he saw all the cameras and all the people lined up. He asked what was happening and why the cameras were up there. Then he looked back at his family, and they couldn't answer him.

I said, "It's because your aunt was a really special person. That is why everyone is out here."

He said, "okay," and then he was quiet. The closer we got to the site, the quieter he became.

When we got there, they unloaded all of the families. The coroner was there to talk to the families as much as they wanted. They asked him questions about where the plane parts went, how the trees got burned, whatever.

Then they were free to walk around wherever they wanted. It was overgrown and family members were wading through bushes waist and chest high. They were kicking dirt and leaves around, looking for things.

A lot of family members brought teddy bears and flowers and pictures. They had some hay bales set aside back by the trees where family members could put things, a designated area for each person who was on the plane. People went from hay bale to hay bale to learn about the other passengers with whom their loved ones had died.

I remember this little boy's family disappeared and I was left with him. They kind of got caught up in their grief and the experience of being right there where the plane went down.

He got really energized. They had some golf carts there, and he wanted to ride a golf cart in the worst way. But they needed the carts to get some elderly people down to the site. He couldn't wait. He got more and more anxious the longer we were there. He started dragging me. "We have to go now. We have to do this now."

The coroner gathered everyone around, and the little boy looked at me and said, "I don't want to hear what he's going to say."

So, I said, "Now's the time. Let's go see if we can find a free golf cart."

He and I rode around on the golf cart in a circle. He just started laughing and having so much fun. Right there, where the plane went down, I'm with this little boy whose aunt was killed and I'm riding around in a golf cart with him.

I looked at the hundreds and hundreds of people there. It took my breath away to think about what each family had gone through.

We rode around for about fifteen minutes, until the coroner was done talking. I said, "We need to get off now. They need to take this back for the elderly people now."

We were at the site for several hours. The family members would go on the bus for a break and then come back out. But Juan and I were holding hands and walking through all of this commotion. I asked him, "Do you want to go down there and look at your teddy bear?"

He did. So, he took me down and looked at his aunt's picture and his teddy bear. Then he said, "I'm ready to go."

We got back on the bus to ride back to Hidden Valley. He was a lot more quiet than on the way out. Everyone was hot and tired. They were emotionally drained from being there.

Periodically, I would touch him and say, "Juan, I'm going to go back and check on these people and be right back."

I tried to touch base with the family members who were on the bus. "What can I get you? Do you need more water? Are you cool enough? Is the air conditioning okay with you?"

They were really appreciative of that, and they thanked us profusely. They said that if this crash needed to happen anywhere, Somerset County was probably the best place that something as crazy as this could happen.

On the way back, I was able to ask Juan about his aunt. He was wearing a pin with her picture on it. We talked about how pretty she was and how proud she would have been that he was there. He appreciated that.

He asked, "Are you going to be here tomorrow?"

I told him I was.

"Will you ride my bus?" he asked.

I told him I would see what I could do.

Bender: Some things from that day I remember vividly. There was a parent of someone on the plane who took a kite out and began flying it. I heard later that it was symbolic for him because the Taliban had banned kite flying in Afghanistan. It was an act of defiance and freedom.

Some of the family members wanted to go right to the place where the plane went down. Some were crying. Some wanted to be with other people. Some wanted to just be alone. Like a funeral. People grieving. It was a time for them just to be together with the other families with nobody else around. We had been briefed beforehand to stay out of the way.

I took this elderly couple, one on each arm, and we walked in the grass awhile. They didn't say anything until they wanted to go back to the bus and sit down.

I just remember it being really quiet, other than the wind. After being at the crash site, we went to the temporary memorial. Down at the crash site, it was unspeakable, I think. Then, when we were up at the temporary memorial, it was almost more solemn, seeing everything visitors had written and left.

I rode back on the bus with someone who identified herself as Debbie Welsh's best friend. She was from Connecticut. She wanted to talk about Debbie, so we talked and she held my hand and cried.

The ride back into Somerset with her had a big impact on me. I think that made it even more real to me than it had before. The year before, I hadn't really been in contact with any of the family members. I was there for the workers.

Ed Root and other relatives of Flight 93 flight attendant Lorraine Bay arrived in Somerset County the day before the anniversary.

Root: We all stayed up at Hidden Valley. It was a very moving experience to meet some of the other family members for the first time. I had never really met any of the other family members until then.

Lorraine's husband, Erich, is a very private individual; he really stays away from any type of publicity. Most of the time when we come out, it is just a private visit. We come out and pay our respects.

I think all of the ambassadors know Erich because he is out there so much. He and I come out a couple times a year, or he's out with Lorraine's friends, or he'll just come by himself.

He'll call a Somerset florist. They know his voice. He usually stops by to get flowers. Up at the temporary memorial, he puts flowers at the angels of all the flight attendants.

Chapter 28

First Anniversary

Shanksville was quiet except for heavier than normal vehicular traffic at 4:00 a.m. on September 11, 2002. However, the new media village, which had materialized a few hundred yards from the 2001 site, was bustling. The sunny, warm weather of the previous day had turned eerie. Gusty, cold winds were interrupted by rain showers and periods of calm.

Two hours before dawn, all traffic was banned by the State Police on the roads leading to the temporary memorial. The only way for the journalists to get to the site was shuttle buses. Security was so tight and the buses were swept so frequently for weapons and explosives that many media personnel waited in line for over an hour. After dawn broke, the drenched and angry journalists finally boarded buses and the media village cleared out. Those who remained to man the trucks for satellite feeds watched the rain give way to ferocious gusts of cold that flapped tents and moved clouds rapidly across the sky.

In Shanksville, many residents began to assemble at the post office for a ceremony announcing a stamp commemorating 9/11. A color guard of girl scouts raised the flag, state representatives and USPS officials offered remarks, ministers prayed, the local television stations filmed and volunteers circulated refreshments. As attendees milled around afterwards, the buses carrying the family members of the heroes passed on their way to the site. Residents waved and saluted as they had done fifty-one weeks before. Family members returned the salutes and mouthed, "Thank you."

School had been cancelled throughout the county that day in order to utilize school buses for an elaborate shuttle system from pick-up locations throughout Somerset. This turned out to be unnecessary since only three thousand people actually attended the memorial service. Most people in Shanksville watched television coverage at home or at the Shanksville Volunteer Fire Department.

Tom Bender and Terressa Walker accompanied the heroes' families on their trip to the site.

Bender: The Secret Service was at Hidden Valley that morning. There was a heightened sense of anxiety around everything. They came to the buses and said, "Keep moving, keep real tight; don't stop for anything."

As we got out on the road, the families started to see all of the local residents out on the roads, saluting and with flags. It got real quiet. There was no talking on my bus.

We got over to the crash site, and the security was just beyond belief. They had metal detectors set up. As we were getting off the bus, I walked over to the edge of the road. I was looking down into the woods and saw something move. Then I realized that it was a man in camo with a rifle. The more I looked, the more armed people I saw down in the woods. Up on a little dirt pile, there was somebody with a rifle on a tripod and another person next to him with a spotting scope.

There was a long line to get in. The Secret Service searched everything. We got into the fenced-in area, and they told the families where they were going to be able to sit. They had room for 150 people on straw bales, and the rest of us had to stand behind them about twenty feet back.

There was a podium set up and a little stage area with cameras and some cameramen. There were a few sets of straw bales behind the podium, out to the sides. They had camouflage netting behind them. I walked up and was looking around and didn't know what they were.

The grass was moving. I thought there was a groundhog. There was a guy on his belly in camo with a rifle on the ground. Later on, I realized that those straw bales in the front had probably three-eighths inch steel behind them. Someone said that they saw guys come out of the woods with rifles and go under the camo net.

So there we were with people behind us and in front of us with weapons, jets flying over periodically and helicopters hovering above us, in and out of the clouds.

Walker: The day of the memorial was so different from the previous day. It was windy and cold. It was just so eerie.

We met them early, about 6:00 or 7:00 in the morning at Hidden Valley. Again, just checking with everybody. "How are you? Do you have everything you need? What can I do for you?"

At that point, we were trying to make sure people were going to be warm enough. Families were loaded onto the buses. I got panicky because one of Juan's uncles is in a wheelchair and I couldn't find a handicap bus. I said to my co-workers, "I have got to get on this kid's bus."

It was really chaotic for everyone: the bus drivers, the people involved, the families.

Finally, I found Juan's family's bus and we headed out for the memorial service. I think the families were ready for it, ready to pay respects to their loved ones. They knew the world was watching them. They knew there were rumors that the President was going to be there. They wanted that. They wanted to have him touch their lives. I heard them speak to one another about it.

When we got to the site of the memorial service, Juan kept saying, "Come on. You need to sit with me. You need to sit up here with me."

I tried to explain to him, "You go be with your family. Go up with all of the other families. I'll be back here if you need me. I'll check on you. I'll look for your bus and get on your bus on the way back."

We made sure all the families were seated together and got blankets for everyone. The Governor and his wife were coming through, shaking hands, thanking us. That was really weird. I'm not sure if I liked that or not. This little boy was so much fun, and I enjoyed meeting him and his family. It didn't seem like I should be thanked for anything.

Ed Root and other members of flight attendant Lorraine Bay's family rode on Tom Bender's bus.

Root: I remember all the State Troopers saluting as we went past. I think that stuck in everyone's mind. There were so many people on the bus with us.

My father, who was in his 80's, was quite chilly, and Tom Bender kept getting blankets and coats for him. We weren't dressed warmly enough; we weren't as familiar with the weather out there as we've become since.

That first anniversary, it was very cold out there on the field. The starkness; it was beautiful but cold. You wouldn't expect that kind of weather that early in September.

I remember looking around and seeing the jets going over and the State Police on horseback, security all over the place.

The speakers were great. The visit by President and Mrs. Bush at the crash site was very moving. I think we all felt that the President and Mrs. Bush were very genuine and very kind.

Governor Mark Schweiker was one of the speakers that day. He belatedly added something to his prepared statement.

Schweiker: One little person, a student from a nearby elementary school, walked up to me and said something that was profound in its simplicity, and I repeated it during the program. "If God brought you to it, God will get you through it."

It was just a simple but profoundly remarkable phrase that accented the value of prayer and the presence of God. How, just when you think you might not persevere and feel overwhelmed, "God will get you through it."

The commemoration proceeded without any problems. A beautiful service was televised live to millions of homes and offices across the nation and around the world. One of the highlights for Somerset County was when the heroes' families spontaneously rose and saluted towards the local residents who watched the ceremony at a distance.

After the service, the buses rolled again to carry onlookers away from the site while the Secret Service began to plan for the arrival of the President. Terressa Walker and Tom Bender again accompanied the families to the Presidential visit.

Walker: After the service, the families left first and went down on the buses to another area.

We got off and went through a security gate. They were searching everything. There were guys in fatigues with guns. I thought, "This is for real. The President is coming."

There were some chairs up front and some people coming around saying, "You need to pick."

I can't remember what the number was, maybe six, family members would actually go up front and sit. The rest had to stay behind those hay bales. I'm sure it was difficult to choose which six were going to go up there with the President.

So, we waited. We listened for helicopters.

The families waited for a good while for him. At least a half hour, forty-five minutes. All of a sudden, he came. He appeared.

I'm assuming he came in a chopper. All of a sudden, you look, and the people are saying, "There's the President. He's coming. He's coming."

There was a long line of people coming, and you looked and you thought that you could see him. Then, all of a sudden, he appeared right in front of you. I'm thinking, "What just happened here?"

They distracted us and brought him in from another direction, him and Mrs. Bush. I thought he was the guy coming towards us with a red tie, but he came from the other direction and had on a blue tie.

It was so weird to be a part of something like that.

The President and his wife brought a wreath of flowers for the victims. Then, they went around and shook the family members' hands. It was wonderful to see the amount of time they spent with each family member. The family members really appreciated that. Afterwards, they were all saying how remarkable it was that he took so much time to hug them or shake hands or pose for the pictures.

I kept looking and thinking, "I hope Juan gets a picture with the President." Sure enough, he did, with both the President and Mrs. Bush.

I was thinking, "Good for you, little boy." That was really good for me to see. Actually, I took a picture of it. I was just so relieved.

Juan doesn't know, yet, the impact of what happened. One day he will. He doesn't have his aunt, and this will never take the place of his aunt, but he will have that moment he will be able to talk about with his kids and grandchildren.

I was able to see Juan and his father before I left to say goodbye to them. He hugged me and kissed me, and I told him how sorry I was that this was how we had to meet, how grateful I was that I got to know him for a short period of time. His father was very nice, very gracious.

It was Juan's father's sister who had been killed.

Bender: We were getting ready to leave the site after the President left. There was a family that still hadn't gone toward the buses. They were behind the podium, near the trees.

I went over to them to see if they needed help with something, and here they had found a piece of airplane, a large piece of airplane skin. So I tried to call the coroner on his cell phone. Of course, I couldn't get service. They wanted to talk with him to see if it was okay if they took this piece of airplane away.

They were digging it out of the ground. They didn't know how big it was. A cameraman came over, and he was going to try to find a shovel for them. He couldn't find a shovel, but they got a chain or a rope or something and four guys pulled it. They actually ripped it out of the ground. It was a piece of aluminum airplane skin.

They took it with them.

After the President left, family members reboarded their buses to return to their hotels. Some disembarked in Shanksville and went to the VFD. NBC had set up a large television stage in the fire truck bays for live interviews. Other radio interviews occurred by way of telephone from the parking lot.

As afternoon dissolved into evening, the focus shifted from Shanksville to Somerset. At the Somerset Alliance Church, a memorial concert was held. Every seat was taken. Television stations continued to broadcast from the church parking lot. However, most of the family members remained at their hotels to

227

watch televised specials of the commemoration. Even those specials contained familiar Somerset County faces such as Jill Miller of Somerset Ambulance.

Miller: I got a phone call. "This is so-and-so from NBC, and we are doing this special at the Kennedy Center for the anniversary. We are having somebody from New York and Arlington, and we want somebody from Somerset to carry the flags during the beginning of the show. We got your name. Will you do it?"

I talked to my husband and said, "Yeah, sure. I'll do it."

I had to get a little dressier uniform than what we wear because we really don't have dress uniforms. We don't march in parades. I wore the same shirt, only with long sleeves, like a dress shirt. Then I got some pants, but not the cargo ones with all the pockets that we normally wear. And I got a nice pair of shiny dress uniform shoes.

I went a little over the edge. (Laughs.)

We went down on Sunday night, and it was filmed on Monday. We came back on Tuesday.

So, there we were, at the Kennedy Center, and there are a zillion people. We practiced all day and the filming was at night. I had to walk in from the side, carrying a flag. I had to learn how to do it properly because you don't just carry a flag. An official flag is carried in an official way.

Then there was the camera. They advised me that the camera was going to be right in my face and that I shouldn't run into it. They talked us through it.

I carried the flag onto the stage and stood as the national anthem was sung. Then we walked off, and we got to go back out for the finale with all the stars and sing. I didn't really sing because I can't. Well, I can sing, but nobody wants to hear me sing.

I got to meet the President and his wife and a lot of big-time people: James Earl Jones, Gloria Estefan, Alan Jackson, Josh Groven, Reba McIntyre, Ted Kennedy, Caroline Kennedy, Frasier ~ what was his name ~ Kelsey Grammer, Hilary Swank, Lance Armstrong. Colin Powell introduced me, but I never got the chance to meet him.

They did my hair and make-up. I was there with Kelsey Grammer, Hilary Swank, and Caroline Kennedy. It was too much!

There I was, getting my hair and make-up done. Little old me from Somerset sitting there with all these people. Just chatting. Going, "All right, here we are. How are you doing?"

They were all really nice and unpretentious. They signed autographs for us. It was fun.

Those things are filmed in different parts. So, the beginning and the end were filmed together. Then, after that, we went out and watched in the audience for a while. We came back into the green room for a long time and just hung out with the stars. My new best friends. (Laughs.)

On September 11, we were asked to provide EMS support at the memorial service at the site. We were asked to provide an extra ambulance and have it available for the President.

We were also asked to attend the opening dedication ceremony of the Flight 93 Chapel. We had a citation given to us there.

Personally, I didn't want to go to the site and wanted to spend more time with Steve and my daughters. So, we went together as a family and to represent the ambulance company at the chapel. We attended that service and received the citation. Then, I was interviewed and that was really bad. It all hit me. I was talking to this reporter on camera and boom! It was terrible because I couldn't get it back together. It went about ten minutes until I finally got it back together again and went on.

I can't explain it. There wasn't a trigger. If there was, I don't know what it was. I was in the middle of a sentence, answering a question, and boom! That was bad.

I got over that, and we just milled around there a little while and talked to people. We met a lot of nice people. Actually, one lady we met still sends the kids stuffed animals in the mail. We ate a little bit and then went home and just focused on being together and blocked the rest out.

I let the kids stay up to watch the special that night. They knew I was going to be on TV. What they didn't know was that Alan Jackson was on and we met him and had our pictures taken with him. They are big-time Alan Jackson fans. We had 8 x 10's made and framed with the autographs.

When he came on TV, we gave them the pictures, and then we took pictures of them holding their pictures.

That evening, at Hidden Valley Resort, the heroes' relatives organized the Families of Flight 93, Inc. Among the charter board members were Ken Nacke and Gordon Felt.

Chapter 29

Memorial Design

Visitors continued to make pilgrimages to the temporary memorial after the first anniversary of 9/11. Family members returned to pay their respects. Flight 93 Ambassadors assisted anyone who came to pay homage.

The second anniversary of 9/11 was distinctly different from the first. The crash site was in the process of being transferred from Somerset County to the federal government. No events were officially scheduled for the temporary memorial on September 11, 2003. Still, at 10:03 a.m., over a thousand people felt the persistent winds calm briefly. Afterwards, on the concrete pad down Skyline Road from the temporary memorial, Secretary of Interior Gale Norton swore in the Flight 93 Federal Advisory Commission.

Throughout the day, journalists searched for a story. Some visited the totem pole in the Shanksville community grove next to the school. A Native American tribe in the northwest sent this symbol of peace across the United States.

Others observed an awkward confrontation during which officials stopped a visitor from flying a kite. Some looked on as State Police searching for suspects in a wallet theft surrounded Ida's Store. The arrival of the troopers freed from duty the neighbor guarding the store with a shotgun.

That weekend, Somerset Trust President and CEO Henry Cook had the opportunity to meet some of the heroes' families.

Cook: On the second anniversary, the families were beginning to organize themselves for different things and looking for a meeting room. They asked if we would be willing to let them use our recently renovated bank building. Of course, we were very happy for them to make use of it. They asked if I would come and speak.

Flight 93 Federal Advisory Commission

LAWRENCE R. CATUZZI– Father of Flight 93 Passenger, Lauren Catuzzi-Grandcolas; Retired Investment Banker, Financial Security Assurance Corporation; Member, Board of Directors of the Houston-Harris County Sports Authority and Co-chairman of the Flight 93 Memorial Task Force; Houston, Texas

JOHN T. FELT– Uncle of Flight 93 Passenger, Edward Felt; Retired Director of Planning for the Town of Cortlandt, N.Y.; formerly Chief Planner for the Department of Housing and Community Development, City of Baltimore, Md.; Member, American Institute of Certified Planners; Kinderhook, N.Y.

DR. BRENT GLASS– Director; National Museum of American History, Smithsonian Institution; former Executive Director, Pa. Historical and Museum Commission; Washington, D.C.

DONNA GLESSNER– Community Member; Flight 93 Ambassadors Coordinator; and Chair of the Temporary Memorial Management Committee, Flight 93 Memorial Task Force; Friedens, Pa.

GERALD GUADAGNO– Father of Flight 93 Passenger Richard Guadagno; Retired Personnel Director, Mercer County, N.J.; Veteran of World War II; Ewing, N.J.

DR. EDWARD LINENTHAL– The Edward M. Penson Professor of Religion and American Culture and Chancellor's Public Scholar, University of Wisconsin Oshkosh; and author of The Unfinished Bombing: Oklahoma City in American Memory; Oshkosh, Wis.

KENNETH NACKE– Brother of Flight 93 Passenger, Louis Joseph Nacke, II; Chair of the Family Memorial Committee, Flight 93 Memorial Task Force; Police Officer of the Baltimore County Police Department, Baltimore, Md.

JOHN J. REYNOLDS– Retired National Park Service Executive; currently Senior Fellow of The National Park Foundation; Member, Board of Directors, Student Conservation Association; and active member of the American Society of Landscape Architects; Castro Valley, Calif.

GARY A. SINGEL– Superintendent, Shanksville-Stonycreek School District; Chair of the Finance Committee, Flight 93 National Memorial; Shanksville, Pa.

JERRY L. SPANGLER– District Attorney of Somerset County, Pa.; Co-chair of the Memorial Ideas Planning Committee, Flight 93 Memorial Task Force; active in local historical societies; native of Stonycreek Township, Somerset County, Pa.; Somerset, Pa.

DANIEL J. SULLIVAN– President and Chief Executive Officer, FedEx Ground; Moon Township, Pa.

PAMELA A. TOKAR-ICKES– Commissioner, The County of Somerset, Somerset County Board of Commissioners; Somerset, Pa.; Friedens, Pa.

GREGORY A. WALKER– Vice-Chairman, Stonycreek Township Supervisors; Secretary, Somerset County Municipal Co-op; and Member, Flight 93 Memorial Task Force; Friedens, Pa.

MICHAEL WATSON– Vice President, Director and Trustee of the Richard King Mellon Foundation and Director of the R. K. Mellon Family Foundation; Ligonier, Pa.

CALVIN EDWARD WILSON– Family member of Flight 93 First Officer Leroy Homer; and Senior Engineer of Turner Construction Company, New York, N.Y.; Herndon, Va.   *from National Park Service News Release 9/11/2003*

232

I found myself with the problem I've had ever since with the families of Flight 93. I am so pleased to have met these people. They are such an interesting group of people. And yet I'm sorry about the underlying necessity of getting to know them. So, it's great to meet you, which is absolutely true, but meeting them is based on the most horrendous thing I've been close to in my life.

The third anniversary found the site controlled by the National Park Service. A large tent at the temporary memorial housed a service. Family members, National Park Service personnel, newly elected PA Governor Ed Rendell and Homeland Security Secretary Tom Ridge participated. Nearly two thousand visitors and county residents attended.

Afterwards, the Park Service held a news conference on the concrete pad. They announced to the press and invited guests the details of an international design competition for the permanent memorial.

Among the visitors to Shanksville that weekend were Larry and Jeannie Eickhoff. Their cargo was a large painted crock carrying 69 river stones, one to represent each of the Congressional pages whose lives may have been saved by the Flight 93 heroes.

Larry: If they had hit the Capitol, the pictures of the dome burning would have sent a message around the world.

Jeannie: It would have taken out the pages and anybody who was there. There were all those young kids working there.

Larry: That's why we're here. We just want to see the place. We want to understand how it all happened here, what the people are doing now. We don't necessarily want to talk to the families because I'm not sure how they feel.

Jeannie: We just wanted to show them the rocks.

Larry: We wanted to support their loss.

Jeannie: So, there are 69 rocks in there. Maybe the pages will come here.

Larry: What we're hoping is that this would be a reason for them to come. Maybe they'll think, "There's a rock there and we have to sign it to honor..."

Jeannie: The courage of these people of Flight 93, that they were able to take action..."

Larry: Even if you know that you're going to die, still... to get up the courage to go against the knives... You know, the immediate threat of people killing you versus the thought that...

How often do we sit there and cower, hoping that what we see in front of us won't happen?

Ed Root was also in Shanksville that weekend. He had become more involved in the process of building a permanent memorial.

Root: I guess it was a gradual process. My relationship with Lorraine's husband, Erich, actually has gotten stronger over the years.

When I first started going out to Shanksville with him, I didn't want to do anything that he wouldn't agree with. As we got to know each other better by going out there all those times, I discovered that he and I were pretty much on the same page about the way we felt about everything. It's just that he is uncomfortable in a public setting. So it kind of evolved; that's why it took a couple of years for me to start getting more active out there. I wanted to make sure that if I did get involved, he would be okay with what I did on his and Lorraine's behalf.

So, I guess I evolved into the family spokesperson.

I really didn't start to become involved until the anniversary in 2004. That was around the same time that they were looking for volunteers to join one of the two juries to judge the memorial design competition.

I thought about it and talked to Erich about it. We went on a tour of the proposed memorial site. National Park Service Project Manager Jeff Reinbold was on the bus, and I got to ask him more about the project. That was when I decided to throw my hat into the ring as a candidate to sit on one of the juries. It was around the same time that I had expressed an interest, through Carol O'Hare, Hilda Marcin's daughter, about further involvement with the family board.

The design competition for the memorial attracted over 1000 entries. Those entries were publicly displayed. The Stage I jury appointed by the Flight 93 Advisory Commission narrowed those entries to five finalists.

Flight 93 National Memorial Design Competition Stage I Jury

SARAH WAINIO, Maryland	Family member
CAROLE O'HARE, California	Family member
RICHARD HAAG, Washington	Landscape architect, professor emeritus
DAVID HOLLENBERG, Pennsylvania	Associate Regional Director for Professional Services, NPS
DONNA GRAVES, California	Arts and cultural planning consultant
MICHAEL ROTONDI, California	Architect, educator
W. CECIL STEWARD, Nebraska	Educator
SUSAN SZENASY, New York City	Design journalist
M. PAUL FRIEDBERG, New York City	Landscape architect, designer, educator, writer

Pennsylvania State Police Corporal Bill Link provided security at the 9/11 anniversaries and other Flight 93-related events.

Link: You see these folks, not only at the anniversaries, but every once in a while at different events, like the memorial judging. Certain people, you may not remember their names, but you remember a face. Maybe you helped someone from the impact site to his car or someone needed something.

You know and they know, even if you don't remember names. There is a bond there, not just with me but with all of our guys.

Ken Nacke has returned to Somerset County many times as a member of the Flight 93 Task Force and the Flight 93 Federal Advisory Commission.

Nacke: Sometimes I run into some of the State Policemen and others we met during those first days after 9/11. It is good seeing them and rekindling that bond. They remember me, as well. There is a special bond between the area, the people and the families.

It just happened. That's the beauty of it. I don't think anybody can take credit for it. I just think 'good will toward men' supersedes it all. Coming from the family side as well as the community side. It was what our country is truly supposed to be about. If you look at what Americans are, just look at the local people of the Somerset area, they are the caretakers of our loved ones memories. No one asked them to do it but they are doing it on their own because it is the right thing to do.

Just like the people on Flight 93.

It's amazing what they did. Only they know what happened that day. We can all speculate. No one truly knows because they are not here to tell us. It's fitting that all 40 of them are recognized, and I think they should be honored, remembered and cherished forever.

They gave their lives so you and I and the rest of this country can continue to live in the way that we know. Our way of life has changed, but it didn't change as much as if a plane actually reached the Capitol Building or hit the White House.

Think back and imagine what our country would have been like if the plane reached its target. What a different world we'd be living in today.

That's why I chose to get involved in the process of building the memorial. I'm not saying our country would forget. I'm not going to give our country the opportunity to forget. It's worth reliving the pain so the country doesn't forget.

When I come back to Somerset, I feel at home. I truly do. I've made a lot of good friends. I always say it's easier for me to make the trip up than to make the trip home.

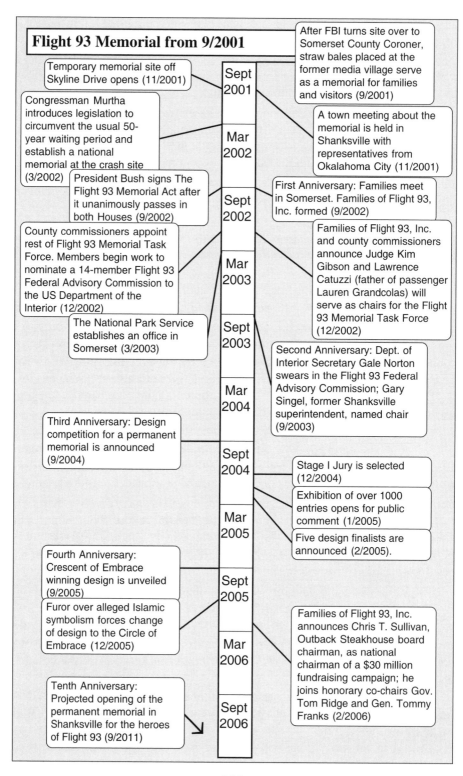

Flight 93 Memorial from 9/2001

Temporary memorial site off Skyline Drive opens (11/2001)

Congressman Murtha introduces legislation to circumvent the usual 50-year waiting period and establish a national memorial at the crash site (3/2002)

President Bush signs The Flight 93 Memorial Act after it unanimously passes in both Houses (9/2002)

County commissioners appoint rest of Flight 93 Memorial Task Force. Members begin work to nominate a 14-member Flight 93 Federal Advisory Commission to the US Department of the Interior (12/2002)

The National Park Service establishes an office in Somerset (3/2003)

Third Anniversary: Design competition for a permanent memorial is announced (9/2004)

Fourth Anniversary: Crescent of Embrace winning design is unveiled (9/2005)

Furor over alleged Islamic symbolism forces change of design to the Circle of Embrace (12/2005)

Tenth Anniversary: Projected opening of the permanent memorial in Shanksville for the heroes of Flight 93 (9/2011)

Sept 2001
Mar 2002
Sept 2002
Mar 2003
Sept 2003
Mar 2004
Sept 2004
Mar 2005
Sept 2005
Mar 2006
Sept 2006

After FBI turns site over to Somerset County Coroner, straw bales placed at the former media village serve as a memorial for families and visitors (9/2001)

A town meeting about the memorial is held in Shanksville with representatives from Okalahoma City (11/2001)

First Anniversary: Families meet in Somerset. Families of Flight 93, Inc. formed (9/2002)

Families of Flight 93, Inc. and county commissioners announce Judge Kim Gibson and Lawrence Catuzzi (father of passenger Lauren Grandcolas) will serve as chairs for the Flight 93 Memorial Task Force (12/2002)

Second Anniversary: Dept. of Interior Secretary Gale Norton swears in the Flight 93 Federal Advisory Commission; Gary Singel, former Shanksville superintendent, named chair (9/2003)

Stage I Jury is selected (12/2004)

Exhibition of over 1000 entries opens for public comment (1/2005)

Five design finalists are announced (2/2005).

Families of Flight 93, Inc. announces Chris T. Sullivan, Outback Steakhouse board chairman, as national chairman of a $30 million fundraising campaign; he joins honorary co-chairs Gov. Tom Ridge and Gen. Tommy Franks (2/2006)

PART 3

MOVING FORWARD

Chapter 30

Final Selection

The Stage II jury pondered the final five entrees to select a winner. Ed Root and Somerset Trust Company President Henry Cook served on the Stage II jury.

Cook: I was asked if I would serve on the Stage II jury. I was really taken aback because at no point had I been asked to get involved at any level. Heaven knows I don't know much about architecture and design. I like things that look nice, but that's all I know.

They sent some literature and I also read some other books about Flight 93 and 9/11. *Courage After the Crash* was the most important. It speaks most to what I consider a spirit that exists in the middle part of America. Middle America is about volunteers caring and stepping up in times of hardship. I felt that was part of the reason that it was important for them to have local representation on that jury. I don't know that I was the best choice, but I was certainly honored that they asked me. My two colleagues from Somerset County were Connie Hummel and Charlie Fox.

Without too fine a point on it, I think the local representation on the second jury was an afterthought. I think they were primarily focused on family and a core group of professional landscape architects and people involved in large earth design.

I have a sense that the committee was being put together and someone said, "You know, you better have someone from Somerset County."

We got together the first four days of August. Those were four of the most intense days I think I've ever spent in my life. I have had meetings dealing with things that were more intense, certainly. But, I've never been through four days of that intensity.

It started at a dinner meeting at the county club. There were three of us representing Somerset County. Virtually everyone else was a stranger to us. The professionals all knew each other and networked. The family members all knew each other. So, here we were, in our hometown at a gathering of people, and we were the biggest strangers. That hasn't happened to me many times in my life in Somerset County.

We got together at 7:30 a.m. the next day. We went out to the Historical Society, and they showed their video. Then we drove out to the site itself. They took us to various perspectives and said, "Remember this point because we're going to use this as a reference point."

After that, we went back and began the process of reviewing the five finalists.

We talked a little bit. Our instructions were reviewed again. We wandered around, looking at the five designs. Some with each other, but mostly individually. We didn't know each other real well at that point.

In three of the designs, the central theme was very easy for me to comprehend; two of them were not. I chose to really focus on the two that I didn't understand. I did not want to be unfair to them, that somehow my lack of understanding would cause me to overlook them.

We were constantly reforming groups and then going out individually. The facilitators did an exceptional job every time we combined as a group. They were really good at knowing when a person was ready to speak. I found, except once, when they came to me, I'd just completed my thought and was ready to go.

The meals were where we really got to know each other a lot better. What an extraordinary group of people!

The family members were kind of a group apart. They were sometimes approachable, and sometimes not. They were dealing with things that I could only guess. I liked all of them, but it was hard to relate to them all the time.

The professionals were a bright group of people. They were very approachable and had a surprising degree of interest in Somerset County and what we were like.

The two facilitators were real nice people and very approachable. They name-placed us at each meal so that we would move on a steady basis and encounter different people. I'm not quite sure if they were placing people to create a sandpaper effect or to create a grease effect.

The second day, each of the professionals on the jury was assigned one of the designs to explain what they were seeing.

Afterwards, we went to each station, and each of us would present our commentary on it.

We then sat away from the designs in one of our group meetings and had a discussion about the process. The facilitator asked us to describe our feelings about what we were seeing. That was very interesting. That was actually the only thing that I wrote down. I wrote down a brief synopsis of each person's comments. It became apparent to me that this was a real emotional high point.

Tuesday afternoon's last activity was a straw poll. My recollection was we could vote for two. Two of the designs virtually had no votes. A consensus was reached that we focus our conversation on the residual three.

The next morning the press was there. They wanted family members. They wanted tears.

We got down to the final three, and the third one was dropped fairly quickly. So, we were down to two.

We spent a very, very long time to get to the final design. Consensus was not easily forthcoming. We were all going back and forth, moseying between them. You'd find yourself next to one person, and then you'd find yourself standing next to another person, and you'd find yourself overhearing a conversation. This was very, very fluid. Everybody was trying to do things right.

Eventually, some people were wearing out and just plain sitting down. They had made their decision, and they were not going to walk around much more. But, I was still walking back and forth between the two, trying to become comfortable with the differences.

One or two people pointed to the interface, where this long walkway touches the sacred ground, and I had not looked at that aspect of the design. I began to look at it, and one of the professionals who pointed but didn't say a lot nudged me to see the elements there. I began to find something substantive there. The point where the bowl touches the sacred ground was potentially very powerful.

I started backing up. I began reevaluating that particular design. I realized what it's doing was very special. It doesn't intrude on the bowl. The whole design surrounds and embraces the bowl. What you look at is only slightly altered from what you see today, and you're going down and actually touching the sacred ground. You have the opportunity of a direct personal experience.

I felt bad for the group who still felt strongly about the other design because their case was strong and powerful. But it was a minority opinion.

I feel that, if properly done, this will be the place where the whole war on terrorism is remembered. The Pentagon doesn't want it. It's not going to work in New York. Yet, our young people who were in Afghanistan and Iraq, and even to some degree our young people who went to the Gulf the first time, deserve to have their efforts remembered.

Pearl Harbor didn't asked to be bombed. The crossroads of Gettysburg didn't ask for two armies to meet there. It just so happens that Flight 93 crashed in Somerset County. We are now the caretakers of that site, and that site may represent the proper place to memorialize this whole era of American history, as Gettysburg does for the Civil War and Pearl Harbor does for World War II.

Root: Being on the Second Stage Jury was an amazing experience. It was a combination of family members, design professionals and local people from the Somerset area. That is where I got to meet Henry Cook and Charlie Fox and Connie Hummel. I was selected as the recorder, a non-voting member of the jury, so I was involved in all the discussions and a member of the jury for all purposes except voting. But, as it went on, one of the design professionals was initially delayed and then ultimately unable to participate. I was elevated from recorder to voting member of the jury.

It was an interesting and fascinating experience. Through the whole process, you got to know everyone's opinions on all the five finalists, what they liked, didn't like, their feelings toward what they thought was behind each entry.

By having a group with such wide-ranging backgrounds, you really got a wide view of how to look at the designs. It was a tough job. I think all of us would look at something and change our minds about what we liked and didn't like.

Of the five final designs, I cut it down to three in my mind. I think most of the others felt the same way. We would go through and have votes and cut things down. I changed my mind a couple of times. Not because I didn't like any of them. It was more that I kept taking elements and thinking this element is stronger than that one. It was an on-going process. I don't think I was alone on that, either. I think everyone kept an open mind.

My background is being someone who is interested in history. I've been very active in historic preservation all my life. I've been on two different boards of preservationist organizations over the years. In the book that Jeffrey Stocker and I just completed, *"Isn't This Glorious!"*, half of the book is about the postwar memorial period at Gettysburg and what the veterans went through to memorialize themselves and their comrades.

I felt that my background enabled me to look at things from a historic standpoint, not only what is important today, but what will be important a hundred or two hundred years from now.

It's important to preserve the feel of the actual impact site. It's always so calm and serene down there. Even when it's cold, you seem to be below the wind line. While the temporary memorial at the top of the hill can be so bitter sometimes, below, it just seems so quiet. There's very little, if any, noise at all, just the wind. Everything seems to fit in; the whole atmosphere of that place is just peace and quiet.

It has that special feeling about it. Different places that I've been to over the years seem to have that aura about them, like in Gettysburg on the battlefield or in Normandy at the cemetery.

The winning design, Crescent of Embrace by Paul Murdoch and Associates of Los Angeles, was formally announced at the fourth anniversary. Fundraising efforts for the $30 million needed to build the memorial were also announced to the several thousand people crowded into and around the large tent erected by the Park Service on the concrete pad.

Jeannie Eickhoff returned to Shanksville for the fourth anniversary. Accompanying her were the first two Congressional pages to sign their stones, Nicole Eickhoff and Patrick MacDonald.

Nicole Eickhoff: Last year my mother came here to the Flight 93 site and had this basket full of rocks designed to represent the 69 House pages working in the Capitol on 9/11. Her idea was that we would come someday in the future, sign our rock and pay tribute to the families that saved our lives and in many ways saved our country. We decided that this year we could finally come.

MacDonald: Today is easier than yesterday. We were up here yesterday, too. It's a humbling and moving experience. The television showed so many shots of this place, but to actually step onto this ground…

We read about and heard about the bravery that those people displayed on that day, but to actually be here is an experience I can't really describe. It touches me very personally and haunts me a little.

What they did on the plane that day…

Eickhoff: We feel motivated by them, as well. I'm just a college student, but someday I hope to mimic their bravery. I feel it has motivated me and obligated me. It obligated all citizens of the United States to mimic their bravery in some way.

I've been crying a lot and it's been very emotional, but I feel like this great burden has been lifted off my shoulders, this feeling of the unknown. I don't usually talk about 9/11, as a matter of fact. I hadn't talked about it for four years until talking with the families. I feel comfortable now. After four years, I am capable of talking about that day and how horrible it was and how wonderful their sacrifice was for us.

MacDonald: We love being here and we love being with the family members. They are all great Americans. I hope that all of the pages can share a moment like this. To be able to say, "We love your brother. We've been praying for you. We've been thinking about you, your sister, your son…"

Eickhoff: God bless these families. Thank you to Shanksville for protecting this place and for creating that beautiful Flight 93 Chapel.

MacDonald: We will be back.

Eickhoff: And there will be more of us!

The families of Flight 93 publicly embraced the winning design. However, comments regarding alleged Islamic symbolism created a national controversy.

Ed Root found himself immersed in that debate.

Root: I wasn't shocked that there was a problem in that we had the ability to read public comments as part of the jury process. There was one vitriolic, hateful thing that was part of the public comments. I remember reading it and thought that I just didn't agree with that person. I thought they were way off base, going in directions that really weren't there. I think we were sensitive that there might be a viewpoint like that out there. This was only one out of the hundreds that we read.

When we got to Shanksville for the anniversary, I saw the first newspaper article and started talking to people. I really didn't expect the bruhaha to take off the way that it did. But, in the world of the internet, it's easy for that kind of thing to happen. Of course, controversy sells much better than cooperation.

If you think about the Vietnam Memorial, initially there was a lot of concern; many people didn't like it. Now it's one of the most respected and honored memorials in the country. I think it would be naive to think that somebody wouldn't have a complaint, given all the things that were happening in New York and all the controversy about that memorial.

After I got home from the anniversary, I was listening to a talk show on my way to work. The host was not trying to be critical; he was mostly being informative and talking about the controversy. I got to work and called the station. I left a message for the producer and told him that I was related to Lorraine Bay and on the jury.

Two mornings later, I was at the station, in the studio. Then, three weeks later, we took a bus trip out to Shanksville with listeners from the radio station. We met Jeff Reinbold out there. Most of the people on the bus were people who had called in with some negative comments about the design.

We went to the temporary memorial first, and one of the ambassadors did a great job explaining things to the people. Then, we took the bus down to the concrete pad where the memorial service was last year. Jeff had the storyboard of the memorial design. He went over everything and answered questions. Most of the people changed their minds and understood the whole design selection process a lot better.

The host of the radio show, Mark Schmekonish, has a column in the *Philadelphia Daily News*. He wrote a nice article that concluded by suggesting that, before you criticize the memorial, you should go out and see what it will look like at the site.

He was very complimentary about Somerset. He wanted to buy some kind of souvenir and said, "Where are the shops?"

Well, the only two shops I can think of are Ida's and Duppstadt's General Store. He was shocked that the place wasn't overrun with tourist traps. I think they were very impressed with the people of Somerset County, the way they embraced this whole event as more than just a money-making opportunity.

Several months later, two more pages visited Shanksville. Tyler Rogers and Julia Owen remarked about their crash site visit while they signed their stones.

Rogers: One of my favorite things is how the guardrail has become part of the memorial.

Owen: It was almost like there was a degree of... I know that the word 'closure' is an overused term, but, for lack of a better word, closure. To get up close and have that connection with those people who saved my life.

Rogers: I was very impressed with Shanksville and the surrounding area. It's just a very down to earth town. To see the way the people around here reacted to everything is just inspiring.

When I was in Shanksville, the fire alarm went off. I'm just not used to that. I mean, these guys are in the shower and they hear it and they jump on a truck. I know those guys don't need or want the recognition, but they sure deserve it.

Gordon Felt has returned to the crash site many times since his first visit during the week after 9/11.

Felt: When I come back, I always like to go out to the site on my own. I've been there with all the press, like during the anniversaries, but I really enjoy just going as an anonymous person to the temporary memorial. Just sitting quietly, chatting with the ambassadors, who are just such wonderful people.

When the press is there, you don't get much privacy. That's fine. I don't mind doing interviews, and I don't mind sharing my loss with people.

I understand that there's a role that we all play in this memorial process. People are interested in hearing how the families are doing. I think that when we first realized the magnitude of this event, we realized we had to give up a bit of our personal privacy.

We are sharing the memories of our loved ones with the nation. I'm very proud of that. Knowing that my brother played a role in the history of our country is a good feeling. Obviously, I wish that the story didn't end the way it did, but it is an important story that has to be shared

I can't speak enough about the people of Somerset County and how supportive they've been to the families. They go out of their way to make us feel at home, make us feel a part of their family. They are so genuine that it makes it much easier to go back.

In many ways, I'm glad that when I visit my brother, I'm going to rural Pennsylvania.

Flight 93 National Memorial Design Competition Stage II Jury

EDWIN ROOT, Coopersburg, PA — Family member
Cousin of Lorraine Bay

GERALD BINGHAM, Wildwood, FL — Family member
Father of Mark Bingham

THOMAS E. BURNETT, SR., Northfield, MN — Family member
Father of Thomas Burnett, Jr.

DOROTHY GARCIA, Portola Valley, CA — Family member
Wife of Andrew Garcia

BARBARA V. CATUZZI, Houston, TX — Family member
Mother of Lauren Grandcolas

ILSA HOMER, Hauppauge, NY — Family member
Mother of LeRoy Homer, Jr.

SANDRA FELT, Matawan, NJ — Family member
Wife of Edward Felt

ROBERT CAMPBELL, Cambridge, MA — Architect, author,
educator, critic for Boston Globe

DR. GAIL DUBROW, Minneapolis, MN — Dean of Graduate School
and Vice-Provost, University of Minnesota

JONATHAN JARVIS, Oakland, CA — Regional Director
Pacific West Region, National Park Service

LAURIE OLIN, Philadelphia, PA — Landscape architect, Founder
Olin Foundation, professor, School of Design, University of PA

THOMAS SOKOLOWSKI, Pittsburgh, PA — Director
Andy Warhol Museum, Carnegie Museums

CONNIE HUMMEL, Garrett, PA — Principal
Shanksville-Stonycreek High School

CHARLES FOX, Somerset, PA — Flight 93 Memorial Task Force
Historic Site and Museum Administrator, Somerset Historical Center

G. HENRY COOK, Somerset, PA — President and CEO
Somerset Trust Company

Moving Forward

Chapter 31

Epilogue

Ira Levy is a professor at Wright College in Chicago, Illinois.

Levy: I was born and raised in New York City. My family still lives there. My nieces go to school a couple of blocks from where the World Trade Center stood.

When this happened, I really wanted to go back and do something, to volunteer. Because I was teaching college, I couldn't go back.

I was supposed to pedal my bicycle the summer of 2002 from Amsterdam to Paris. I decided I wasn't going to do that. Instead, in late October 2001, I decided to pedal my bicycle across the United States and raise college education funds for children who lost at least one parent in the attacks.

I planned, as part of the 4800-mile trip, that we were going to visit every crash site. One of our stops was in Shanksville. David Mapes handled everything for us. We were supposed to get quite a bit of media coverage. All of these media outlets were actually in town, and the only organization that ended up covering us was the *Daily American*. That's because the day we arrived was the day the miners got trapped.

We spent a day and a half in Shanksville and Somerset. We did a bike safety clinic for kids. We made a lot of connections ~ David, Shanksville Mayor Ernie Stull and his wife ~ a bunch of nice connections.

I teach Media Criticism. I decided to build a research class on 9/11. I spent three years collecting everything I could get my hands on, waiting until the right texts and articles came along. I realized that the right texts and articles came along when the *9/11 Commission Report* came out and other books such as *False Alarm*, *Never Forget* and *Among the Heroes*.

I didn't want the course to deal with the blunt issues of terrorism, why everyone hates us so much. I also wanted to get away from the surface issues of 9/11, ones that all the young, beginning research students would tend to gravitate toward. So I thought, "What do I know?"

Well, I know a lot about what's going on in Lower Manhattan because I'm from there. But then I found *Courage After the Crash* and the course concept came to me. I decided to build the course around the impact that 9/11 had specifically on the residents who lived in lower Manhattan and the residents who lived in Shanksville, PA. Not so much the victims of the crash and the families, but the people who live there. What role did the news media play in covering and impacting their towns and neighborhoods? Also, what role the media plays or doesn't play or should not play in the healing process of these people? That's been the basis of the course. I thought, what better way to round out my students' course experience than to visit Somerset County.

They are learning things and viewing these events in a way they hadn't thought of before. Just by reading *Courage After the Crash* as a textbook, they are hearing about stories that they wouldn't have even considered. Stories outside what the news media reports to us.

That's really important.

The Wright College journalism students sacrificed part of their spring break to visit Somerset County. They started Saturday morning at the historic Somerset Trust Company where they met Barbara Black.

Black: I joined the National Park Service about a year and a half ago. They hired me to take care of this full time.

I'm still saving mementos people leave at the temporary memorial. They are being saved for the future so the world will know fifty years from now or one hundred years from now how people reacted. What were their thoughts? What were their feelings? What did they do after this happened?

Once the memorial is built, they will be used as part of an exhibit that will be in a visitor's center. We have over 25,000 objects and many more messages. We can't possibly put them all on exhibit. They may have rotating exhibits.

I brought a couple of things with me. They're in plastic. This one says, "When you got on the plane, you thought you were regular people, but now you are heroes. Thank you."

This one was placed there in December of 2001. "The people of Washington, D.C. owe a debt to the passengers of Flight 93 that can never be repaid. Rest in peace."

We get many, many people from Washington, many people coming up and leaving something, leaving a message or an object that symbolizes their thanks for saving their lives.

We get a lot of military. (This was written in 2004.) "Shortly after September 11, the fall of my junior year in high school, I joined the Army and became a volunteer firefighter and EMT because of all the heroes of September 11. I leave for Kosovo soon. I will serve with pride to defend our nation, our freedom and our flag. I know I'm there defending the families of the people who died to save others, the passengers of Flight 93 and those who died in New York City and Washington, D.C. God bless."

We get a lot of men and women on their way to duty and on their way back from duty. Some people haven't even seen their families yet, and they are making a stop at Flight 93 to pay their respects before they go home. This person said, "I went to Afghanistan August 2002 to January 2003 to help support the prevention of this happening again. This patch is the coveted U.S. Army's Combat Infantry Badge. It was awarded to me for combat infantry ground operations during Operation Enduring Freedom. It is hoped it is a strong representation of the least I could do to honor your memory of the tragic day of September 11."

It is signed by a First Lieutenant, and he has a note at the bottom that says, "Laid here on 14 January 2004, on my way home after finishing my U.S. Army commitment."

Sometimes we have objects that do have messages attached to them, so we know what the object is supposed to mean. This is a compass that they may have had in their car because the message attached to it does not look like something they prepared at home. It looks like something they hastily put together, maybe after they got there and saw some of the other things being left behind. It reads, "Let these courageous people show us the way."

This is a letter from a family in Washington, D.C. "My husband is a D.C. firefighter and was working on that day, September 11, just a few blocks from the Capitol. We talk often about what would have happened if Flight 93 had made it to Washington."

She talks about her children then, ten, three and one. It's written by the wife. "Your heroics personally affected our family, and we would like to extend our most heartfelt sympathy and gratitude to your families and send our continued thoughts and prayers to them."

Many of the messages are written directly to the families, or they are written to the passengers or crew as if they were there, as if they could read these. "We have come to know some of your life stories through the media and

247

feel very honored to know how you lived your lives. Your spirits will remain with us. You have inspired us to live more passionately with deep conviction, according to what is right and good in this world. You have made this world a better place for having been here."

So, these are some of the things that I pick up off the ground or removed from the fence.

We thought that this might only last until the weather got bad. Now, four and a half years later, close to the fifth anniversary, visitation is still strong. We have about 130,000 people coming each year to a place that is not well marked and doesn't have a lot of National Park Service signage.

But they come. They find their way.

We are in the planning stages for the permanent memorial. We just completed an international design competition to design the memorial.

When you go to the site, you'll be able to see how well the final design fits on the land. We wanted something that did not distract from what had happened there.

There will be a visitor's center where you will be able to learn the story of Flight 93 and have a chance to leave a message and sign your name.

This design embraces the sacred ground. It provides a circular walkway so that while you're walking down to the sacred ground you're focusing on it. When you get down to the sacred ground, there is a plaza right in front of it. We are not allowing the public to walk on the area where the plane crashed, but right at the edge of this area there will be a granite plaza and people will be able to look. We wanted to give people the opportunity to continue to leave things if they want to. So there are niches for that in the plaza wall. I'll still be down there every day collecting the things that people leave.

We're still developing the interpretation, which is, perhaps, our greatest challenge.

Historians generally take time to look back on things, to see change over time. Journalists write the first draft of history. Had you been writing on September 11, you would have been writing about what happened right then, and you would have been shaping people's minds as to its importance.

As historians, we need a bit of perspective. We need to step back from the event and see what happened and have enough time to analyze it. So, we decided our first exhibit in the memorial and our first interpretation of the memorial will be transitional. We can't, yet, even after five years, know the complete importance of this event or how it has impacted our world.

We'll start moving ground in about 2008. We're trying to do a zoning study to help control development along the corridor to the memorial. The memorial boundary itself is 2200 acres. We want to bring people off Route 30, a major highway, rather than bringing them down country roads. Last year we had 320 motor coach tours that came along these country roads. They're destroying the side roads, so we will be bringing them in off the highway.

We plan on purchasing about 1300 acres. The rest will be in easements. We will have agreements with the landowners not to develop that land into gas stations and T-shirt shops and things like that. Just keep it the way it is.

How do I feel? I would never have wished this on anyone. Now that it's here, well, we can't deny that it happened. The thing to do is to make it the best and welcome people.

The students then met with two local newspaper reporters. Kirk Swauger, of the Johnstown *Tribune Democrat*, described how he covered the Flight 93 story since the day of the crash. Bob Leverknight of the Somerset *Daily American*, explained how, on September 11, he was on Air Force Reserve duty. He came to the crash site in uniform and helped the FBI.

The students' bus then carried them to the Flight 93 Memorial Chapel, where they met with Rev. Al Mascherino.

Rev. Al: Judy Baeckel had the first memorial for Flight 93 where people were coming to pay tribute immediately after the crash. State Police stopped everybody at an old abandoned church in Shanksville. They had to turn around. Where they turned around was Judy's yard. They stopped and started dropping their flowers and their tributes right in her yard. They wanted to leave something there in Shanksville.

In Judy's yard, the overwhelming response of the people was one of faith. God bless America. People wrote messages like that on the painted plywood sheets in her yard. I knew if the government would get a hold of that memorial, you would never see the God bless America or anything having to do with faith. So I thought of how to preserve that.

This church is 100 years old. It came up for sale October 2001. I was driving by and saw the "For Sale" sign and said, "Wow."

I pulled over and tried to buy it, but it was already sold. About ten days later, they called me and said the church was available. I had $300 in my hand. They held it and I finally bought it in January 2002.

From January to August, it was completely stripped. Nothing was left on the walls. I used to go down to 84 Lumber and buy things $50 at a time. Finally, I said this is for a church, and the manager called a corporate higher-up and said, "There's this guy here trying to build a church $50 at a time."

84 Lumber gave me a check for $23,000 to buy lumber. When they came to the chapel to give me the check and saw it, they decided to finish the work.

Ten days later it was finished.

It's really an all-faith chapel. What I want the chapel to be is a testimony to faith, a recognition and celebration of the faith of those forty people on that plane, whatever religion they practiced.

In those thirty minutes, they figured out what they were going to do, and I'm sure they didn't ask each other what church they belonged to. They believed in their hearts, and the most important things that were dear to them brought them together.

What's amazing was, those terrorists had planned their attack on America for years and they knew every inch of that plane. They knew it so well they could fly the plane themselves. And, here you have forty ordinary people, no famous people, no politicians, no world leaders, no sports stars and no Hollywood stars. Just ordinary people who became heroes in thirty minutes. It took them thirty minutes to thwart the plans of those professional terrorists. Mothers and fathers and grandparents became heroes that day.

They prayed together, and three minutes later, they died. In those three minutes, they changed history forever. Forty people changed the direction of history. How much could 275,000,000 Americans accomplish if we have the rest of our lives? But, we waste our time sometimes. How many times have I wasted three minutes? Three minutes are very precious. In three minutes, they changed history.

After the stop at the Flight 93 Chapel, the students visited Shanksville. They stopped at the Shanksville Volunteer Fire Department and listened to Fire Chief Terry Shaffer and 9/11 Fire Ground Commander Rick King recount their stories. After a bag of chips and drinks from Ida's Store, they visited the memorial gardens at Shanksville-Stonycreek High School.

Their motor coach's next stop was at the crash site, where they met with Sherry Stalley and Keith Hoffer. Stalley and Hoffer were one of the two reporter-photographer teams to actually reach the site of the crash on September 11, 2001.

Stalley: We're just trying to get our bearings. This is actually the first time that we were back here together at the crash site since it happened.

When we got the call to come out, we had no clue where we were going. We were told that there had been a plane crash and to head to Shanksville, and that was it. Actually, we got to the site because people were outside and they pointed us in the right direction.

Hoffer: See the dragline? We stopped in the vicinity and I walked out near that ridgeline over there, set up and started shooting. Those were the pictures you saw of the crash site. Ours were the first pictures out everywhere. The other stations didn't have a crew there yet.

By the time we came back to our truck, they wanted to do a live feed. We had talked to some of the local police that we knew, and they were kind of pushing it, letting us stay as long as we could. Finally, they said, "Sorry. You guys have to leave."

That's when we moved over to the dragline. We were trying to feed our video back to the station and, before we knew it, the state policemen had surrounded us. They said, "You guys have to leave right now."

That's when Jon Meyer was out there talking to the police, so we had time to get all of our video sent back.

Stalley: We really had no clue what had happened. As the nation was learning stuff, we were learning it. When you looked at the scene, honestly, it looked like a small plane crash.

All we could do was tell them what we saw and whatever information we could get. We just kept feeding it. We went live maybe twenty times until they kicked us out because they didn't know if there were chemical or biological weapons on that plane.

They put us in a cornfield. So, we started living right in the middle of a cornfield, with the hundreds upon hundreds of media from around the world that converged here.

Hoffer: We interviewed three coal miners the day after. They were working in a coal pile on the other side of here, and they saw the plane coming in. They were each in a different position, and we filmed each one from where they saw it. Some of the wild stories you heard about Flight 93 being shot down and all that, we knew it wasn't true. You knew these guys saw the plane going in.

I just have so much respect for the people that were on the plane and how they fought these terrorists just so another tragedy in Washington didn't have to happen.

Stalley: I have trouble coming back to the scene. Driving out here, I didn't want to be back. It's very emotional for me even to think about coming back here. In fact, besides the first anniversary, this is only the second time I have been back. Even now, if I turn around and look back there, it makes me want to cry knowing what happened on this site and the impact that day had on the nation. Not just on us, but on everybody.

The media changed that day. Everybody worked together. It wasn't a competition about who could get the juiciest story. We were all there for something much bigger than we were. I think everybody realized it.

Also, every photographer and reporter that covered this story lost it at one point or another. You would see a photographer put a camera down right in the middle of an interview. That is unheard of. Someone would put his camera down and walk away and then come back a half hour later. You knew they had been crying.

Before you do a live shot, normally, you brush your hair, put your make-up on and you make sure you look decent. No one cared. I remember going on with my hair not being brushed for 6 hours. It was hot and I was sweaty, my shirt was dirty and I had dirt on my face. No one cared.

It was down to the nitty gritty of what journalism is all about. Telling people what was going on. For a lot of people, we were all they had to find out what was going on in their own backyard.

I would go home at night and couldn't sleep. It was that way for everybody ~ the police, the EMS, reporters.

The day they brought the families in and lined the street with police officers is burned in my memory forever, the respect that you saw that day.

After they left, they allowed us back to where the families had been to the straw memorial at the command center. I remember a bag of M&M's, hats, things that were for the heroes of Flight 93 from their families. That was one of the hardest days. After that I wanted to go home. I have never wanted to leave a story and say, "That's it. I've had it. I can't do it."

Hoffer: That was the hardest day, in my opinion. That was the day I lost it. Seeing all those mementos. Usually everybody is running around and trying to get pictures. Everybody was silent. It was very reverent, very respectful. When I went back to get a live shot, I just had to walk off into the cornfield and cry.

Stalley: As journalists, stories you cover are just stories. You cover a house fire. It's a story to you, and you go home. You are supposed to leave your job behind. It's a story. This wasn't just a story and it never will be. It became a part of us.

Hoffer: When this happened, I had been a news photographer for maybe 25 years. I saw some things that affected me deeply, like a little girl being killed in a fire. That was really hard on me. But this, by far, was the worst that a story affected me.

Stalley: What was amazing is that we didn't see the crash site. We didn't see any remains. We didn't see any of that stuff. But we could feel it. We could feel everything. Being over the hill, on the other side, seeing the faces on the people, knowing what had happened.

I had nightmares two weeks before the first anniversary. I was to the point where I told my news director that I didn't want to come back down. I didn't want to do it. That's how much it affected me. As we got closer, I found myself crying at the thought of what we were doing. The day of the anniversary, I remember waking up physically ill. I had not been back out to the scene since the last day we left the year before.

When I got out here, I realized we weren't there to remember the bad things, the terrorists and the whole scenario. We were there to remember and to honor and to never forget what had happened. When I got there and realized that, I was okay with it. Although it was still hard, I would find myself looking at something and remembering and having to regain my composure.

Every time there is a story here, I ask not to go.

Hoffer: I remember the six-month anniversary a lot. I remember being able to talk to some of the families, which I considered to be a huge privilege. I was able to talk with them, have them tell me stories about their family member. The families were so gracious. How thankful they were to Somerset County and the people here.

The emotions, by that time, had kind of died off because I had been out here time after time after time, just because that is part of my job as a photographer. I can't say no, I don't want to do this. Most of the time, I'm too busy doing my job and worrying about getting what I need to tell my story than worrying about the emotions. If I would come out by myself and sit and stare out there where the crash happened, it still would bother me.

I think there was a special bond that the four of us who covered the story shared. It's still there to this day. I think we relied on each other a lot to talk and share feelings.

Stalley: You hear about post-traumatic stress and how it affects people, and I think we all went through it, to some degree.

I don't think I'll ever get over it, and I don't think I want to. I don't want to forget. My children, they both know. My little girl was just itty-bitty. It was my first day back from maternity leave when this happened. My little boy, in the past couple of years, has asked what happened. I want him to know what we, as a nation, experienced that day. It happened in our own backyard.

I let him watch the last Flight 93 TV movie. Also, I have an air check tape of that very first time we went on air that day, the first 12 hours. I let him watch it. He wanted to come out, and that's the reason I came out here. I brought him out, and I explained to him what happened. It made him cry.

As a mother, you don't want your children to cry, but I want him to know; I don't want him to forget. When he grows up and has kids, I want them to know that this wasn't just a story. This was history and something so amazing. The families, Shanksville, and everyone pulled together. That's what I want him to know, and that's what I want him to remember.

That's what I want to remember.

Donna Glessner, founder and head of the Flight 93 Ambassadors, provided a guided tour of the temporary memorial to the students.

Glessner: When we first started, we noticed that people coming here seemed kind of lost, not geographically lost, although that was also a problem because there weren't any signs to help them find the place, but they were also disoriented as to what they were seeing. There wasn't even a flag on that fence down there, so you really couldn't pick out the crash site.

Many people were making the incorrect assumption that this pond was connected with the site because it looks like an excavation. Some people assumed incorrectly that the scrap yard at the top of the hill had something to do with it; that the pile of metal up there was the remnants of the plane. Or, they would jump to the conclusion that these draglines over here on the hill were brought in to bring out pieces of the plane. Some thought that the whole clearing was created by the crash of the plane.

We felt it was important for all people who visit to know what and where everything happened.

People come here from all over the world.

In the summertime, almost every month, there are people from all fifty states and usually as many as fifteen to twenty countries. I've met people from countries that I never even knew existed. I had to go to an atlas and find out where these places are.

International visitors are very well informed about the events of September 11 and very respectful of Flight 93, in particular, and the heroics on board the plane.

We get a lot of military, both active duty and retired. We get a number of people who are going to or coming back from Iraq. We've had people ask us to fly flags here at the site that they can take back to their base. They also take pictures here and take them back to their buddies at camp.

The main question we get is, "Where did the plane crash?"

The crash site is just beyond the American flag at the edge of the trees. The plane came over Lambertsville and the scrap yard at the top of the hill.

There were seven people working there that day, and this plane went right over them so low that one of the gentlemen remarked that he felt like he ought to duck. It was flying about 580 mph. It must have seemed huge going over them that low and that fast.

It wasn't like a gentle, attempted landing; it was a case of a plane driving into the ground. It created an explosion as the jet fuel ignited, and a smoke cloud rose in the sky that you could see for miles. The trees were burned right behind the crash site.

There was an area of about a hundred trees that have since been cut down. The coroner commented that these trees had so much debris embedded in them that he felt they needed to stay on the site with the other unrecoverable remains. He had the trees chipped. The wood chips from these trees are that little bump that's right behind the American flag.

The larger mound of dirt off to the right looks important but it's not. It was here before the plane crashed; it's dirt left over from when they were mining here. Its only function now is when a family comes to visit. They are permitted to go inside the fenced area. Often, they will climb up on that mound of dirt so they can get a view down at the crash site.

254

Visitors ask about the benches. The seventh and eighth grade students at a school called Spring Valley Bruderhof are making them. The Bruderhof is a communal religious society. They have a community about an hour and a half from here.

They embraced this place from early on, feeling the need to reach out to the people coming here. Many people who came here early on came here as a surrogate for New York or Washington. For various reasons, they felt they couldn't go there.

There were family members coming here, grieving. All America was grieving, really. This Bruderof community came here every Sunday afternoon. They were very warm and friendly to the people visiting.

As an offshoot of that, they realized it would be nice if people had a place to sit. They made a bench with the name of Deora Bodley on it because they made contact first with Deora's father. Other families saw the Deora bench and really liked it. They began making a bench with each passenger and crewmember's name on it.

There are only thirty-five right now. They don't put someone's name out there until they have made contact with the family and the family says yes. The families let them know what they want the name to look like. That's why some of them have only the first name. For instance, there is one that just says "Edward" for Edward Felt. His wife, Sandy, said she felt like if it just said "Edward" anybody who had an Edward could think, "Gee, that could have been my husband, brother or dad."

The angels are made of slate. A husband and wife from Reading, Pennsylvania brought the original set. They just brought them up one December day in 2001 and asked if it was okay to put them out. Anything is okay here, as long as it is in good taste. That's been our only rule.

So, the angels were put out and became, sort of a tombstone, if you will, because at the time there was no marker and no other place where all forty names were written.

The granite marker between the two flagpoles has a plaque with the names on it but was not put out here until February 2002. The angels were important, and the families kind of adopted them as the place where they leave individual tributes to their loved ones. You'll see on the angels that some people left pictures or trinkets that meant something to them.

The German flag is on Christian Adams' angel. He was a citizen of Germany and was here to attend a wine conference in California. The Japanese flag is in honor of Toshiya Kuge.

Plans for the permanent memorial? This is the land that we're talking about acquiring: the crash site, the debris field behind here in the woods, and this strip-mined area that extends behind you out toward Route 30, about two and a half miles out that direction. It's all strip-mined land that looks a lot like the field that you see around you. Grass and little seedlings.

When you enter the park from Route 30, the first thing you will see is a tall tower that is ninety-three feet high and will house forty wind chimes. That is beyond the dragline that you see out there, too far away to see from the temporary memorial. Then, you will drive down into this area where we are and go to a circular walkway up where the scrap yard is, on the top of the hill. At that place you will have a view right down the flight path of the plane to the crash site.

Then, you'll have the opportunity to go into a small visitor's center and see exhibits and learn about the events of that day and the people on Flight 93.

The designer said he felt like after you came out of that visitor's center, you'd have a lot to think about. He didn't want you to proceed quickly to the final resting place. He wanted you to take your time and make this slow, thoughtful walk along this one-mile-long path and eventually get to the sacred ground. There will be a sloping black granite wall around the crash site and a little plaza area for reflection right at the edge.

I hope we can keep the temporary memorial open right up until they cut the ribbon on the permanent one. Hopefully, they can build around us. This temporary memorial has meant so much to so many people.

As for the ambassadors, they say there will always be a need for volunteers. We'll continue on as what they call VIP's, Volunteers in Parks, which is the official name for National Park Service volunteers.

The Wright College students also met with Terry Butler at the temporary memorial. In his usual soft-spoken manner, Terry Butler recounted his view of Flight 93's last minute in the air. He then walked over to his blue pick-up truck for pictures. As a personal memorial, Terry had the names of the forty heroes painted on the bed cover. He also changed his official Pennsylvania license plate to "UAL 93."

On his way back to the temporary memorial, Terry spoke of another more personal remembrance to the heroes.

Butler: I don't come up here that much. It's too hard. Mostly, I come for the anniversaries and Christmas Eve. I know it sounds silly, but I bring a card up for them every Christmas Eve.

I want them to get something. I want them to be remembered.

Wright Students Share Their Thoughts

Hector Rizo

I did not expect to feel something out there on the crash site; you can feel what people were feeling on that day. What got to me most was the story of the heart made by the little girl.

Joey Morales

The thing that surprised me the most was when the people reflected and were recounting those events; it felt as if they were taking us back with them to that day.

Anthony Armando

This experience helped me to personalize not the events so much as the impact the events had on everyone in the town. I wish I could take with me the emotion and genuine sincerity that everyone has with them when they talk about that day.

Paula Campo

For the first research paper in class, we had to write about two Somerset residents that appear in the book *Courage After the Crash*. They only seemed as characters in a book. After coming to Shanksville and talking to some of them in person, I realized how real their experiences were. I also found very interesting the fact that for some people it is still hard to think about September 11.

Tony Loster

The best part of the trip was meeting Terry, Sherry, and Keith. The emotion they feel being at the site affected me. Everyone was so open and honest; it was refreshing.

Nicole Serrano

Going to visit the memorial chapel had an impact on me, especially the room with the pictures and the information about the people on the plane.

Edith Vazquez

It's different reading these residents' experiences and then hearing them tell it themselves, seeing the emotions on their faces. I felt connected with them as if I knew the pain and trauma they endured.

Elizabeth Fitton

I felt the chapel is a great and emotional representation. The painting of the planes flying into the hands of God was incredible. If there is to be one image that explains 9/11, that should be it.

Wright Students, continued

Ron Heine

I can see what brings people to Shanksville. The people are easy to talk to, approachable, and respectful of those who visit. I hope to bring the family next time.

Steven Kararo

Meeting Terry was the best experience of the trip. Talking to him in person was different than reading about him. Meeting and talking with these people was a life-changing experience. When you stand there and look out at the empty field and close your eyes, I felt, like Terry said, a presence out there.

Jenine Stallard

I learned that Shanksville is not just a place where a plane crashed or a place of death, but a place where ordinary people did extraordinary things in times of need. The people there helped, more than we realize, to shape the face of the coping mechanism for the entire country. I will be forever grateful to all of those that I met.

Nefertitti Muhammad

What impacted me the most was listening to Barbara Black speak about the objects and letters from people who visited the crash site. As she spoke about preserving the items, I felt a compelling emotion that connected me to the heroes of Flight 93.

Aidee Jardan

This trip to Somerset helped me to understand that I was not the only one trying to avoid reality. Also, I find unity is so important.

Carlos Martinez

I learned that one of the passengers, Waleska Martinez, was Puerto Rican and went to the same university as me. My friend and I left a card with a message for Waleska at the memorial.

Walter Alvardo

This experience is unforgettable. I came here with a state of mind that the plane was shot down, but after listening to everyone and watching and comprehending the real facts, I changed my view. I was so surprised at how such a small community made a difference by showing the families of these heroes that they did, and still do, care. Also, by inspiring others, like myself, to enjoy life day by day and that I can also make a difference to a person I may not even know.

ISBN 978-0-9721031-6-9
Library of Congress Card Number 2002141281

Courage
After the Crash

by Glenn J. Kashurba, M.D.

The story of the aftermath of Flight 93 told through unique photographs and oral histories of witnesses, first responders, investigators and crash site workers.

Courage After the Crash is hardbound with dust jacket and retails for $34.95.

"*Courage After the Crash* is an extraordinary personal and regional tome that will touch hearts across the globe. This is the story of Flight 93 that you have not yet seen and heard!"
John E. Schlimm II
Autograph Collector Magazine

Courage After the Crash is 200 pages and features over 100 unique, full color photographs.

Author's royalties donated to 9/11 and children's charities.

"Kashurba's book is an extraordinary account. It is intelligent and cohesive. As a student of history, I find *Courage After the Crash* speaks volumes about the people of rural Middle America."
G. Henry Cook
Stage II Juror for Flight 93 National Memorial
CEO of Somerset Trust Company
Fundraiser for Flight 93 National Memorial

For more information, or to buy *Courage After the Crash*, go to:
www.sajpublishing.com

For additional information, go to:

www.sajpublishing.com

- Interviews with the author, Glenn J. Kashurba, M.D.

- Author's notes from *Quiet Courage: The definitive account of Flight 93 and its aftermath* and *Courage After the Crash*

- Author's contact information and availability for book signings, media events, speaking engagements

- Flight 93 updates

- Photo gallery

- Somerset County history

- Other books on 9/11 and Somerset County

- Links to 9/11 and Somerset County websites

- Upcoming books and projects

- Purchasing information

About the Author

Glenn J. Kashurba, M.D. is a Board Certified Child and Adolescent Psychiatrist and nationally known writer, speaker and advocate for children and families.

Dr. Kashurba volunteered with the American Red Cross after the crash of Flight 93. He accompanied the heroes' families when they visited the crash site in the days following 9/11. He dedicated the next year to research, write and publish *Courage After the Crash*. All profits from the book are donated to 9/11 and children's charities.

Dr. Kashurba was honored for his 9/11 work with the prestigious Catcher in the Rye advocacy award at the American Academy of Child and Adolescent Psychiatry's Annual Meeting in San Francisco, California, on October 26, 2002.

In 2005, the American Psychiatric Association recognized Dr. Kashurba for his contributions to the field of psychiatry by bestowing on him the title of Distinguished Fellow.

Dr. Kashurba is the co-chair of a panel of nine experts who writes the enormously popular parenting series, *Facts for Families* for the American Academy of Child and Adolescent Psychiatry (AACAP). This information has been translated into many languages and is read by millions around the world. It is available to download, free of charge, in English and Spanish at www.aacap.org.

Dr. Kashurba lives in Somerset, Pennsylvania with his three teenage children. His leisure time pursuits include coaching youth sports teams.

For more information, go to www.glennkashurba.com.

Author Glenn J. Kashurba, M.D.
with his children Alex, Joe and Sophie